Christine Müller
Local Knowledge and Gender in Ghana

Christine Müller (Dr. rer. soc.) has recently become a scientific transmigrant being a Post-Doc at National Centre of Competence in Research North-South (NCCR North-South), University of Berne (Switzerland), and a lecturer at Sociology of Development Research Centre, University of Bielefeld (Germany). She has switched her research focus on virtual governance in Southern Africa and South East Asia.

CHRISTINE MÜLLER
LOCAL KNOWLEDGE AND GENDER IN GHANA

[transcript]

The book is based on a doctoral thesis »Coming out of our Shells – Local Knowledge and Gender in Ghana« *(Prof. Dr. Gudrun Lachenmann/Prof. Dr. Joanna Pfaff-Czarnecka) conducted at the Sociology of Development Research Centre (SDRC), University of Bielefeld (Germany) with the financial support of the Friedrich-Ebert-Foundation, Bonn/ Berlin.*

Bibliographic information published by Die Deutsche Bibliothek
Die Deutsche Bibliothek lists this publication in the Deutsche Nationalbibliografie; detailed bibliographic data are available in the Internet at http://dnb.ddb.de

© 2005 transcript Verlag, Bielefeld

All rights reserved. No part of this book may be reprinted or reproduced or utilized in any form or by any electronic, mechanical, or other means, now known or hereafter invented, inlcuding photocopying and recording, or in any information storage or retrieval system, without permission in writing from the publisher.

Cover layout by: Kordula Röckenhaus, Bielefeld
Typeset by: Christine Müller
Printed by: Majuskel Medienproduktion GmbH, Wetzlar
ISBN 3-89942-378-X

Distributed in North America by:

Transaction Publishers
New Brunswick (U.S.A.) and London (U.K.)

Transaction Publishers	Tel.: (732) 445-2280
Rutgers University	Fax: (732) 445-3138
35 Berrue Circle	for orders (U.S. only):
Piscataway, NJ 08854	toll free 888-999-6778

CONTENTS

1. Knowledge between Globalization and Localization — 9
   1.1   Introduction — 9
   1.2   The Emergence of the World-Wide Women's Web — 14
   1.2.1 The "Discovery" of Women for Development — 18
   1.2.2 UN Conferences as Vehicles of Movements — 22
   1.3   Global and Cross-National Networking — 26

2. Doing Research and Writing Wor(l)ds — 35
   2.1   Setting of Research — 35
   2.2   The Interview Partners and Situations — 40
   2.3   From the Process of Fieldwork to the Process of Writing:
          Politics, Representation and Reflexivity — 43

3. Conceptualising Local Knowledge — 51
   3.1   Agency-Orientation in Sociology of Knowledge — 51
   3.2   The Concept of Space/Time and Empirical Operationalisation — 54
   3.3   Research as an Explorative Process — 57
   3.4   Methods: Chances and Limitations — 59

4. Knowledge Transfer over Generations: Continuity and Change — 65
   4.1   The Old Generation: *"The young ones will not listen"* — 66
   4.2   The Process of Knowledge Generation — 67
   4.3   The Mediation of Knowledge: Symbolic Spaces
          and Practices in the Everyday World — 73
   4.3.1 *"At first there were gods in town"* — 74
   4.3.2 *"To drive the sickness out of town"* — 76
   4.3.3 Worshipping at the River Susuan — 78
   4.3.4 Symbolic Spaces in Transition — 81
   4.4   The Young Generation: *"Nowadays we are Christians"* — 83
   4.4.1 Different Strategies in the Process of Knowledge
          Generation — 86
   4.4.1.1 The "traditional" type: Afia — 86
   4.4.1.2 The "mixed" type: Kofi — 88
   4.4.1.3 The "educated" type: Akosua — 89
   4.4.2 The Meaning of Formal Education — 92
   4.5   The Emergence of Ambivalences in Gendered Relations — 93

5.	**"Traditional" Institutions as Arenas of Knowledge Struggle**	**95**
5.1	Asymmetries within "Traditional" Institutions	96
5.1.1	The Queenmother's Dilemma	99
5.1.2	Loss within the Political Spaces: From "Complementarity" to Asymmetry	102
5.2	Challenging of Spaces: The Subqueenmothers	106
5.2.1	"*We are not too shy*": The Long Way to the Palace...	109
5.2.2	....and how to get into the Palace	110
5.3	Discourse about Political Spaces: "*Due to Beijing*"	113
5.3.1	The Negotiation of Tradition "*They want us to live like in ancient times*"	116
5.3.2	Creation of New Spaces: The Queenmothers' association	118
5.3.3	Moving in Different Spaces: Nana Ama Serwaa	121
5.3.4	Self-Organization: Female Economy, Social Security and Public Sphere	122
5.4	The Knowledge Pillars	124
6.	**Social Networking between Women's Organizations**	**127**
6.1	The Women's Forum at Sunyani: A Platform for Change	128
6.1.1	Organising Development: The National Council of Women and Development	135
6.1.2	The Women's Forum at Accra: Another Platform for Change	137
6.1.3	The Organizational Structure of the NCWD	139
6.2	The Pan-African Network Women in Law and Development Africa (WiLDAF)	141
6.2.1	Initiating WiLDAF: From Local Realities to Transnational Networking...	141
6.2.2	The Organizational Structure: Struggling for Power on the Ground	144
6.2.3	WILDAF 1999: Backwards and Forwards	145
6.2.4	...and from Transnational Networking back to Local Reality	146
6.3	Networking as a Knowledge Bridge	149
7.	**The Migrating Knowledge**	**151**
7.1	Becoming a 31st December Woman	151
7.2	Every Human Being is a Political Person	157
7.3	Women doing Development	161
8.	**Decentralised Political Institutions: Knowledge between Bureaucratising and Lobbying**	**165**
8.1	Processes of Decentralisation	166
8.2	The Unit Committee Council in Susuanso	167

8.3	The District Assembly Man: Linking Politics		170
8.4	The District Assembly		171
8.4.1	Planning Development-Development Planning		171
8.4.2	The Policy of the District Assembly		173
8.5	Planning at Regional Level		175
8.6	Reflecting on Women's Organizations: Changing Gender Ideologies ?		176
8.7	De-bureaucratising Development Knowledge		177

9. Glocalised Practices: Towards a Knowledge Society   183

Bibliography   189
   Homepages: Web Addresses   205

List of Abbreviations   207

1 KNOWLEDGE BETWEEN GLOBALIZATION AND LOCALIZATION

1.1 Introduction

To conduct a study on local knowledge in a small village of an African country seems rather inconsistent with the ongoing process termed globalization. The sociological description of "the globalization of a knowledge society" mainly refers to the construction and production of knowledge in universities, research institutes, consulting firms and think tanks, which have expanded in all parts and regions of the world (Evers 1999: 7-11). The relevance of knowledge in general and in the context of developing countries in particular has become a discourse not only in the scientific arena and within development organizations[1], but also outside those institutions in everyday conversations and discussions such as one between two young men sitting under a shady tree in the small Ghanaian village of Susuanso discussing the kind of maize they should plant next season, having to choose between the "traditional" or improved new variety. In current development paradigms as well as in social theory, knowledge in its different dimensions and forms is considered as an important – or even the most important – factor for present and future social change[2] in comparison to other factors such as capital, time or labour. In the context of development discourse and politics, the meaning of knowledge in southern countries has been labelled as "local" knowledge[3], which has resulted in a large body of literature, especially about agricultural, environmental, technical and medical knowledge systems. The discussions among academics, development experts and politicians on the relevance and

---

1 The current discussion deals around the notion of knowledge management. Knowledge management refers to the internal organization of knowledge within development organizations such as the proper storage of knowledge, expertise and experience as well as its dissemination among, and utilization of development experts. In sight of a growing competitiveness between organizations, knowledge management as an innovative strategic concept is supposed to strengthen the (economic) capacity of organizations (Evers/Kaiser/Müller 2002).
2 Many studies such as those of Weingart (2001), Stehr (2000), Knorr-Cetina (1999) argue along the socially determining effect of knowledge in present societies.
3 The term "local" knowledge is a derivative from Clifford Geertz's essay collection *Local Knowledge* (1983) who claimed for an interpretative explanation of cultures. The term entered the broad discussion in sociology of development through Richards (1985) and Hobart (1993).

appropriate use of local knowledge within development cooperation taking place in Germany during the 1990s (vgl. Honerla/Schröder 1995) raised my personal interest in the topic, inspired me to undertake steps for scientific investigation and finally pathed my academic career.

The worsening of living conditions in the southern countries, the failures of multiple development programs and projects after three decades of development cooperation have gradually led to awareness and to a "new emphasis" (Geschiere 1995: 170) on the importance of local knowledge. Two shifts were responsible for this change in paradigm: first, the change in perspective towards local was strengthened by demands by participatory movements in Latin-America since the 1970s for a definition of their own development and by NGO's[4] in Africa, who demanded from the donor side the integration of local people and knowledge in the formulation of development concepts and realization thereof. Participatory under those paradigms was strongly aimed towards the transformation and politicization of development. Second, a major shift tended away from the dominant technocratic-oriented discourse on development towards the integration of social scientific knowledge within development institutions (Geschiere 1995: 171)[5] and the rhetoric recognition of local knowledge as a relevant resource for practical development cooperation. These double shifts could not, however, resolve the problem that the majority of social anthropological studies on development or case studies within development projects result in an indigenisation and mystification of knowledge and people, with less consideration of the broader context and negligence of power problematization and politicization of world-wide knowledge production as a whole (Moore 1996: 2-3). Those studies further strengthen the conventional view that knowledge at local level is static, homogenous, easily applicable for development and more or less cut off from the rest of the world (Geschiere 1995: 171; Lachenmann 1995a: 132). The term local is not unproblematic in itself since it, at first glance, implies a geographical spatial arrangement. As a sociological term, however, I intend to broaden its meaning for describing the processes of production and of construction of meanings which characterize a locality. Arjun Appadurai (1998: 178) defines locality as relational and contextual, rather than as scalar or spatial. His definition of locality is close to the definition of space, which also has a spatial and a contextual component. A local space is, according to these preliminary characteristics, not absolute, but relational in its constitution.

---

4   In 1990 about 500 representatives of NGO's met in Arusha (Tanzania) making a claim for participation, transformation and a sharing of power in development planning (Nelson/Wright 1995: 3).

5   One of the first studies within the German development context which dealt with the negative consequences of modernisation on the transfer of medical knowledge within developing countries such as Namibia and Benin was conducted by Gudrun Lachenmann (1982).

The terms local and global initially indicate two isolated or dichotomic spheres without any interaction taking place. But this is not what this study is aiming for. More relevant than the construction of new boundaries and the continuation of dislinked spheres is the focus on the connection between the different levels and the linking of localities. In this theoretical approach the topic deals with the "interface" of knowledge (Long/Long 1992: 6) between the global and the local and both terms have to be utilised in a relational sense as "[...] the fluid ends of relations between cultures" (Nederveen Pieterse 1995: 62).

The flow of knowledge does not necessarily have to come from the global and flow to the subordinate periphery in a linear one-dimensional direction as described in Wallerstein's "World-System" or according to Giddens' definition of globalization as a consequence of modernity and therefore as a product or project of the Western world (Giddens 1995: 214-215). Nor is globalization a convergent amalgam of multiple processes leading to a "single world society" or "global society" (Albrow/King 1990: 9), which means that the globe will ultimately be covered with a homogenous web of knowledge. The flow of knowledge is rather situated in a complex web, which connects the local with the global level and vice versa. From this point of view the theoretical concept of globalization in its different dimensions is not a floated or one-directional phenomenon, but a process of linking localities and local actors. This complex configuration of social relations and the density of interrelations of different actors at the horizontal and vertical level is defined by Robertson as "Glocalization" (1995: 26) indicating the dynamic interplay of flows not towards homogenising, but towards homogenising and heterogenising. Global and local are in this sense relational, whereas the relationship is based on mutuality, and has implicitly overcome the dichotomy and the counter-position of local versus global.

I do not deny that the global order of knowledge is an unimportant issue nowadays: on the contrary, it is. The difficult and complex interrelations between locations, actors and power as well as the multifarious interplays along and within the different levels also imply discontinuities, contradictions and asymmetries. Critical questions regarding the location and structures of knowledge production in science come from various directions. Feminists especially from the North and South, anthropologists as well as scholars within the discourse of postcolonial studies have questioned and challenged the dominance of Western theory and science as a whole.

Sandra Harding, for example, focuses on the production of knowledge within institutions and organizations in the West which has to be seen under male-dominated conditions. The implementation of women's knowledge is therefore not enough. The structures of organizations and institutions need to be changed in order to transform social relations. "What is progressive about organizing heroic campaigns to "add women and gender" to the social structure and the subject matters of the sciences without questioning the legitimacy of science's social hierarchy and politically regressive agendas?" (Harding 1991: 47).

To set the statement into analogy with local knowledge, one can ask, if the incorporation of local knowledge into development programs is sufficient to change the power structures within the development discourse and within social and political relationships. The main field of interactions between the South and the North is still the politics of development. The field of development politics is about the organization of space, where different actors (NGO's, GO's, institutions, individuals etc.) interact at the different levels. Knowledge within research, policy-making and within the different types of organizations at national and international levels, manifests itself practically in development programs and projects and discursively in development language. According to Mark Hobart, Western scientific knowledge remains a focal point of reference for the definition of development/underdevelopment and for the formulation of its solutions. As "world-ordering" knowledge it ignores indigenous knowledge and constitutes itself as developed by defining indigenous knowledge as underdeveloped (Hobart 1993: 2). Despite the sharp contrast Hobart is drawing at the theoretical level and the fact that local knowledge has gained recognition by development organizations, the practical relationship between development experts as carriers of Western knowledge and local people as carriers of local knowledge is, in most cases, intended or not organized in a hierarchical manner. Although recent approaches under the heading of participation should lead to an equal listening and mutual sharing of knowledge, the crucial question remains as to whether within participatory relationship local actors can define their own agenda of development based on their own knowledgeability or remain objects of development planning by reproducing discourses and instrumentalising their local knowledge.

In such a complex web of unequal relations indicated above, knowledge can also be a factor for change and for the transformation of social relations (Berger/Luckmann 1966: 92). My perspective is not to analyze how politics and planned interventions in the form of development projects are implemented at local level[6]. Although development rhetoric find expression through different channels in the official language. I have taken up a bottom-up perspective by analyzing how women use their knowledge to bring about social change. One research question was, how women exchange knowledge, transmit it, and combine it with new innovative elements or new strategies. A second question focused on women's organizations, the existing forms of organizations and their potential for transformation. Since Berger/Luckmann (1966: 168) have already indicated that men and women can inhabit different social worlds within one society, the central question is how gender relations and interlinkings between gender-relations and gendered knowledge are organized. The relations among gender and the (re-)structuring of space is used

---

6 This topic has already been well discussed by Long/Long (1992), Long (1996), Hobart (1993).

here as the core theoretical concept for an alternative approach to development. Space as a theoretical and analytical concept (Chapter 3.2) is gaining importance in sociological and social anthropological theory, in particular since the claim of universal valid knowledge has been challenged in the progress of feminist, deconstructivist, post-structuralist and post-colonial approaches (Gupta/Ferguson 1992: 6). By following the sociological tradition of phenomenology, one guiding question was, how knowledge becomes reality. The process of "becoming reality" is conceptualised as a dynamic social process, which turns the research focus to processes and relations among those involved.

Glocalization also challenges the perspective of empirical research. The claims for a new "global sociology" (Robertson 1995: 25; Nederveen Pieterse 1995: 63) or "transnational anthropology" (Appadurai 1998: 48) should no longer focus on society in its hegemony and exclusiveness, but on established social networks, which operate across boundaries whether in virtual, face-to-face or discursive interactions. Knowledge is in itself locally bound and produced, but the relational reach can expand and create new forms of knowledge. To talk about local in a global context means that processes across cultures are a necessity for analysis. The links between localities in their translocal or transnational dynamics demand a perspective which goes beyond the village level. Local particularities do not disappear nor are they absorbed or abolished by the dynamics at national and global level, but on the contrary remain an important aspect of analysis.

Those actors constituting locality have to be seen in a wider context while they are contributing to it: they can be part of small formations such as neighborhoods or families and/or at the same time part of larger formations such as associations which can be based on "modern" or "traditional" structures, or be engaged in social movements or translocal networks. In contrast to Arjun Appadurai (1998) whose focus is stronger on the permanence of the fluid character of local-global flows, my perspective focuses more on the emergence, implications and consequences those flows have for the social organization of knowledge in a specific locality. A locality results out of translocal interactions *as well as* constitutes new translocal dynamics. For the empirical research process this also means, that the borderlines of fieldwork vanish and have to be opened, depending on the dimensions of interactions and locations of knowledge production. For example, discussions at the Beijing World Women's Conference in 1995 influenced the discussion about "traditional" political structures and the results of a research project on Women in Public Life in Ghana conducted at the University of Legon are now used as arguments against unequal gender relations in public life.

The challenge for a researcher nowadays is not only the combination of a local and a translocal perspective, but also the extension of it to the end of dimensions of interactions, which in view of global networking can become endless. For this more or less arbitrary act of defining research boundaries, I have taken two things into consideration: first, the encounters at which practices at local level are transformed into abstract political formulations; and second, the ongoing process of decentralisation in Ghana with the restructuring of political power relations leading to concrete everyday reality.

After these general theoretical clarifications, I would like to describe and specify what constitutes the global. It is not only the conceptual perspective, which forms the framework of my analysis, but also the practices that currently make up this framework. Therefore the emergence and genesis of this framework need to be explained as its make-up is of importance for the following chapters.

1.2 The Emergence of the World-Wide Women's Web

Women in this study are defined as the actors in the interplay between local and global dynamics[7]. Although their formation into groups and organizations as well as connections across distances can be traced back to a long history, the new quality of intensification in the continuity of long- and short distance interactions and the density of communication evoked new forms of social power. A Subqueenmother in Ghana perfectly described in an interview the present state-of the-art of women's movements as initiating a turning point of socio-political marginalisation and of knowledge order. She emphasized, that *"Now, we are coming out of our shells"*. *Coming out of our shells* is a metaphor indicating two movements: the process of going into the shell and the process of coming out of the shell. The process of going into the shell symbolises the partial marginalisation of female knowledge. The process of coming out has already began, but is not yet completed and if it is fulfilled, continuation will be a slow movement similar to the movements of a snail which leaves symbolic trails. Snails also put out their horns for orientation similar to an electronic antenna and function as mediators of the translocal flow of knowledge by crossing local boundaries. The flow of knowledge is in practice translated into interactions, which take place at different levels of society and can result in the transformation of spaces, the creation of new room for manoeuvre, new power structures, identities, alliances and a new knowledge repertoire (Long 1996: 46).

When using the term global I refer to the global women's movements which have been formed in almost all parts of the world and operate as arenas where knowledge is produced, negotiated and disseminated. The international connections between women are not really a new phenomenon however as they

---

7   Several studies indicate that women are a constitutive part in the formation of local-global linkages whether as migrants between Lebanon and Ivory Coast (Peleikis 2003), as long distance traders between Ghana and Hongkong (Amponsem 1996) or in the environmental movement of Mexico (Rodenberg 1999).

already existed in the second half of the 19th. century[8]. As early as 1863 the Swiss feminist Marie Goegg founded the first international women's organization: the International Association of Women. In 1888 women's activists from New Zealand, India and Egypt formed the International Council of Women as a unit of all national women's associations, perpetuated through meetings such as that held in Chicago in 1893 and attended. In 1902 women from England, Russia, Norway, Sweden, Germany, Turkey, Australia and Chile attended a suffrage meeting in Washington D.C. The conference resulted in the International Alliance of Women which after the founding of the UN had consultative status within the UN Economic and Social Council (Fraser 1987: 5). Women also established networks in the southern hemisphere such as the Pan-Pacific Women's Association in 1928 located in Honolulu or organized meetings as in 1931 when women in Lahore (Pakistan) joined the All Asian Women's Conference[9]. The topics discussed in those cross-boundary networks were mainly peace, women's rights and their bodies. The main concern of the meetings was the exchange of experience, mobilisation and self-organization (Wichterich 1999: 111-113; Wieringa 1995: 12ff.).

The chronology of this early formation of women's movements in its pre-global form was not consistent, but followed a period of fall-off by women's movements in the North and struggles within anti-colonial and liberation movements in the South. In various African countries such as Cameroon, Nigeria, Namibia, Somalia and Mali, women were active by mobilising and organising political actions, fighting against colonial practices or showing acts of resistance, which in some cases led to a weakening of colonial power structures or even to the downfall of political regimes[10]. In Ghana and in the form of collective military attacks, the famous Queenmother Yaa Asantewaa, (who is still well known today), fought in 1900 against the British army but could not prevent the continued process of colonisation (Arhin 1983: 96). Market women in urban areas also supported anti-colonialist, non-violent actions against European companies via strikes and boycotts (Klingshirn 1971: 234-235). At an individual level, unmarried women adopted strategies to maintain their autonomy and independence from colonial rules of being officially forced to marry or being imprisoned[11] (Allman 1996: 204).

The diversity of activities against colonial power structures did not, however, correspond to equal political participation after independence and did not result in self-determined development at the onset of development cooperation in the early 1950s. The biased process favouring men in national

---

8   Those organizations were established out of a variety of movements as socialist or peace movements (Rupp 1997: 88).
9   For a detailed description see Wichterich (1999).
10 Aidoo (1981), Grau (1989), Lachenmann (1995), Wieringa (1995).
11 The official explanation was, that unmarried women would be the reason for the spread of veneral disease through prostitution. The fact was, that women outnumbered men. Their economic independence in farming and trading was seen as suspicious by colonial rulers (Allman 1996: 208ff.).

and international politics has its roots in colonial politics by concentrating on the establishment of a political administration headed by male leaders, a government bureaucracy as a labor market for mainly male servants, or the support of export-oriented cash economies, which after the introduction and expansion of cocoa in the turn of the 18th. to the 19th. century, increasingly favored the cash crop industry and neglected the subsistence and market production of "traditional" agricultural products. Despite the mostly female workforce in the cocoa production, little efforts were made in terms of agricultural training and in the agricultural sector (Mikell 1985: 17). In her recent study on gender-relations and agricultural innovations in Northern Ghana, Martina A. Padmanabhan suggests that this perspective leads to the consequences of male-dominated research and extension services being directed to male farmers. Women were mostly ignored when it came to the structures of new innovative knowledge distribution, e.g. of new technologies or new forms of crops, a practice which continues today (Padmanabhan 2002: 27ff.), indicating the ongoing gender blindness in institutions towards research and policy.

Women, however, continued to be active as "hidden" subjects. Those forms of organizations of women which existed in precolonial and during colonial times within the traditional setting and pursued social, ritual or military purposes, gradually lost their meaning while new forms of women's associations emerged during colonial times as women's clubs and built up intellectual, western-oriented elite, labor associations, self-help groups in the urban areas or monetary, market or trading associations in the rural areas of Ghana (Little 1972: 275-288; Tsikata 1989: 75; Klingshirn 1971: 234). A first step towards a national umbrella organization, the Ghana Women's Federations, was taken in 1952 and boasted 2,300 people members in 1957. Less is known about the internal structure and the relationship between rural and urban women. A strong relationship between women's organizations and the state was set up in the year of independence (1957) when the first President Kwame Nkrumah annexed the renamed National Council of Ghana Women as part of the Convention Peoples Party (CPP).

At a time when the leading ideology was towards modernisation, industrialisation and the establishment of a modern nation state, it can be assumed that the interests of rural women and of women such as the Queenmothers were not taken into consideration. The enforcement during Nkrumah's time (1957-1966) of participation by women in politics and public life was, in reality, rather limiting as the tasks of addressing women's issues as well as improving women's living conditions were restricted to social indicators of a basic education or legal reforms. Women leaders in larger organizations held political seats in regional parliaments and were influential in political power processes (Little 1972: 280) but the negative attitudes towards women in government limited any room for manoeuvre within the overall political context. Although the limitation of articulation within the political system hindered the political power of women's organizations, some organizations did manage to orient themselves towards international issues as in 1960 when two women's leagues, the Ghana Women's League and the Ghana Federation of Women, protested against French plans to test atomic bombs in the Sahara (Tsikata 1989: 78).

Between 1966 and 1981, women's movements in Ghana were "hidden" from the political context, which was in particular due to changing (military) regimes and a declining economy. Both reasons made it almost impossible to engage in active political and social movements at a national level or to channel individual concerns into a common body. The activities of different associations and organizations were split up into diversified fragments and tied to the articulation of particular interests for self-help and charitable purposes (Tsikata 1989: 80).

The political environment for mobilisation and organization during the 1980s changed slightly when Nana Konadu Agyeman Rawlings, the wife of president Rawlings, who took political power in 1981 via a coup, engaged herself in women's issues and founded the 31st December Women's movement (Tsikata 1989: 83), which is officially an independent NGO, but is really a wing of the ruling party and a channel for government politics. Her personal engagement definitely contributed to making women's issues a popular topic in the media and politics. Tsikata states however, that she adopted the issue of gender politics without any constitutional or institutional basis and hindered the establishment of a strong independent political movement (2001: 266). The engagement of "First Ladies" in gender politics is mixed, and ranges between instrumentalising and popularisation of women's issues, where Ghana is not, however, an exception as similar effects can be observed in Nigeria and Mali (Tsikata 2001: 267).

Internal state relations and particularly the relationship between the women's movement and the ruling party influence the national politics as regards gender issues in law and policy and to a certain degree the effects of individual women's organizations and their specific policies. Despite the possible controlling function of co-optation, it has not prevented the emergence of present transnational relations and the gradual spread and density of linkings among women's organizations as well as their motivation to change social and political conditions. This aspect of the emergence requires consideration of two main context reasons:

1. The "discovery" of women for development in international development politics.
2. The interconnectedness between the women's movement in the North and the women's movement in the South during the Decade of Women (1975-1986) and during UN conferences.

Both context reasons stand in mutuality and are described below as they also reflect the turnaround of women from being regarded as objects as opposed to subjects of development in international politics. Instead of only responding to development approaches defined in national and international development politics, women made themselves visible through the formation of their own separate capacities of knowledge production within the World-Wide Women's Web, through the formulation of their own development concepts and through disseminating knowledge gained along the local-global scale of interaction. This specific process of capacity-building went along with the creation of an new epistemic culture on issues of development and gender, which can be defined according to Karin Knorr-Cetina, as a culture that "creates and warrants knowledge" (1999: 1) by emphasising and legitimating the setting of knowledge in practices, processes, symbols and structures. Knowledge is, according to this definition, not a individual or intellectual property, but permeates social life, transforms social institutions and symbolically structures societies.

1. 2. 1 The "Discovery" of Women for Development

With the end of the first development decade in the 1960s, development planners, funders and practitioners recognised the failure of many development projects and goals. Up until then, development had been defined under Western episteme as modernisation, urbanisation, industrialisation and the expansion of education. Under these paradigms grounded in a binary/dualist view of a developed and underdeveloped world, the knowledge availed of by people living in the South was considered "non-scientific", "irrational", "traditional" or "risk-averse" (vgl. Parpart 1995; Silitoe 1998: 211). Development co-operation was conceptualised as a transfer-of-knowledge approach from the North to the South, oriented towards the implementation of Western standards and models with the aim of forcing development to play catch-up. Meanwhile the realization of projects was mainly addressed to men – which also implies an instrumentalisation of their labour and knowledge – whereas women were completely neglected as subjects of development. It was assumed that with the growth of the economy and its inherent trickle-down effect, women would automatically benefit equally to men (Rathgeber 1990: 500).

With Esther Boserups study[12] on *Women's role in Economic Development* published in 1970, the economic achievements of women in Latin America, Africa and Asia were highlighted and made "visible" for the first time as well as revealing the negative influences of development projects towards forcing inequalities in gender-relations. The book was of particular importance, because it was one of the first studies to explicitly deal with the lives of women in the Third World and the impact of development projects thereof. On the basis of Boserup's findings and the world-wide struggle by women for emancipation, feminists in international development agencies sought to make women "visible" as a category for research and policy, resulting in the first

---

12 Her study was highly criticised, since it stuck to modernisation thinking. For further discussion see Beneria (1981).

approach to women known as the Women in Development (WID) approach (Kabeer 1994: Xi).

Under the WID approach, the disadvantage of women's lives was simply seen as a matter of exclusion from development. Programs in the form of income-generating projects or credit schemes specially designed for women were elaborated with the major aim of enhancing economic capacities of women. Accompanied by the approach of basic needs and equity formulated by the International Labour Organization in 1976, the worsening of women's livelihoods, the increasing poverty and women's workloads were supposed to be suspended by welfare measures. Women were furthermore seen as mediators for social development within households by eliminating the identified problems and issues of hygiene, literacy, welfare and childcare (vgl. Rathgeber 1990). Those efficiency, equity and welfare approaches were embedded within modernisation and evolutionary thinking, without giving any thought to the possibilities of alternative forms of development or to development concepts, ways or goals defined by women themselves.

One slight change occurred in the organization of development cooperation at national and international development agencies. Various programs were added with a women's component and were actually staffed by women. But those who were active remained marginalised within their own society and institutions, and their capacity to direct policy by themselves was reduced accordingly. As Naila Kabeer has stated, the act of including women was institutionalised in the form of women's desks and in most cases represented nothing more than a mere symbolic recognition of women (1994: XIII). Newly created jobs were also abolished within a certain period or remained weak within the development context (Wichterich 1984: 68). While it was anticipated that women as a "target-group" would be the solutions for development, and therefore conceptualised as a "logistic" category, measures for the advancement of women and different forms of implementation were less efficient in terms of structural change. The concept of integration was taken up and deconstructed by German feminist circles, which adamantly criticised the isolated one-dimensional promotion of women within the WID approach, demanding instead, integration of women in decision-making processes within development programs right from the very beginning, as well as integration in processes of realisation and evaluation (Wichterich 1984: 66). Integration and addition to predefined concepts were not regarded as the solutions, but rather the ideal that women themselves are active (Wichterich 1984:67). Gudrun Lachenmann commented on integrationist approaches to the effect that integration is more a form of implementation and intervention from outside, making external knowledge the central reference of programs with the accompanying increases of dependence on external knowledge. Implicitly it is an externally driven devaluation and marginalisation of local knowledge (1996: 1).

The marginalisation of knowledge remained, even within the Women and Development Approach[13] (WAD), which conceptualised women outside the mainstream development arena and claimed that if women were to have their own development projects, they could overcome structural inequalities. Rooted in marxist/dependency theories, this approach still adopts the paradox of thinking that the solutions of development are in the hands of experts. Efforts by women in any area of their live were thought to be dependent on external knowledge. The knowledge of women was not seen as a resource, but rather as a barrier to development (Parpart 1995: 229).

Neither the "integration" (WID) nor "isolation" (WAD) approach changed the living conditions of women. In its theoretical conceptualisation they did not grasp the complexity of women's lives, the complex relations of power and the hierarchical structures within the development arena. Women living in the South continued to be construed as passive beings, who were not knowledgeable in international donor agencies such as the World Bank, which as recently as 1989 published that

"Women are bound to tradition and gender based difficulties [...] to improve women's nutritional status, women themselves must be convinced of the need. Women's lack of self-confidence is a major impediment to the success of maternal and child health programs. It often shows up as "silence" or extreme denial as self and dependence on external authorities for direction" (World Bank, 1989).

Research within social sciences conducted by Western researchers contributed to this construction. The perception of the "traditional" role of women in the given society was maintained by many studies focusing on customs and institutions such as bride-price, polygamy, marriage or fertility. Conceptual and methodological approaches were based on household or domestic levels, e.g. on decision-making processes between couples, which biased the multiple responsibilities held by women within their community beyond the household[14] (Goetz 1991: 137). By mainly analysing the role and status of women measured at macro level or in terms of descriptive studies, women's worlds

---

13 The WAD approach was formulated at the end of the 1970s with its theoretical assumptions on dependency theory grounded on the binary concept of centre-periphery. To overcome structural inequalities, development should take place outside from and separated from dominant structures and from male dominated institutions (Parpart/Marchand 1995: 12). This approach reduces the complex economic relations between and within societies.

14 The models of household are oriented towards the Western understanding of a nuclear family, as well as the functions of mothers as childbearers, rearers and homemakers (Goetz 1991: 137). Household studies are also conducted by non-Western researchers, continuing to count social change in numbers and factors as Haddad on women and poverty in Ghana did (1991: 5-16). Instead of taking processes of the emergence of poverty into consideration, the study emphasises basic need poverty indicators, which in its interpretation rather leads to further questions than to answers and to a deeper understanding on poverty processes.

were caught up in social indicators and the overlapping and multiplicity of worlds reduced to a static number. The amount of figures, data and statistics at least resulted in the powerful political slogan that women constitute half of the world's population, fill two-thirds of its work hours, receive one-tenth of its income and own less than one-hundredth of its property (Newland 1991: 127).

This methodology of research of homogenising Third World Women did not go unanswered. Chandra Talpade Mohanty's influential article from 1984 *Under Western Eyes* examined the fact that many feminists from the North take themselves as the focal point of reference and as subjects while continuing to construe Third World Women as passive objects, and through this establish a discourse of victimology. The inherent structure of discourse of victimology exercises authoritative power over "powerless" Third World Women (1991: 3-6). But in turn within Western feminist circles the differentiation of women's worlds also created new approaches. Early Bielefeld feminists, who took the relations between and among women in the North and the South together in a main analytical frame of reference analyzed local contexts of women from a global perspective. The writers of *Women: The Last Colony* (Mies/Bennholdt-Thomsen/Von Werlhof, 1988) followed the methodological perspective of examining the relations and linkages between women in different parts of the world which was used to analyze aspects of uniting and separation with special reference to the interlinkage of forms of economic production as between the market and subsistence production. This analytical approach of overcoming the isolation of women's worlds by taking the relations between and among women in the South and in the North together overcame dichotomies and divided worlds. The interest to continue in examining the complex relations and to come up with new insights had been given, as academic women in the German context formed working groups on different aspects of development such as technology, education, economy, credit and marketing and tried to influence national development politics (Rott 1992: 7). At least one common result of the women's struggle was the challenge of a male-dominated science by women's units at universities, research and documentation centres[15] in the North as well as in the South, which deal directly or indirectly with women and the issue of development. The flow of information and resources however did not bring about change in the realities of women living in the South, whose living conditions actually worsened (Wichterich 1984: 4).

The process of the "discovery" of women can be characterised as an ambiguous process between the search for solutions of development and the stepping out of mainstream concepts in international development politics by

---

15 In 1976, the UN founded INSTRAW (International Research and Training Institute for the Advancement of Women), which in 1983 moved to the Dominican Republic. In 1976, the Fund for Women and Development was set up, which in 1985 became the autonomous organization UNIFEM (Braig 1999: 114; Newland 1991: 124).

some women in formulating their own approaches. This stepping out signified a major *epistemic turn*: the "discovery" of women *for* development turned into a discovery of development *by* women. Thereby turning away from the symbolic recognition to an active articulation and politicisation of their private lives. Despite heterogeneous methodological and practical concepts of development – which still exist nowadays – the "discovery" process laid the common ground in its initial stage for the building up of its own structures of knowledge production and for the gradual mutual exchange of new insights and knowledge cross-culturally. This exchange has a common ground in UN Conferences to which I will turn next.

1.2.2 UN Conferences as Vehicles of Movements

With the international Year of Women announced by the UN in 1975, the fragmented women's movements that existed all over the world gained recognition in international politics. Coming under the auspices of a global institution, the UN, these movements became part of inter-state relations, which opened the possibilities of influencing international and national politics. The umbrella function of the UN institutionalised women's politics on a common platform, with common agendas and statements which, however, were products of official delegations and less reflective of the diverse interests of women and especially those living in rural areas. Political issues were discussed in a general form, e.g. New International Economics was the main discussion point in Mexico at the first World Women's Conference. Special topics on women were kept separate from main political issues, summarised as "equality, development and peace", themes which had already been formulated at the 10th meeting of the International Women Suffrage Alliance in Paris in 1926 (Fraser 1987: 11).

The resolution of the first UN Conference was a Plan of Action. Political strategies aiming at enhancing the status of women, full and equal participation by women in politics, strengthening peace, abolishing inequalities and eliminating discrimination. For the process of implementation a setting-up of national "machineries" was recommended (Fraser 1987: 26), which took place in Ghana in 1975 with the founding of the National Council of Women and Development. During its first few years the NCWD had little influence on the national political context as regards to the mobilisation of women in particular due to limited material, a rudimentary infrastructure and a small budget. As in Ghana, many other African governments such as Ivory Coast, Cameroon, Kenya and Sierra Leone also established ministries of women's affairs or women's offices. On the one hand, these bureaucratic institutions established a new relationship between women and the state, on the other hand, its top-down mechanism influenced by the Women in Development (WID) approach was not designed to question or change power structures. In many countries the newly formed institutions remained politically weak, instrumentalised women and/or gradually were abolished (Lachenmann 1992: 203-205).

Outside the complex bureaucratic procedures of the United Nations, a parallel structure in the form of NGO forums opened a space for the articulation of women's politics among each other and became "centres of crystallisation" (Wichterich 1999: 115) of the women's movements by establishing discussion meetings and workshops and continued in its permanence towards global networking, which I will call the World-Wide Women's Web (WWWW). The solidarity of women across cultures and national boundaries emerged out of this context, which took a long time and a great deal of effort. Women attending the first NGO forum in Mexico, which was organised by volunteers, used it for discussing urgent issues such as women and imperialism, which the government delegations at the UN were not willing or open enough to debate. The women or groups participating formed a loose coalition of academics, national and international civil servants, peasant organizations and trade union women (Newland 1991: 127). Despite the common platform, differences and conflicts among women from the North and South dominated the forum. The claim of northern women of a collective gender identity, of universal suppression and a world-wide structure of patriarchy was denied and opposed by women from the South (Wichterich 2000: 258). Similarities between women from the South and the North were displaced by differences between the social, political and material situations and living conditions. Apart from the obvious differences among women, the common grounds for learning from each other were taken seriously and the movement was strong enough to listen to each other and to learn from each other.

The political visions and actions of women were less concentrated on common goals and more focused on the process of "how to influence politics" within the particular social context. Fraser describes the meaning of the first NGO forum in Mexico as a "highly sophisticated lobby, aiming in the short term at influencing the conference and the world's media and in the longer term at influencing national governments and the public" (Fraser 1987: 12). The process of lobbying[16] became a powerful medium for influencing politics and is used in the preparation processes[17] of major UN conferences, through

---

16 Lobbying took place at almost all UN conferences such as in 1992 on environment (UNCED) in Rio, in 1993 at the UN conference on human rights in Vienna and in 1994 at the UN conference on population and development in Cairo.

17 Before the conference at Beijing, viewpoints of women living in the south were integrated within the preparatory process of German NGO forum by common conferences held together trying to influence national government representatives (Ruf 1996: 20). Resolutions prepared for the UN preparatory meetings were built on a connection between visions from the south and from the north. For the first time, women all over the world communicated through electronic media with each other, elaborated regional documents, created regional platforms of actions etc.. This was not unproblematic: during meetings the fissures between women

caucus mechanisms and the increased contact with the media and national delegations of international conferences (Lachenmann 1996: 2; Clark/Friedmann/Hochstetler 1998: 13).

The importance of the first NGO forum did not only lie in the creation of a common institutionalised platform outside the UN system and on influencing national and international politics, but in the process of networking within and across national organizations as well as the founding of new alliances and new organizations. With the process from informal, independent or amorphous groups towards networks and organizations, the women's movements can be analyzed as a social movement. According to the definition by Ute Gerhard (1996: 4-6) social movements are carriers and catalysts of social change, which have the ability for further mobilisation, and the establishment of a public sphere. By taking up and politicising private topics or social contradictions towards the public sphere the women's movement is not only restricted to a pushing through of women's issues as isolated topics, but to further transforming social relations and challenging power relations.

During the second conference in Copenhagen in 1980 recommendations from the UN were affirmed and the thematical frame extended to education, employment and health. In 1980 the importance of women's organizations at the NGO forum was highlighted by pointing out the increase and growing importance of women's organizations at all levels of society. It became obvious, that women had pragmatized, professionalised and politicised their work (Fraser 1987: 159).

At the final conference of the women's decade in 1985 in Nairobi, a new quality of solidarity appeared. Women from the South determined most debates (Wichterich 2000: 259). They criticised the dominant WID/WAD approaches, pointing out the instrumentalisation of women, governmental control and the increasing working load of women. At the end of the women's decade, the goals of the Plan of Action of 1975 had only been partially achieved (Fraser 1987: 175) and in many countries the living conditions had actually worsened. Out of a situation in which women in international mainstream development politics were declared "vulnerable" or "disadvantaged" and many African countries were hit by structural adjustment programs implemented by the World Bank and by the International Monetary Fund, women became aware that policies should not be imposed on them, but they have to do it by themselves. The constant rise of poverty and the ongoing constant destruction of their environment, drew the attention of women in searching for their own alternative solutions formulated by themselves. In this sense mainstream politics and programs cannot give power to them like recipients, they have to take it themselves (Fraser 1987: 169). Out of a situation of such negative tendencies, with the "empowerment" approach of DAWN[18]

---

living within one country and the existing forms of discrimination became visible (Ruf 1996: 20-26).
18 DAWN was founded in 1984 by 22 women in Bangalore such as Neuma Aguiar (Brazil), Zubeida Ahmad (Pakistan), Peggy Antrobus (Barbados), Lourdes Aripe

(Development Alternatives with Women for a New Era) a new concept for development from a women's globalised perspective by combining global economic, political and social contexts with everyday lives, and new insights into the international debate on development were set. It is the first theoretical approach developed from actual experiences and research by women from the South and was first presented in Nairobi in 1985. The approach of DAWN overcomes the idea that women should be added or implemented into development as it is practised in most development approaches. Development as a process should be carried by women at local level and strategies have to be developed by women themselves. As central actors they are able to formulate their own concepts of development according to their specific context of living. With the self-definition of women, they turn the picture of women as a passive, unknowing "object" into "knowing, active subjects" (Knorr-Cetina 1981: 4). Development should not only be carried out by women themselves, but the strategies of women should focus on structural change at different levels of society. The core issue is the change in unequal gender-relations, but goes beyond this by transforming and restructuring social institutions such as the market, the state and civil society (Sen/Grown 1987: 10). In particular women's organizations in their different forms as traditional, worker-based organizations, externally founded organizations, grassroots associations, with affiliation to a political party and research organizations have the capacities for the constitution of civil society (Sen/Grown 1987: 90-92). Not isolation, but rather co-operation through networking between women's organizations is expected as the main force in empowerment processes (vgl. Sen/Grown 1987).

The approach of DAWN was innovative and remains a vision and exceptional today in its formulation. With the production and dissemination of their knowledge, the women of DAWN expected inspiration for transformative processes at the local, national and global level. The "empowerment" approach became a central holistic strategy in feminist agendas in the North and in the South, and is meant more as a paradigmatic and less a normative or dogmatic approach. Development implies the notion of diversity instead of difference as well as the acknowledgement of a multiplicity of feminisms. In mainstream development politics as of the World Bank, the empowerment approach has been taken up and reduced to gender-planning, therefore depoliticised leaving power aspect in development planning aside (Kerner 1999: 104).

At the end of the decade the World-Wide Women's Web itself had gradually become a product and a motor of globalization. The number of partici-

---

(Mexico), Nirmala Banerjee (India), Carmen Barroso (Brasilien), Ela Bhatt (India), Noelen Heyzer (Malaysia), Hameeda Hossain (Bangladesh), Devaki Jain (India), Kumari Jayawardene (Sri Lanka), Isabel Larguia (Cuba), Ranghild Lund (Norway), Geertje Lycklama (Netherlands), Lucille Mair (Jamaica), Kaherine McKee (U.S.A.), Fatima Mernissi (Morocco), Achola Pala Okeyo (Kenya), Marie-Angelique Savane (Senegal), Gita Sen (India), Claire Slatter (Fiji).

pants increased from 6,000 at the first NGO forum, where 114 NGO's joined the official conference, to 14,000 at the third NGO forum. The fourth World Women's Conference in Beijing/Huairou in 1995, more than 30,000 people and 3,000 NGO's participated (Clark/Friedman/Hochstetler 1998: 9; Fraser 1987: 58). At the beginning of the 21st century the World-Wide Women's Web covered extensive parts of Africa, Asia, Australia, North- and South America, the Caribbean and Europe, while the dynamics of expansion and the process of networking is still going on at all levels.

Not only is the number of participants an indicator of the growing density of global interactions; the mutual perception and cultural stigmatisation based on binary concepts between women from the South and the North has changed. During the first conference in 1975, the concepts of autonomy of women from diverse cultural backgrounds dominated and hindered communication. In 1980 cultural separation was articulated and worked on as a boundary of cross-cultural exchange and communication. With the abandoning of the "myth of a global sisterhood" (Basu 1995: 3) and the holistic approach of DAWN in 1985 a common basis for further co-operation and communication with the articulation of common grounds *and* diversity was established (Von Braunmühl 1998: 93; Wichterich 2000: 259).

In Beijing in 1995 the North/South, East/West relationship was overcome, but new conservative and religious trends were splitting the movements (Lachenmann 1996: 11). Between the common platforms at the "big" conferences, multiple "small" but no less important women permanently formed networks and new organizations via workshops, forums and meetings and established spaces of interaction between and across short and long distances. The process of interaction between the global and the local can be characterised as a vertical going into culture and a horizontal crossing of cultures. The actors nowadays are women from the North, South, East and West as ethnic minority women, immigrant women, academics, rural women, women refugees, women belonging to different religious faiths, political ideologies, social classes and cultures (Mc Laughlin 1995: 83).

To summaries: the original development of the World-Wide Women's Web started under the auspices of the UN from which it has gradually freed itself. The UN system did not function as a vehicle for change but rather as a vehicle, which is now driven by women themselves. The original international relation is, nowadays, institutionalised on a transnational basis between organizations, which implies the continuity of density of collaboration.

1.3 Global and Cross-National Networking

The networking of local, regional and national women's organizations through linking nation-wide towards global horizontal networks has developed a dynamism of its own and has become institutionalised through organizational structures without having lost its innovativeness: in 1974 women founded *ISIS* focusing on health, population politics and empowerment, which was initially based in Geneva and Rome and later dispersed into decentralised organizations to southern locations such as Manila, Santiago de Chile and Kampala. Under the name *WLD* (Women, Law and Development) in 1979 an organization of women dealing with the field of women's rights was set up with its main office in Washington, D.C. As already indicated, set up in 1984 *DAWN*, was initially attached to the University of Barbados acting as an organization of academics and politically active women concerning the broad issue of empowerment and transformation processes. Meanwhile it too has decentralised structures within five regions of the world. With the approach of the UNCED process, women all over the world founded *WEDO* (Women, Environment and Development Organization) located in New York, but attached to many women's organizations such as the Greenbelt movement in Kenya. As a northern institution located in Brussels and concerned with the issue of women's economic rights since 1985, *WIDE* (Women in Development Europe) operates by lobbying national and international politics. The perspective is oriented to changing trade and economic processes within and between Northern and Southern countries. World-wide relations are not, however, structured by the North-South collaboration alone, the relations between women's organizations in the South-South context and particularly within the women's rights movement are also involved: *CLADEM* (Comité de America Latina y el Caribe para la defensa de los derechos de la mujer) headquatered in Peru, *WiLDAF* (Women in Law and Development Africa) based in Zimbabwe and *APWLD* (Asian Pacific Women in Law and Development) located in Thailand. These transnational relations are also connected to regional organizations such as *APWIP* (Asian Pacific Women in Politics), a network established in 1990 between women from Korea, Thailand and the Philippines. Since the recent political transformations in Eastern Europe, women have begun to take up political issues by forming networks and organizations such as *Ecojuris* focusing on aspects of the environment and law in Moscow.

Those glocal organizations have built up their own research capacities and/or are affiliated to universities or research institutes, which transforms the organizations into female "think tanks" by developing their own context-specific approaches to development and by realising projects and programs based on their own scientific knowledge production. The variety of themes reflect the need of women to articulate their particular local experience by transcending it onto the global level and by hybridising and homogenising it at the global level to formulate global programmatic strategies for alternative forms of developments. The production of knowledge within those global organizations is channelled into a mechanism based on cycles: the integration of lifeworld knowledge is transformed at a global level and disseminated through decentralised structures by splitting the organizations themselves into regional offices such as DAWN[19] or ISIS, regional focal points or through structural collaboration with national or regional networks. Lifeworld knowledge becomes, as Giddens has called it, "disembedded" (1990: 21) through the lifting out of social relations from local contexts of interactions and "re-embedded" into new social relations at a global level.

The continuity of this global-local circulation is further manifested through the internal organization. Members constituting the global board of directors are at the same time members of regional organizations in different parts of the world. For example: the board of directors of Women in Law and Development International (Washington, D.C.) is composed of 18 members from the USA, Ghana, Trinidad and Tobago, Bulgaria, Sudan, Colombia, Pakistan etc. At an individual level Noellen Heyzer is, in addition, a member of DAWN, executive director of UNIFEM and working for an NGO in Malaysia. Or Akua Kuenehiya, Dean of the Law Faculty at the University of Ghana, is also a member of WiLDAF Ghana.

The form of communication within and between the levels differs: at the global level, the use of electronic media such as the Internet transfers the locality into a de-territorialised space. Almost all glocal organizations and networks have their own home-page and use the Internet as a technical medium for social interactions and for supporting communication[20]. Women's organizations in South America currently use the Internet to pose their virtual common agenda, which substitutes for personal meetings and also reduces expensive travel costs. In Russia women's organizations established a common virtual platform in 1993, the "Open Women Line" for exchanging information on women's movements, rights, gender studies and social issues[21]. At national level and towards local level, meetings, workshops and forums are platforms, where women meet on a regular basis. In addition, women are using different channels of communication such as radio or theatre, through which "connected" women dispersed information to "unconnected" groups (Farwell/Wood/James/Banks 1999: 106).

The current tendency of women's movements to be local and global at the same time shifted the current perspective to political activities now at local level. After twenty-five years of networking and organising towards global level, women have realised that change has to start at the bottom. ISIS when

---

19 In the year 2000 DAWN has offices in five regions: Caribbean, Asia, Latin America, Africa and Pacific (www.dawn.org.fj).
20 In 1990, the Association for Progressive Communications (APC) set up a Women's Networking Support Programme financed with grants from the International Development Research Centre, Ottawa, to support the women's organizations world-wide with new electronic media and to facilitate communication (Fawell/Wood/James/ Banks 1999: 102ff.).
21 Personal notes at the conference "Zukunftswerkstatt: 25 Jahre Internationale Frauenpolitik", Heinrich-Böll-Stiftung, 13./14. Oktober 2000, Bonn.

Figure 1: The World Wide Women's Web

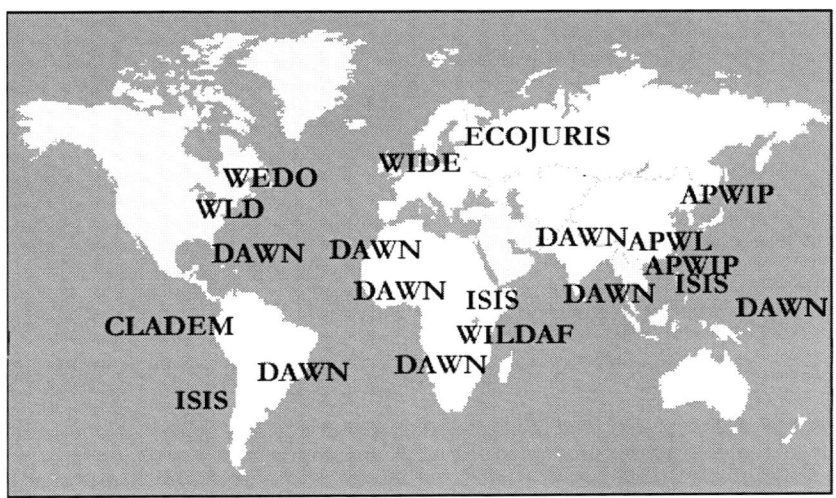

moving from a northern to a southern context exemplifies just how difficult the work of such a glocalised network at the bottom can become. In 1993, the head office of ISIS moved from Geneva (Switzerland) to Kampala (Uganda). The objectives, strategies and actions were embedded in a global feminist perspective. With the move to Kampala the aim was to strengthen the link between local women's organizations. While searching for funds, the argument put out by international donor agencies for refusing it was that the international orientation did not fit into their local projects. The global perspective does not correspond with mainstream local development perspectives. Similarly the organization was labelled as local which made it only acceptable for funds from national and regional offices. "Being rooted in a Southern situation, we were discovering, it is not any longer possible to be international" (Porter/Verghese 1999: 139). The stereotyping of a women's organization in the southern context as local means that it cannot work with a global perspective. "Here lies the tension: the donor definition of what constitutes acceptable work in gender and development risks effectively silencing the voices of international organizations in the South" (Porter/Verghese 1999: 136), which means that the perception of dichotomic social relationships into divided, disconnected lifeworlds continues by defining the practices of women to an artificially bounded local place. It also exemplifies the contradictions and ambiguities between predefined concepts of development and a social environment which has already changed.

What have the women's movements achieved at international level so far? At international level, statements and resolutions have been acknowledged but are rarely realised. One success is that women are gradually being recognised by international development institutions as subjects of development and not mere objects (Lachenmann 1998: 226). The change of mainstream paradigms and transformation is still on the agenda. Rhetoric has often paid lip service, and programs and projects on the practical side are still – with some exceptions – conceptualised within the WID approach, which means that women are only added to development, separated from men, and remain helpless, "vulnerable" others, with the ignorance of the knowledgeability of women. Evaluations of development projects, conducted in the 1980s and 1990s come to the conclusion that women are silenced or restricted to their "traditional" activities even in gender-analysis (Goetz 1991: 140). When projects are planned and priorities set as regards national development goals, women were almost completely absent. Targeting women for special treatment still excludes them from mainstream development activities. Besides a very slight "blurring" of the borders between feminist agendas and the international development agendas, there exist contradictions and ambiguities which indicate the minimum of reflection on feminist/women's agendas and its incorporation into their programs. At times of a shortcut in expenses, some development organizations such as the Canadian CIDA, known for supporting women's organizations with a feminist agenda (as ISIS) stopped with grants. Up to now, most programs avoid transformation aspects in their work and de-politicize the programmatic and transformative approach of women's organizations (Porter 1999: 9). This policy is highly criticised by Ghanaian women activists and as its argumentation will be taken up in Chapter 8.

Cross-boundary networking in Africa between women's organizations is also a new phenomenon and has emerged out of the context of the World Women's Conferences. In the aftermath of the Third World Women's Conference in Nairobi, which was followed by several small regional meetings and workshops, the issue of networking and collaboration across nations came up and built the frame for the establishment of pan-African women's organizations. Back in 1975 in Addis Ababa, *ATRAC* (African Training and Research Centre for Women) attached as part of the UN was set up and formed a kind of umbrella organization for research on African women dealing with topics such as technology or trade. One of the first pan-African networks was *AAWORD* (African Women's Association for Research on Development) formed in 1977 in Senegal as an autonomous organization which deals with the theoretical and practical aspects of development and is active in the organization of seminars, publicity and in supporting research. Research on environment and transformation is also the object of *WEDNET* (Women, Environment and Development Network) which was launched in 1989 and has set up a research program in eight anglo- and francophone countries[22] with regard to women's knowledge in the management of natural resources (symbolized in figure 2 with a tree). This approach combines scientific research with a policy agenda and the publications of WedNews (Jommo, 1993:

---

22 These countries are Burkina Faso, Ghana, Kenya, Senegal, Sudan, Kongo, Zambia and Zimbabwe (Jommo 1993: 162-163).

155). In addition *REFAD* (Réseau Sous-Régional Femmes Africaines et Droits Humainés) in Burkina Faso was set up in 1993 with the objectives of publicity, research and publications in the field of women and law. Nowadays *WiLDAF* (Women in Law and Development Africa) based in Harare/Zimbabwe is one of the biggest networks, having evolved in 1990 and meanwhile expanding to cover 26 African countries.

In recent times academic research networks reach out beyond Africa such as those between Ghana, Pakistan and Switzerland dealing with studies on gender, resource management and social reproduction. The fruitfulness of cross-cultural exchange lies in the comparison of similar situations, such as on the issue of land rights, e.g. women in Switzerland hardly have access to land since it is mostly inherited by men compared to Ghana where both men and women are entiteld to have access to land (vgl. Harcourt 1997). Knowledge partnerships to build up a mutual exchange of research experience between the Humboldt-University (Berlin) and Ahfad University for Women (Khartoum/Sudan) dealing with topics related to gender and development are institutionalised. In a common workshop[23] on aspects of methodology and problems of empirical field work in urban and rural settings conducted by foreign and local researchers on topics such as women's reproductive rights, career patterns, micro-credits and social security systems in Sudan (Klein-Hessling 2000: 7-16) it became obvious that academic knowledge itself is becoming a globalised product as it is no longer bounded to the exclusive production of knowledge in a national context, but transcending instead national and continental borders.

Finally reaching the national level in Ghana, two glo*c*al organizations as FIDA (Federation of Womens Lawyers)[24] and WiLDAF are institutionalised. The NCWD (National Council of Women and Development) as the umbrella organization of all national women's organizations, has offices in all regions as well as the 31st December Women's Movement with branches in rural communities. At the first monthly meeting of the Women's Forum organised by the National Council of Women and Development and which I attended in the capital of Ghana, Accra, and – here is the beginning of my fieldwork – the range of women's representatives from different organizations came as a surprise. Women came from religious groups such as the Church of the Mother's Union in the Anglican Diocese of Accra, the Ahmadiyya Muslim Women's Association, from unions such as the Powerqueens of the Electricity Company of Ghana, the Ghana Medical Women's organization, beadsmakers, mar-

---

23 The Workshop had the title "Methodology of Gender Research and Local Development Concepts" and took place on 11.-12. November 1999 at the University of Bielefeld, organised by the Gender Division of the Sociology of Development Research Centre at University of Bielefeld (Klein-Hessling 2000: 2).
24 I have not taken FIDA into consideration during my research, since its exclusive focus on law would have given my topic another direction on the complex issue of law and women's rights.

Figure 2: The African Women's Web

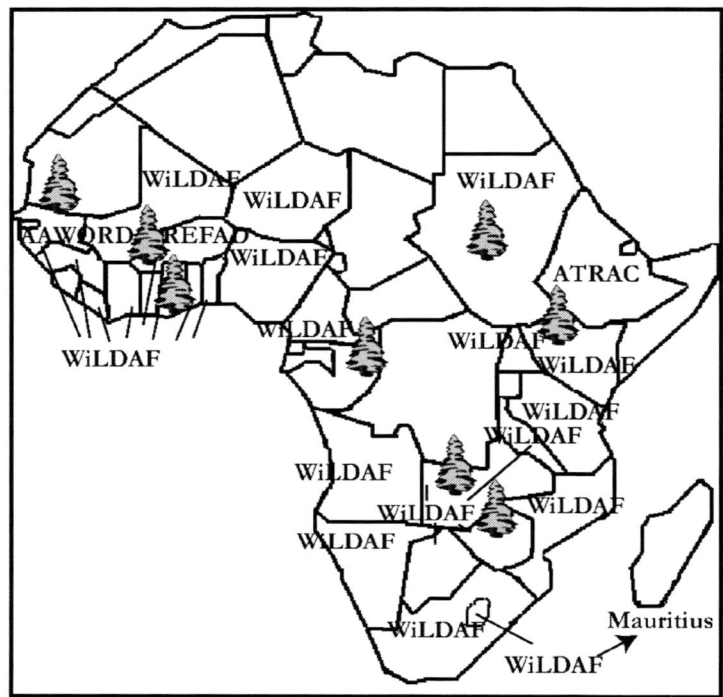

ket organizations, the African Women's Bank, universities, research institutes as well as women representing suburban organizations in Accra such as the La Women's Organization or the Teshi Women's Society.

Aware that those Women's Forums are an important platform for discussion, after I had visited twice, I thought that the urban setting and the closeness to ministries and international NGO's would be the reason for the number of organizations. When I went to Sunyani, the capital of the Brong-Ahafo region, about 300 kilometres away from Accra, and visited the office of the National Council of Women and Development, the representative told me that she had just started by organising a monthly Women's Forum. At the first meeting I attended there, the sheer number of women coming from more than 30 organizations was even more astonishing.

The picture was rather different in the rural town of Susuanso, where I stayed for 10 months from November 1998 to August 1999, and where I was also expecting forms of formal organizations. In fact I started off wondering why there seemed to be no other association in town apart from two church groups, such as the Christian Mother's Association and the Presbyterian Women Fellowship. The existing kinship ties at village level are the main context for collective activity, assistance and daily interactions. But informal gatherings across kinship women, who are the female heads of their families, established a local social movement, something which takes a longer time to "discover" than the formal organizations referred above.

Now that I have reached the local level, I would like to briefly summarise the descriptions above. The frame of reference for the flow of knowledge goes along the different levels of organizations which connect the local with the global level and vice versa. Those organizations or informal gatherings are the framework for interactions between women. However, it is not the frame which defines the practices, but the practices which define the framework, while size and form thereof remain flexible.

2 Doing Research and Writing Wor(l)ds

2.1 Setting of Research

Doing research is a complex arrangement between researcher and actors in the field, which is expressed in mutual perceptions, daily interactions, and the location of the researcher in the social context of the field. As one of the first social anthropologists who conducted research in Melanesia, Rhodesia and Hollywood, while comparing and reflecting on the different research situations, Hortense Powdermaker suggested in 1966 that "a scientific discussion of fieldwork should include considerable detail about the observer: the role he plays, his personality, and other relevant facts concerning his position and functioning in the society studied" (1966: 9). Research arrangements considerably depend on positioning oneself in the field, the aims of study and daily interactions outside the defined aim. The classical issue of *Women in the Field* (Golde 1986) is not necessarily restricted to aspects of sex and gender, but also takes class, marriage status and ethnicity into consideration. The importance of a discussion of the mutual constitution of the "context of discovery" (Knorr-Cetina 1991: 19) encompasses the researcher's location in the specific locality, the process of information accessibility, gathering and textualisation which makes the discovery a social process instead of a singular one. A discussion on entering the field and my positioning reveals some logic of the field. The subjective position not only puts the researcher into a relative position, but also turns the interaction patterns to deal with it in an objective way (Schütz 1962: 43). This follows the methodological postulate of Schütz (1962: 43) to the effect that inquired data is always influenced by the researcher's aim, as well as social sciences and the results are constructed out of and refer to subjective meaning contexts: the ones of the actors, who have their own pre-interpreted world in everyday life, and one's own position.

When I came to Ghana, the decision about where to conduct my fieldwork was not clearly made. What mainly influenced my arbitrary decision to choose the Brong-Ahafo region was the institution of Queenmothers. Although it is a common institution in southern parts of Ghana, it is non existent in the three northern regions of Upper East, Upper West and Northern.

When I contacted the German Technical Co-operation office in Accra, they advised me to get in touch with their office in Sunyani, the capital of the Brong-Ahafo region, where Elisabeth Poyari, a politically active woman in 31st DWM, working in the field of improving post-harvest-systems, introduced me to the administrative team and to several politicians at the regional ministries and offices as well as at the district assemblies in Sunyani and Bechem.

But more importantly, she took me to three villages and introduced me to the group of farmers with whom she was working. Of these three villages I chose Susuanso. The town did not appear to be either too rural or too urban with a well-developed infrastructure as regards electricity, water wells and public transport links. About 3,000 people live in Susuanso and the town is built almost symmetrically on the left and right of the main street. The Susuan river, which is dry for most of the year, "flows" close to the town. With two schools – the Roman Catholic and the Presbyterian Primary Schools – several churches, a market, some small shops such as a drug store and some kiosks along the street sides, the town does not distinguish itself from many other towns I have visited in the region.

The economy of the Brong-Ahafo[1] region is based on agriculture and timber production. The main food crops are yam, cassava, plantain, tomatoes and garden eggs with maize as the main cash crop. Since 1984/85 when a drought and bushfire destroyed almost all of the cocoa-farms in the region, the production of cocoa has declined. While it was once the most important cash crop, nowadays it has virtually lost its significance and has, to a certain degree, been replaced by maize. With the government implementation of structural adjustment programs and economic recovery programs during the 1980s, accompanied by a decline in agricultural production, the rise in the cost of living has led to increasing poverty. Although an inhabitant of Susuanso told me that people in town did not actually consider themselves "poor" until the government started with its poverty alleviation schemes in the 1990s.

Most people in Susuanso are farmers and only a few are employed as civil servants such as teachers working in one of the two schools or in a government department in Sunyani or Bechem. Women are taking over labour-intensive farming tasks[2] and trying to cope with the severe economic conditions by supplementing their daily activities through trading, selling crops, preparing and selling food, sewing, storekeeping, hair-dressing etc. Despite women having multiple jobs, the income often remains very small. Many young men and husbands are absent, partly because of daily, seasonal or constant migration, whereby they search for jobs in other rural agricultural parts of Ghana as labourers, in the bigger cities such as Kumasi and Accra, or even migrate to foreign countries such as Canada, Great Britain, Austria or Italy. Some husbands leave their families behind; some have them follow at a later stage. It was a common feature for most families to have a relative somewhere abroad, whether a son or daughter with whom they are staying in more or less intensive contact.

---

1 Land of the Brong-Ahafo region is supposed to be the most fertile in Ghana, terming the region the "food-cradle" of the country.
2 Figures present a percentage of about 70 % of all women (2.8 million) working in the agricultural sector (Tsikata 1989: 57).

During my first visit to Susuanso, I made contact with Mr. and Mrs. Mensah, both farmers, who supported my decision to reside in Susuanso. I then had to ask the Chief and the elders for permission to reside in the town. During a meeting, which is usually held on Tuesdays, I explained the reason for my mission: that I was from a German university and wished to do a study on "women's knowledge and culture". For their part, they were interested in my reasons for choosing Ghana from so many other countries. I explained that I had studied in Switzerland, where I had obtained my first degree and during which time I had often gone to the library and the archives of the "Mission-House" in Basle, where I read a lot of books about Ghana and gradually became interested in the country. My interest therefore was awoken by literature and I wanted to know more about the people.

Some days later I received the message that I was welcomed to stay. Meanwhile they had organised a place for me to stay and I finally moved to the house of Yaw Boakye and Nana Ama. At that time Yaw Boakye was working for the Ghana Cocoa Board and Nana Ama was a hairdresser with her own shop. Both had gone to secondary school and were fluent in English. I had a very close relationship with Nana Ama who was just two years older than me. Born in Susuanso, Yao Boakye had spent almost his whole life there, whereas Ama was originally from Dormaa-Ahenkro, a town near the Ivory-Coast border and had moved to Susuanso where she was brought up by her grandmother. Their house was newly built and comprised of several rooms. I had my own room with electricity and a porch, and I could make myself comfortable. The house was some distance from the town but you could still hear and see what was going on yet it was far enough to withdraw to a quiet place when I was tired and wanted to rest or be by myself. During the entire time I spent there, I was not once burdened with the preparation of food or cooking. *"As part of the family you have to eat with us"*, Ama proposed on the first day. Whenever she prepared food for herself, her husband, her grandmother and the two fostered girls who also stayed in our house, she included me. Ama also advised me on how to dress properly but there was never any social pressure on this. My preferred Western style T-shirts and trousers gradually changed to Ghanaian clothes, in which I did not feel too comfortable at first, because of the multi-color designs. But I gradually got used to it and the positive reactions of other people made me realise that they liked it, especially when I went for an interview at government departments or when I was attending meetings.

It was not a personal problem for me to be a single woman in town. Being enclosed in different personal networks and in Ama's family, I never felt lonely. Neither my unmarried status nor that I had not yet given birth to a child had any influence from my point of view on the research process. To overcome the "lack" of not having a child and because I was often seen together with the eleven-year old daughter of a friend, people started referring to Eva as "my daughter". My unmarried status was a subject of entertainment for some women and a reason for joking. One day when I was sitting at a corner on the side street, a woman came to me loudly accusing me of being in love with her husband. Before I even realised what her accusation was about, she left. Once I had collected my thoughts, I ran around the corner where I saw her standing. I went over to her and explained that it was not possible for me to be in love with her husband, as I did not even know him. My explanation was just another reason for her to laugh at me again. Even Ama tried to convince me to marry her brother, which involved me in another struggle to maintain my unmarried status. Because the topic of marriage was sometimes so prominent, I thought for a long time, that my unmarried status would be an obstacle. So I was all the more surprised, when I met a female American Ph.D. student who was researching some miles away and we discussed our various experiences. She told me that her status dropped when her husband came to visit her from the USA. She was no longer seen as an independent woman, but as his wife who was financially dependent on him!

During the research process I worked together with male assistants. Most people in town could hardly speak English and my understanding of the local language Twi (a tonal language, whose words sound very alike) was not sufficient to conduct an interview by myself, particularly when I commenced my fieldwork. At the beginning I was working with a younger man who was a relative of Mr. Mensah and was asked by him to assist me. After two months we stopped our cooperation, owing to the difficulties and problems arising during the working process and which, unfortunately, could not be solved. After a research break of two weeks, my language teacher, who gave me lessons in Twi, took over and we worked together until the end. Mr. Asante-Dompfe, who was an inhabitant of the town, had studied European History at the University of Cape Coast and was now working as a teacher in a secondary school. He was also the president of the Roman Catholic Church and a well-respected person in town, to whom people went for advice and help. Because he did his own research on fetish priests for his diploma at the university he was, to a degree, familiar with the methods and the research process as such. He adopted the role of my teacher while I became his pupil or young innocent student. With the ignorance of a stranger, I was in a position of advantage and able to ask naive questions or beg for clarification. To a certain degree, he also influenced my work, suggesting whom I could further interview or what I should also take into consideration. For example, he advised me to go to a female fetish-priest who lived some miles away from the town to do an interview with her.

During the interviews, he asked questions that he was interested in or what he thought would be of importance to me. Gradually every research step was discussed between us. He was also a personal adviser, as for some unknown reason, my moods tended to be up and down.

At the beginning I was skeptical about working together with a male assistant. I feared that the women interviewed would withhold secrets because of the presence of a man. Therefore I also conducted an interview with Ama's grandmother with Ama acting as the interpreter. I asked the same questions as in an interview the day before and to my surprise the content of information did not differ. Gendered co-operation with an older man was in this case not a disadvantage but rather created a fruitful working situation permitting an exchange of mutual experiences across cultures and gender. We both learned about the historical past of the town and its cultural changes and he often admitted that he had not known "*this or that*" before, reacting in a more astonished way than within a negative attitude towards the past and "tradition". At the end he asked me for my tape recorder in order to conduct a study on the history of the town. And I have to be honest that I learned more about the past of his town, than he learned from my knowledge about German or European history. His questions such as "*What was it like under Bismarck ?* " or "*Tell me something about Napoleon*" were only partially answered or I avoided answering then while searching for excuses for my ignorance. The people in town regarded me as a student conducting a study on "*our culture*" and working at a university. For most men and women my purpose was understandable. They defined my interest in "*our way of living*" which encompassed all aspects of life including agriculture. Although it was the most exhausting work I had ever done, I accepted offers mainly from women to go with them to their farms to weed or collect food. I then took advantage of such situations to hold informal conversations about topics on land-ownership, inheritance, methods of cultivation, changing food situations etc.

With my status of as a student, a single woman and my often-underestimated age, I was not really considered "rich". When questions were posed regarding my financial support and I said that I received some money from the government, people mostly answered "[...] *but you are a student, and because there is no husband around, so you do not have any money*"[3]. Of special importance was the way gifts were exchanged. Often when I came home, I found some fruits or food on my porch. After finding out who the donor was, I went to thank him/her and availed of the next best opportunity to respond with a gift, e.g. in the form of bread or photos I was asked to take. Sometimes I knew the donor, sometimes it was a stranger. The exchange of gifts is not only a form of establishing relationships and reciprocity. The contact and approaches often assume a one-sided process of "going native" by the researcher alone, a mutual process of making a stranger an inhabitant of the town with the result that it sometimes difficult to maintain some distance. I never heard any remark about myself as a female researcher, and when I asked friends if they had heard anything about this they denied it. Gender as such did not – at least from my point of view – influence my access to information in any negative way. Apart from the Chief's palace, where special secret meetings are not open to women, there were no public or private restrictions on me or for any Ghanaian woman. Nor even is there any clear cut division of gender in public or in private spaces or forms of seclusion. During the

---

3   It was only once that somebody asked for money. Apart from the way I was perceived, it is not polite to ask a white person for money.

day, the domestic sphere is opened to the public. Most rectangular houses have big open doors, which lead to the central compound. Just by symbolically knocking (expressing of some words) or by calling somebody, one can go inside or pass the door to take a quick look at what is going on inside. The compound is the main working area for washing and drying clothes, cooking and preparing food for consumption and sale. Only at night do people withdraw to their small rooms, which are usually stuffed with a bed, a table, some chairs, a wardrobe, a refrigerator, a radio and sometimes a TV.

During the day, women dominate public spaces. Whether in the market, at the water pipe where women use to collect money, along the streets, where women sell food as kenkey, fried fish, or porridge, they are more present than men in terms of number. It is common to see women sitting in bars, pubs or under a shady tree, drinking beer or spirits such as local gin or soft drinks like Coca-Cola and it is not a topic for local discussions. The presence of women in public was striking at the beginning and almost scared me. In a letter[4] to a friend in Switzerland I wrote enthusiastically that I had discovered a women's town, so I felt comfortable there. On the other hand, I kept wondering "how to find the gender aspect". The atmosphere of openness and freedom of movement created lots of space for interaction and communication. For the aim of my research and for my own personal freedom, movement and contact were not limited and I could move without any barriers within the village and its surroundings.

2.2 The Interview Partners and Situations

Although people in the town were not use to interview situations, nobody refused an interview or showed any negative attitude towards one. Most of the interviews were conducted in the interview partner's compound during the evenings when people had time after finishing their supper and after they had finished their daily activities. The atmosphere was in most cases relaxed with situations only differing depending on the number of people participating. Sometimes we gathered with family members who listened in silence or participated with comments.

The older people were especially eager to give an interview with the explanation that people are not usually interested in the past and nobody listens to them. One time when we were interviewing an elderly woman, another older woman, whom we had interviewed the day before came to visit her. Both started talking about the "olden days" and began to sing and dance the way they used to a long time ago. The whole situation changed to an event

---

4 Instead of writing a diary I preferred to write letters. Being back home it was interesting to get to know the reactions of the addressed people on how they perceived my situation. I was astonished on my over-emphasising of negative impressions, as e.g. the beating of children, but I assume that the writing of letters was a way of dealing with personal moments of stress.

which was a lively impression of a past activity[5]. It also happened that an old woman told me that she was not going to answer any of my questions but would rather talk about the history of the people. Being overpowered by her argument, I obeyed and it was only later that I became aware of the importance of her explanations.

It was rather the opposite with younger people who were very shy and nervous. They relaxed during the interview situations and gradually felt more comfortable. In cases when I conducted the interviews by myself, I tried to make the situation more "informal", more like a conversation or by letting them decide where we would sit together and talk. Nevertheless, it was usually impossible to overcome the tension altogether and particularly in the presence of Mr. Asante-Dompfe, they felt shy answering questions which were similar to a classroom situation.

The semi-structured interviews were recorded on tape and transcribed the next morning. I went over the interviews again, looking for open questions or misunderstandings and in several cases I had to go back to the interviewee again.

With people of my own age, I interacted in daily conversations as when gathering in the evening in front of Ama's shop where women in particular met, or at a special corner frequented by males in Susuanso, which we named "Political Corner" because we discussed plenty of political issues: German or Ghanaian politics, "delicate" issues such as the women's movement or polygyny. The place was not restricted to men; women frequently joined it too, but were usually absent due to their lack of time during the late afternoon when women are busy preparing food and cooking. I did notice down those conversations when I was back in my room and although it was "harder" to remember the detailed information and explanations, the informal style of conversation was more open and less exhausting than the formal interviews.

At the district and regional level, the majority of interviewees were men working at government offices. Most of them remembered me from the introductory visit I had paid to them some weeks before in the company of Elizabeth Poyari. Some were already familiar with interview situations and asked immediately for the "questionnaire" which means a standardised guide of questions written on sheet of paper which they just had to fill out. After I explained my interview method, they were skeptical, but agreed to co-operate. I also recorded the interviews. At the end of every interview – after I had stopped taping – I asked my interview partners if they had any questions for me. In most cases they were interested in my eating habits and in my marital status. Having dispensed with the formality of an interview, they started talking much more openly and gave an insight into their personal opinion. Sometimes these sessions ended in long discussions covering political, economic, gender or personal topics.

---

5   The meaning of the dance will be described in Chapter 4.3.2 *"To drive the sickness out of town"*.

I once invited the six Subqueenmothers of the town for a group discussion. As female heads of their families they were restricted to family matters and were not allowed to attend the meetings at the Chief's palace. Based on interviews with individual Subchiefs and Subqueenmothers conducted some weeks before I detected some contradictions in their answers – especially as regards the issue of permission for Subqueenmothers to attend meetings at the palace.

Four of the six Subqueenmothers[6] joined the meeting which took place on a Sunday afternoon in the compound of "my" house. During the discussion they suddenly asked me if I would be able to assist them in obtaining admission to the meetings at the Chief's palace. An issue they had already been pursuing for years without any success. I promised to help them but felt uncomfortable and uncertain. It was not only the situation "Subject-Object" which was changing direction, but I was also asking myself who was to give me the authority to change political structures and "tradition". What would happen if the Chiefs were to ask me why I had come to change things ? What would happen if they got angry ? I was in rather a dilemma trying to help the Subqueenmothers within their intention of "self-empowerment". On the other hand I knew that if they were able to join the meetings, they would be in a position to influence political decisions. But I was afraid to intervene in local issues where I would probably create an atmosphere and bring both them and myself into difficulties. This unintended action[7] was only reduced by the thought that my research would in any case be finished soon. Together we went to the Chief and asked him to organise a meeting with the Subchiefs and Queenmother. We explained the purpose of the discussion which he accepted. The meeting took place two weeks later and the final decision was made at a later stage by which time I had already left Ghana: in future the Subqueenmothers were to be permitted to join the meetings. Their strategy of using me changed my situation as an "honoured guest" (Golde 1986: 8) to a crosscultural broker. This situation indicates that research is far more than a process of pure thinking or a technical means of gathering data. Interactions involve the whole person, in the same way as in everyday life with the mind and the body. The researcher uses him/herself as an instrument with personal features for communication through listening, talking, feeling and acting. This embodied instrument is two-fold: I was not the only person studying people, they were also studying me. This double embodiment of a researcher being

---

6 Two were absent with excuses. One Subqueenmother was visiting a family member, the other Subqueenmother was attending a funeral.
7 This unintended action research turns the researcher into an activist researcher. The German feminist Maria Mies suggests using this approach of "consciousness raising" during the research process as a way of overcoming structural inequalities (Wieringa 1995: 30). From my point of view this approach is highly problematic, because the situation can easily become uncontrolled and by the worsening of the situation can certainly influence the process of further research in a negative way or even lead to its end.

the subject and object at the same time causes a partial "hybrid identity" (Hirschauer/Amann 1997: 26). Not only the researcher studies and analysis, but also the same happens to him/her. This partial "hybrid identity" does not mean the "loss of self or the instability of self" or a "weakness of one' identity" (Moore 1994: 115), but reveals the complexity of fieldwork and through mutual observations and interactions the construction between the "Self" and "Others" which is definitely a process of switching relationship and not a structure. I assume, it is exactly this partial "hybrid identity" which creates the space for dialogue and communication and turns the objects of research into subjects as well. Space in the sense that the outcomes of research are co-determined and to a certain degree controlled by the subjects under research, based on the condition of a more "egalitarian" relationship of exchange within research. The neutral "objective" position of a researcher, who observes the community from the outside with binoculars as it is conceptualised by researchers following the claims of participatory approaches (vgl. Schönhuth/Kievelitz 1993) is a myth and is rather cementising unequal relations instead of dissolving them. And finally it denies the accountability of the researcher to those researched.

I conducted three biographical interviews with women engaged in women's organizations in the Brong-Ahafo region. Despite the fact that they do not live in Susuanso, they strongly influence the lives of rural women through their activities at regional level e.g. in changing inheritance laws. The interviews were extremely intensive and personal, and the interview situations took place after I had met the women several times.

Other interviews with people living outside the region such as in Accra or near Kumasi were only problematic from a logistic point of view as trying to make an appointment on a fixed date via a phone[8] call was sometimes a time-consuming activity and it was helpful to have personal contacts for short-distance contacts e.g. giving a written message to one of the taxi drivers, who passed it on in a snowball system to another driver until it reached the specific person. Even with those persons I met for a single interview only as e.g. the organiser of WiLDAF in Ghana or a former president of the National House of Chiefs the interview situations were open and even though they were busy with other visitors, they took their time to answer my questions.

2.3 From the Process of Fieldwork to the Process of Writing: Politics, Representation and Reflexivity

Stepping out of the field and returning to my university in Germany was accompanied by several difficulties. The daily form of verbal communication

---

8 Since there was no telephone in Susuanso, I had to travel to Sunyani and to call from a communication centre.

and interaction changed to a situation of silent reading and writing. My feeling of loneliness was at first overwhelming and only slowly became a familiar companion. Despite working groups, seminars and colloquia at the university, the rapid change in my personal world made it a burden to start writing. Books written by other people or studies conducted by my colleagues seemed to be much more interesting than my own empirical data. It was like a piece of hot charcoal, which I hardly dared to touch. I required much more time to stop underestimating my own data after my return. The first step into the library was a shock although I had frequented that place regularly for the last eight years. As if I had never read a scientific book before, the language seemed to be so abstract that I wondered how I could ever be able to understand the thoughts of the writer and the meaning of the book. The difficulties in understanding the scientific language made me more aware of the form of presentation of my material and the artificial division between everyday and scientific language. The transformation of language from the construction of reality to a further construction of the construction of reality with our vocabulary of scientific words, made me struggle to find out a way out of the cage of scientific language before I finally realised that I would lose it.

The process of textualisation (Moore 1994: 108), the constant reflection on and criticism of the creation process of a new form of knowledge, which starts with the first fieldnote, suddenly entered a different unexpected stage. Reflection on categories and concepts and the way my perception changed during the fieldwork is a necessity and an important discussion point, but there is a danger of getting immersed in an ocean of self-reflection and self-criticism particularly being back home. Moral and ethical questions came up, which in my case turned "the dilemmas in fieldwork" (Deere 1996: IX) into dilemmas after fieldwork, too. When I discussed this with Mr. Asante-Dompfe during my second visit – a brief return trip which was useful for further distancing myself – he stated that he did not see it as a problem as such that I had "used them" for my own scientific purpose: the only thing I have to do is to make sure that I did not forget them and to keep in touch. But the dilemmas have remained all the same. By locating myself in the institutional structures of knowledge production, I clearly have a weak position in a kind of double marginalisation – personal and institutional: as a woman with a womens' topic within the field of social anthropology. The idea that I may influence discourses within German development institutions seems very unrealistic. Is my entire work ultimately a self-centred product ? Bringing the information back to the field would seem to be one realistic possibility of crossing the bridge by using existing networks and contacts. A good example of closing the cycle from taking knowledge out of the field and bringing it back was displayed by Elizabeth Ardayfio-Schandorf[9], who conducted a research study as part of the WEDNET Initiative in the northern parts of Ghana on gender and forestry resources and brought back the results by establishing

---

9 She is Professor of Geography working as a lecturer at the Department for Geography and Human Resources at the University of Ghana, Legon.

contacts with women's organizations (Mensah-Kutin 1994: 231). The necessity of networking across boundaries and the direct translocal exchange of knowledge is at least a strategic step which could be taken without getting mired down in hierarchical or bureaucratic structures. Academic knowledge in the double reflexive form by theorising everyday knowledge and making it practical becomes translated into a new type of "hybrid" knowledge, re-embedded in the original context, politicised with the collaboration of women's organizations and finally used as a tool for transformation. This form of epistemic knowledge production is not one-way, but is embedded within a circle, which blurs the hegemonic forms of knowledge production and the borders between academic and everyday knowledge.

The additional burden weighing on my shoulders concerned the relationship between the "self" and the "other" in the text. Since Edward Said's opus *Orientalism* and Geertz's statement that the work of an ethnographer is "he writes", the writing process and the creation of text have provoked a "crisis in ethnography" (Berg/Fuchs 1993: 71). Debates within postmodern/poststructuralist anthropology, cross-cultural literature, feminist ethnography and postcolonial studies have shifted the focus from fieldwork encounters to the process of writing and the production of text as a form of representation. A written text can be in its discursive form an instrument of power for establishing dichotomies and authority and for setting boundaries. Globalization with the phenomenon of interlinking local social processes and the creolisation of cultures has contributed to the "crisis" of anthropological writing. Within the search for a new location between globalization and localization, social anthropology/sociology is challenged by conventional categories as culture, nation, community and society. The answer cannot merely lie in alternative categories produced by definition, but rather in a critical process of examination of Western epistemic culture, in particular in a re-evaluation of central sociological and social-anthropological concepts, in a sharpening of analytical instruments as well as in a politicisation of knowledge production and of knowledge order cross-culturally. The entire complexity of knowledge production, the theoretical reflection on categories and concepts is not restricted towards Western researchers, but is yet to be discussed in African academic circles. After a long period of accusing social-anthropology of supporting colonialist or imperialist politics, since the 1980s a process of "accommodating" (Prah 1997: 441) has raised the question of "where is the African anthropology on Africa ?" (Prah 1997: 444) which leads to a multiplicity of problems associated with establishing its own epistemic culture. As a first step, Mudimbe proposes that it would appear to be impossible to capture the African order of knowledge as long as discourses, categories and concepts are based on Western epistemic orders (Mudimbe 1988: X). The problem cannot be solved simply by replacing Western researchers with local ones, who are mostly Western educated academics and whose knowledge is based on Western concepts (Hountondji 1995: 5). The creation of own discourses requires a general step out of the order of discourse based on dichotomies. Mudimbe indicates that the main discourse topics are establishing dichotomies such as between oral and written; agrarian versus industrial; subsistence versus market; or modern versus traditional (1988: 10). The breakdown of dichotomies should open up the perspective for capturing the (re-)connection between scientific innovation and "endogenous" knowledgeability. The scientific and political aim is to make countries less dependent on imported knowledge (Hountondji 1995: 9). The acknowledgement of existing forms of knowledge within the countries and drawing scientific attention towards ones' own knowledge background is something which is difficult to realise[10] in research practice and the example of Elizabeth Ardayfio-Schandorf, referred to above, remains an exception.

Apart from conceptual, methodological, theoretical and practical reconsiderations of a relationship in the process of making one's own culture a foreign one (vgl. Hirschauer/Amman, 1997) and to be interested in research in one's own country, the institutional context of African universities also needs to be taken into consideration. It is not only quelling the effects of a "brain-drain" that low salaries make intellectuals prefer to teach abroad rather than at home, but also the critical African universities which are often political and suspicious of the state, make public critical discourse on knowledge production impossible (Appiah 1995: 119).

The internal and external contexts of research on knowledge strikes the issue of the "self" and the process of "othering" which is summarised in the following manifest by the Ghanaian scientist Kwasi Prah who states, "first we have to learn to look at ourselves, hear others about ourselves and themselves, and above all allow others to speak for themselves" (Prah 1997: 444-445). Kwasi Prah's othering is a manifest which invite reflection on the practices of research by both local and foreign researchers. His claim is a further demand towards Western research to integrate not only the voices of others within the field, but also discourses of non-Western intellectuals. Just how close this space is indicated by the Writing-Culture debate, which paradoxically aims to search for new forms of elimination between the author and those under research by experimenting with different forms of writing a text such as "social performance", "collagen", "fragments" and "ethnographic allegory". Apart from the fact that none of these experiments can eliminate the research arrangement but rather constructs an ethnographic exclusiveness of the other, they justify the absence of non-Western authors in their publications with the argument, that they have not played a significant role in this discussion (Fuchs/Berg 1993: 9).

This cut-off from non-Western debates and the analysis of Western discourses is a major dimension of postcolonial studies, which questions the hi-

---

10 Here I refer to a talk by Dr. Steve Tonah, social-anthropologist and lecturer at the Institute of African Studies, University of Ghana (Legon) given at the University of Bielefeld on 13.07.2001. He clearly mentioned the difficulties with encouraging students to conduct research in the rural parts of Ghana as they prefer the big cities.

erarchical arrangements and textual forms in which knowledge is produced and codified (Williams/Chrisman 1994: 5). Postcolonial studies with its most prominent scholars such as Homi K. Bhaba, Frantz Fanon, Chandra Talpade Mohanty, Gaytari Spivak, Edward Said or Stuart Hall are not exclusively located outside "the developed world" but are also situated within Western academic institutions. Their highly theoretical contributions are not reduced to a reaction or response to Western discussions, but have been formed within "Third World" discourses through transnational dialogues since the 1950s, and have mutually influenced discourses within southern regions[11] (Williams/Chrisman 1994: 4; 16). Historically and politically postcolonialism deals with the step out of the processes beginning with colonialism towards an independence of knowledge production. As a rather heterogeneous and amorphous field of scholarly positions, it goes beyond the discussion of representation and deals with a broad variety of issues such as: migration, slavery, suppression, resistance, difference, race, gender and place (Ashcroft/Griffiths/Tiffin 1995: 16). The fruitfulness of postcolonial discourse theories lies in the challenge of Western concepts and textual description. The analytical field of postcolonial studies encompasses external relations between countries and internal relations within a country. One common concern is the revision of past and present relations with the aim of reconfiguring social relations. Relations are not methodologically conceptualised in the blur between the "self" and the "other", but emphasis thereon lies in the acknowledgement of the "other". To change social relations based on discursive structures, "other" stories, "other" histories, and "other" narratives have to be told, listened to and integrated into textual description.

In the complex relationship between different locations of writing and knowledge production between the North and the South or between people form the South living in the North, gender plays a crucial aspect. Women and feminist anthropologists discussed the issue of "othering" during the entire course of the twentieth century. Early researchers and writers such as Ruth Benedicts, Zora Neal Hurston, Elsie Clews Parsons, Ruth Landes and Hortense Powdermaker dealt with issues of subjectivity-objectivity within the fields and had even experimented with different textual forms of representation (Bachmann-Medick 1998: 30; Behar 1995: 14; Abu-Lughod 1991: 152) long before the Writing-Culture debate has claimed to do so. By emphasising dilemmas within research situations, the debate was extended to issues of methodology and epistemology (Abu-Lughod 1991: 152; Stacey 1991: 117). Majorie Shostak's "Nisa. The life and Words of a !Kung Woman" in particular exemplified the possibilities of opening a text without closing the words of the woman interviewed. However, the writing and knowledge of those early writers can hardly be detected in mainstream discourse, seeing, as the Writ-

---

11 So between African-American thinkers as Booker T. Washington or W.E.B. du Bois who influenced discourses in South Africa as well as South African discourses influenced the ones between African-American, Caribbean and West African scholars (Williams/Chrisman 1994: 16).

ing-Culture debate explains the absence of women with the claim that they have not produced innovative work (Clifford 1986: 20; Clifford 1995: 210).

Feminists argue that many debates on anthropological research in particular are still Western centred as well as male dominated and controlled (Lutz 1995: 14). Cultural poetry represented in the Writing-Culture debate leaves the power relations intact and should be replaced by cultural politics (Abu-Lughod 1991: 147ff.). The claim of "ethnography of the particular" goes alongside the integration of daily practices embedded in the dynamic process of how culture is constructed and negotiated under conditions of globalization (Abu-Lughod 1991: 158).

I think that the neglect of women's writing is symptomatic of the relationship towards women's/feminist writing. By engendering academic discourses, women have contributed to new insights, but are marginalised in the overall discourse which leaves them in an innocent position which is barely worth mentioning. From an approach of sociology of knowledge, the construction of science and reality based on mainstream discourses is still male dominated, which is even more surprising at a time when women like those in the networks I have described in Chapter 1 are already conducting intensive research and producing new insights into global-local development.

The theoretical discourse on representation and the search for new symmetric relations coming out of the text did not really result in a new approach or in a new agenda of representation, but rather sensitises the researcher towards the whole process of knowledge production, the production or reproduction of discourses and the use of language, which has opened the methodological perspective to discourse analysis and towards a new relationship between literature and sociology/social-anthropology. This process is surely a necessity, because the absolute position of the author is put into a relativist perspective. But what cannot be expected and achieved is a "pure" representation. So I stopped the process of searching one by coming out with what I had in mind before: I am not going to be an artist like a dancer on a tightrope, but I will write the text in a conventional way and to centralise those who are sometimes paradoxically forgotten within the debate: the subjects and their daily practices. Instead of working with binary concepts, I am focusing on interactions across localities and cultures and the production of differences and understandings within connected spaces. By using the term "them" or "women" in a homogenous way – depending on the context – I refer to a phenomenological "othering" following the argumentation of Schütz that "[...] the "others" are a question of an objective equalisation, a mutual interrelatedness of my existence and of all the others" (1962: 126), which in its political meaning is identifiable with the theoretical manifest of the postcolonial claim of a – non exclusive – but *inclusive* "*other*". I turn the dichotomy between the "self" and the "other" into a relationship between the "self" and the "other". This aspect should not be confused with the authority of the text, which will still remain in my hands: as the only writer, the one who analyzes the data, the one who chooses the additional literature, quotations and formation of the text. Therefore, the analytical perspective of cross-cultural women's knowledge exchange is the basis of this research and a terrain of articulation. Apart from their exercising discursive power, research and text can also open new spaces. By opening this, it can be a chance for women to articulate, problematise and politicise. It can function as a venue for those women who speak in the text by participating in the production of academic knowledge and theory.

The process of writing therefore encompasses multiple aspects, which should not be cut off from each other and reduced to one or two points, but are ultimately centred around the notion of what I will call "triple" reflexivity: first, continued reflection on the practice of research (institutional, methodological, theoretical and empirical), and second, reflection on knowledge production done by non-Western researchers. Third, reflection as a form of integration in practice, by opening the text to transparency following the claim of how I got to tell "other" stories which definitely contribute to the results and direction of this work. Within the text partial quotations of "other" statements are put in a direct form as well as small details will let the situations "talk". And finally the products of gained knowledge should be transferred to Ghana which can be easily done by using the established contacts at the university.

3 Conceptualizing Local Knowledge

3.1 Agency-Orientation in Sociology of Knowledge

Every empirical study is based on a theoretical and methodological approach towards society, the methods of data collection and construction of the researched field. By following the theoretical approach of phenomenology (vgl. Schütz 1974; Schütz/Luckmann 1979) and social constructivism (vgl. Berger/Luckmann 1966) I have taken the main thesis of a sociology of knowledge into consideration which should be the mutuality of the structural relationship between the individual and the social stock of knowledge, its generation, distribution and memorizing as well as the processes of how knowledge becomes reality, which is the process of legitimation. It is based on the assumption, that knowledge is constitutive for agency and the mutuality between agency and knowledge constitutes a structural relationship (Soeffner 1999: 31; Luckmann 1986: 191). Knowledge can therefore be defined as a capacity for agency.

Agency in its everyday form is embedded in the structures of "lifeworld", a term Husserl introduced and which was subject to solid theoretical grounding by Schütz and Luckmann (1979). Lifeworld is split up in space, time and the world within its reach. Despite the diversity of existing lifeworlds and multiple realities in every society, common structures of relevance enable communication expressed through agency, speech, signs or symbols (Schütz/Luckmann 1979: 26). Agency of subjects is always oriented towards other subjects as well as to the constructed social world, which encompasses the natural, environmental and cultural world. As Schütz indicated, the specific meaning of agency context is dependent and constituted within social relationships, and at the same time connected with the social world through moments of reflexivity, which means that meaning does not lie in experience itself, but it is the way in which the "Ego" regards its experience (Schütz 1965: 23ff.). The meaningful structures of agency and the meaningful structures of the social world stand together: meaningful structures arise through active acquisition and transformation of subjective agency, whereas the actors are oriented in their agency towards it. The term agency refers in a dual manner to the actors. First as a subject, who acts on, proves and transforms and second, who also constructs and interprets it (Hitzler/Reichertz/Schroer 1999: 13). Subjects are not free of structures or are atomised individuals just as structures are never free of subjects, but rather owe their existence to the agency of people.

Seen from this perspective, agency produces or reproduces moments of social structures, whereas the meaning is both a condition and a result. Lifeworld is therefore constituted intersubjectively and the structures of lifeworld knowledge are constituted through a structural relationship with the construction of the social world. The concept of the relationship between the constitution of the structures of lifeworld and the constructed social world was taken up and further developed by Thomas Luckmann and Peter Berger's concept of a humanistic sociology of knowledge (1966) which bridges the artificial and, up to that time in sociology, dominant concept of methodological dualism between the individual and society or micro- and macro-approaches.

Within this social constructivist approach, reality is permanently socially constructed (Berger/Luckmann 1966: 22; Knorr-Cetina 1989: 87): within the lifeworld people develop strategies and actions with processes and mechanisms of habitualisation, institutionalisation and legitimation transform into "objective" facts or a world which is taken for granted. The social organization of society with all its institutions, organizations and order is a product of human agency and therefore man/woman-made (Berger/Luckmann 1966: 5). People have everyday knowledge about the social structure and organization of society, are acting upon it, but they can also transform it (Garfinkel 1973: 189). To define social order as man/woman-made further implies, that it is produced, contested, reproduced or transformed in specific situations. People can avail themselves of different elements of knowledge, depending on the structures of distribution, but also depending on their relevance for the individual. Not everyone has the same knowledge and not everything is shared in the same way. There is no one reality in a given society, but a multiplicity of realities which can stand in contest towards each other (Berger/Luckmann 1980: 124), as for example between experts knowledge and everyday knowledge, among gender or between generations.

For a researcher entering a social world which differs from his/her own familiar social world, the first confrontation is with the different relevant structures of meaning. A first step of the researcher should be to understand the relevant structures of agency. To capture this, interpretation by the actors of their own agency reveals the subjective meaning of agency. Because actors interprete their agency within the social world, the subjective meaning turns into objective meaning, which needs a further interpretation of the explanation by the researcher (Schütz 1974: 153; 310). Schütz has taken up and critically argued with the "interpretive" paradigma of Max Weber[1] which is the understanding of subjective meaning of social action. In order to catch the subjective meaning of agency, Schütz differentiates between act, action, behaviour and the implication of the observer. For analytical reasons, Schütz makes the useful distinction between the interpretation of agency through the subjects and further reconstructions by the researcher (1974: 137ff.). Both

---

1 Schütz refers to Max Weber's interpretive sociology focusing on agency. He developed it further by making the distinction between action as a determinant future goal and act as a completed agency (Schütz 1965: 8).

steps, of interpreting and reconstructing meaningful agency are necessary for intersubjective understanding (Schütz 1965: 113). Schütz refers to Max Weber by calling this methodological approach the explanation of interpretation (Schütz 1974: 34).

From this theoretical and methodological perspective with the emphasis on the social agency of people, the gap between micro- and macro approaches can be bridged. The starting point is at the micro level. As Knorr-Cetina has explained, by "defining micro-elements of social reality as social relationships, power, interactions, macro-phenomen-on can be logically derived from micro-situations" (Knorr-Cetina 1981: 26)[2]. This means that not only social situations at the micro level transcend the macro level of society, but furthermore this constitutes the macro level. The bridge from micro-phenomenon in reference to the broader societal level is of "tacit" relevance (Cicourel 1981: 56), connected theoretically through the complexity of actor-structure relationships and empirically through interactions in social situations and through contextualisation.

This integration of the micro with the macro level of analysis in general and in particular in the context of research in development countries is still controversial issues between and within academic subjects. Macro measurements, which take social indicators of development such as income, access to health clinics, enrolment rates at an aggregate level are trying to capture social reality in numbers and estimations and socio-cultural change at system level. Apart from the fact, that aggregates are less complex than everyday life, the methodological aspect of the relevance of this data's criteria can be questioned. With measurements which are probably not even relevant to the specific society, research can create a "system of ignorance" (Lachenmann 1994: 299), making people unknown and passive by neglecting everyday agency and knowledgeability. Research at the macro- level is often oriented towards Western standards and Western definitions of development and indexes, which implicitly exhibit the "under" or "delayed" development of society and constitutes a sharp distinction between developed and underdeveloped countries. The practical knowledge derived from this data is often inapplicable for specific projects or programs or is irrelevant for the project partners and furthermore undervalues local knowledge (Lachenmann 1996: 7).

The other side of the spectrum reveals participatory approaches such as Participatory Rural Appraisal (PRA) or Rapid Rural Appraisal (RRA), which dominate the design of research on "local" knowledge within the developing context. These standardised techniques narrow the focus on knowledge in a locality towards a polling of information, by splitting it up into pieces. By neglecting the broader social context and wider transformation processes, knowledge becomes disembedded, decontextualised and reduced to a set of

---

2 In general micro-situations are at first glance less complex than macro-approaches. In studies in laboratories, Knorr-Cetina concluded that the closer one looks at the interactions the more complex social reality gets (Knorr-Cetina 1991: 84).

elements. By focusing on the local artificial cut-off context only, which theoretically binds knowledge to a closed space or "box", it pretends to seclude social relations across spaces and confirms the "myth of a village community" (Albrow, 1998 in Noller 2000). Following the argumentation of Cicourel (1981: 56) this means that without paying attention to the broader context, sociologists would ignore their own interests.

To sum up, the majority of research designs are based on a dichotomic understanding of society and by splitting into disconnected levels neglect and isolate social interactions at the different and complex connected levels of society. By taking the connection between micro-macro approaches under the condition of globality into consideration a methodological approach must follow the interweaving of the different levels of interactions along the local-global spectrum. This seems to be a necessity for anthropological research and its theoretical challenge lies in the new formulation of sociological concepts of space.

3.2 The Concept of Space/Time and Empirical Operationalisation

As indicated above, everyday knowledge and social agency are embedded in a complex interwoven relationship within the lifeworld and the construction of the social world. The question arises as to how to conceptualise local knowledge from the perspective of a phenomenological and social constructivist approach by taking the interface of local-global processes into consideration. For the analytical side I have chosen the concept of space[3], which due to different trends within academic discourses has (re-)gained increasing attention in sociological theories in an attempt to capture and explain current social phenomena under conditions of globalization (Noller 2000: 21; Löw 2001: 10). Early territorialised concepts as that of Emile Durkheim referred to space as a social determined order, which reflects the "thinking" of the inhabiting group (1980, orig. 1895). The argumentation of Durkheim's scholar Maurice Halbwachs (1967) went into a similar direction. Space is the expression of "collective thoughts" and an expression of tradition and conservation. Within German sociology, Georg Simmel was one of the earliest sociologists who, in 1903, developed a sociology of space. According to him, the conditions of geographic and political space influence social interactions and shape

---

3   The majority of early concepts on space through their national reference hindered a development of a concept towards a cross-national perspective. Within its nation-boundedness, space became in imperialist politics a highly political contested term and had not lost its negative connotation until recently. Even Foucault, who explicitly dealt with the term wrote in 1980, "I remember, ten years ago discussing these problems of the politics of space, and being told that it was reactionary to go on so much about space, and that time and the "project" were about life and progress about" (cit. Löw 2001:11).

the borders of symbolic differentiation among social groups. The given space determines social relations and mutual social influence between individuums (1983). Only gradually did academic thinking overcome the deterministic effect of space on social life, in favour of approaches defining space as an outcome of social relations and of social agencies and less as its predicament.

In recent social theory the concept has in particular been emphasised by Anthony Giddens' theory of structuration and by Pierre Bourdieus' concept of social space. The aim of both has been to bridge structure and agency. Giddens' approach results in duality of both by overcoming the dualism, whereas Bourdieu conceptualises space as a field of relations and struggle between actors whose agency is determined by the different forms of capital and resources as well as by the constitution of "habitus". While it is not my aim to present an extensive critique of both approaches, it should suffice to state here that both lack crucial aspects of the production and scope of spaces and implicitly the emergence of spaces under the dynamics of globalization processes. In addition: Giddens' approach to space is based only on regionalism, while Bourdieu's concept of space is determined and rather static.

Within its theoretical coherence Henri Lefèbvre (1991) elaborated a more differentiated concept which leaves the metaphorical level to emphasise the processual construction of space while taking practices, knowledge, objects and symbols into consideration. He breaks it down into: 1. cognitive space, which is the space of spatial practices 2. imagined space, which is the representation of space 3. lived space, which he calls the space of representation (1991: 38-39). Drawing his ideas from Marxist thinking, he overcomes the strict economic emphasis and even prefers to replace production with generation of space to avoid dichotomies. With the focus on the process of generation and the multiplicity of meanings social spaces can have in the everyday world, he has definitely influenced my critical analysis of the concept on the micro level in particular. The conceptual usefulness of Lefèbvres lies in analytically breaking space into a spatial, representational and social dimension. The spatial component of knowledge and social agency has been of subordinary interest by constructivist approaches. Berger/Luckmann have prioritised time and only paid minor attention to the aspect of space (1980: 29) seeing it as being taken for granted for agencies, but not as a central category of investigation.

In a first step, I want to note that space consists of different layers and dimensions. Social space is far more than the location of spatial practice. It is a constitutive element of social relations, emerging out of social practices and is therefore not naturally given, but rather an act of processual creation (Lefèbvre 1991: 12). Space is lived before it is conceptualised and theorised by the actors. Through perception, experience and practice social space is the outcome of multiple and durable processes (Lefèbvre 1991: 11): it is produced and maintained through agency and vice versa as space also shapes and maintains social practices. As a locality of interactions and negotiations, social space evolves out of diverse actions which can be discursive, symbolic or face-to-face. Symbolic in the way that meaning is given to objects, e.g. natural things or artificial objects (Blumer 1973: 81ff.). Natural space can therefore become an objective for frames of relevance and constitutive for individual and social agencies.

Two aspects have to be taken into further consideration: first the internal organization of space and second the relationship between interlocking spaces. Both aspects are relevant for the order of knowledge and the power constellation of defining social relations. Space emerges out of social relations between actors and social agencies. As a theoretical definition we can define social space along two aspects:

1. Internal differentiation: Space is produced by and between subjects or between subjects and objects. Space combines spatial *and* contextual (symbolic, imagined, representational) moments, constituted by layers of internal, actual or virtual, horizons and spatial dimensions of interaction. Through mechanisms of social differentiation such as the inclusion into or exclusion of subjects out of social spaces, the relations between and among subjects are defined.
2. Internal-external boundaries: The constitution of social space varies according to the spatial reach of dimensions of interactions. The specific form of openness and closure of dimensions and horizons of social space through its subjects signify the degree of control over social spaces.

On the analytical side the social organization of knowledge can be analyzed through the constitution of social spaces. The social organization of knowledge in social spaces refers to the central processes of: knowledge generation, transfer, memorizing, distribution, innovation and legitimation. As the focal point of my research design I have narrowed social space to women's spaces[4], a term Gudrun Lachenmann (1996: 2-3) introduced to analyze gender-relations along the interface with institutions such as the economy, markets, development politics and civil society. Women's spaces in their diversity and multiplicity on the local level present how women shape it and what significance they attribute in their everyday life as for example in religion, health and environment and in female political institutions. Although I was focusing on women of different generations it shows how the relevance and meaning of lived spaces has changed, how the constructed world has changed as well as the order of knowledge production and transmission. Every social

---

4 Empirical studies, especially in social-anthropology have taken up the analytical category of space. One of the first was Shirley Ardener (1986) analysing how the spatial and social organization is used by women in different parts of the world. Henrietta Moore (1994) took it up in a study on gender relations among the Marakwet in Kenya which has shown how women define gender practices in the household. A recent study of Salma Nageeb (2000) on women and space in urban Karthoum explains, that space is a constitutive element of agency in everyday life, embedded in a complexity of social and political power relations.

space therefore has its own history. By neglecting household or domestic categories and turning the research design on female networks within the matrikin and beyond the family level, the perspective is opened towards processes of informal networking and informal organising which are necessary for an analysis of changing processes in the dynamics of knowledge generation and distribution.

Female spaces can differ at the different levels of society. From an empirical aspect the emergence and existence of women's spaces in the form of women's gatherings or organizations at the different levels of society, demands flexibilisation of the research design and mobility in practice. To capture the dynamics of relations and knowledge circulation on and between the different levels, I moved along those interconnections of female spaces i.e. back and forth between Susuanso, Sunyani and Duayaw-Nkwanta, and less regularly to Accra. This mobility explores the structuration of relevance of local knowledge in its reach and the direct and indirect horizons of experience over long distances. This mobility was also a disadvantage because it prevented me from a going into depth outside Susuanso in particular.

Space is therefore one form of organization of societies, while the interesting point is the expansion of the structures of lifeworld in reach, the growing density of social relations, the intensification of social agency and the overlapping of spaces by taking the multiple locations of knowledge production together. As a sociological category of analysis it reverses the dichotomies of micro versus macro or previously territorialised concepts of rural-urban or centre-periphery as well as of fixed ethnic boundaries and captures the interlinkings between constellations of knowledge flows.

Time is an additional aspect and is used here as a vehicle of social change by taking the relationship between spaces and history into consideration. Time is not separate from space but does function as a dynamic vehicle within spaces. It also challenges the assumption that women are mere victims of social change; instead they are also active in constructing it by defending old or opening new spaces. Seeing the time/space relationship together, it offers a more processual and interwoven pattern of changes in the past and makes discourses in the present understandable. Time as "gendered" time is expressed and used in language and discourses in the formation of gender constructs, identities and relations. In the negotiation of tradition and in the way actors refer to the past as well as to the present and future, time can be used as a tool for the relationships of actors within and between spaces. Time has to be seen as a social flow of simultaneity and dissimultanity, continuity and discontinuity and like space is another contested arena.

3.3 Research as an Explorative Process

The two steps of the explanation of interpretation (Schütz 1974: 34), the methodological entering perspective is emic. The process of "going native" should not mean that the researcher is able to see through their eyes, but to understand and explain the daily practices and the construction of reality. By following the theoretical conceptualisation of the protosociology of Schütz, Berger, Luckmann, "interpretive" sociology has its roots in the communicative process of understanding the other, whereas everyday life, everyday experience and everyday knowledge are taken as phenomenons. The orientation of the researcher lies in specific everyday communication (Schütze 1973: 434) and it is everyday communication, which forms the basis for knowledge arrangement.

The research process is oriented towards the explorative paradigm, in which the actors define further criteria of exploration. In practice I started the interviews with some guiding questions, but the questions were open for narrations and queried data gave rise to new questions. This concept is much more open and flexible than standardised questionnaires and it allows new directions which were not taken into consideration before. When I asked if land had a specific meaning, people turned the question into the direction of the meaning of the river, and this gave rise to a new phenomenon of analysis, which I had not considered before.

The relevance of data and control are already inherent within the emic perspective. Data inquired via a predefined etic approach is uncontrolled in the way that is probably not relevant for the actors. The criteria of objectivity of scientific research cannot be applied within qualitative research, but will be questioned in itself: it is not the methods of science which determine objectivity, but rather the objectivity which determines the methods (Schütze/Meinfeld/Springer/Weymann 1973: 434). The "un"-controlled process requires a degree of freedom for the generation of data evolving from the different steps of discovery during the research process. By following the grounded theory approach of Strauss (1994) the practical research technique of theoretical sampling, intensive reflection on and selection of the explored data, coding and writing memos, structures the research process into a constantly intertwined and systematic exploration and analysis of data. The aim is not to isolate data and knowledge, but the embeddedness which is gained through the contextualisation of data from an outside perspective. The claim of representativity in qualitative research, which is usually a criterion for data generalisation and validation, focuses more on the process of data collection and the process of understanding relevant and typical connections of agency than on the quantity of its characteristic features. Within the research process which has to be seen under the perspective of communication mediated through the process of the construction of social reality, stocks of knowledge stand in mutuality with social structural moments. The aspect of control is inherent in those elements of knowledge which are practised by the members of society (Schütze/Meinfeld/Springer/Weymann 1973: 470). It is therefore the relationship between the method and the structures of becoming reality which controls the process of understanding.

Apart from the process of exploration, the background knowledge gathered during the research process in the field and the experience of oneself within the research process also represent additional information. New theoretical aspects emerge and are "grounded" in the empirical inquired data. Existing theories are not formulated as hypotheses, which have to be "tested" through falsification or verification; they "work" as background knowledge and are used for the process of the integration of data towards theorising it. The discovery and generation of a new theory should not be the goal of research as such, but existing theories function as a "thinking tool" (Hirschauer/ Amman 1997: 37) in the sense of investing it and re-evaluating it in the empirical data to form a new construct of scientific knowledge.

3.4 Methods: Chances and Limitations

As I have already shown in Chapter 2.2 how interview situations took place, I would now like to highlight, from a hermeneutic perspective, the methods I used for obtaining data. Those methods will be further discussed under the aspect of their relevance in the particular context. Knowledge can not always be verbally expressed but can be silenced in daily practices as "practical knowledge" (Giddens 1984: 431). Anne Honer (1989: 297), who combines pure description with phenomenology in an approach to lifeworld ethnography, uses observation and interviews for the discovery of phenomena. I have taken up her approach to situate knowledge and reconstruct the context of meaning. While those methods have proved to be adaptable for the fieldsituation, contradictions crossed my way. In trying to dissolve them, I have contrasted the results in group-discussions, one with women only and one including men and women. Both groupdiscussions additionally revealed the difference in female speech contributions. On their own women talked much more animatedly than in comparison with the mixed one.

Special kinds of interviews are biographies in form of trajectories. The narrated life-history reveals the dynamism between individual lives within the social world. Biography as a construct between the individual agencies in mutuality with social conditions is both, a method and a result. The individual construction of one's history is also a process of self-construction (Dausien 1995: 576), and explains both the self and the outside formation (Luckmann 1981: 60). Because individual biographies stand in reference to other biographies, they open the perspective for individual and collective spaces of manoeuvre of subjects (Dausien 1995: 576). From a gender perspective the "logic of construction" of gender-order (Dausien 1995: 3), the positioning, restriction and moving of gender in social spaces can be analyzed. The movements of women explain the capacity of a changing stock of knowledge, how women develop new strategies and integrate new innovative elements of knowledge. The association of new elements in connection with the biographic interpretation of meaning, explores the potential of changing social structures.

I used Oral History within the framework of topical interviews. Questions concerned social institutions which have been abolished, changed or are still present. My aim was not to reconstruct the history of the town or the history of the Akan, but to focus on transformation processes which were of importance for changes in female spaces. In conversations women explained their lived everyday history from their own particular point of view, which located them between social structure and history (Vorländer 1990: 13; 21). Oral history is therefore less about "how it really was" but with interpretations based on the relevant categories chosen by the narrators, it reveals what was relevant for them in the past and what continuous to have relevance for them now. The narratives are therefore not only a document of the past, but also a result of the present (Vansina 1985: 8). The narratives spanned the 20th century and moments of change were dated by the individual time frame such as "before I was married" or "after the birth of my third child" or by referring to historical circumstances such as "after independence" or during "Nkrumah's time". Using women's oral history reveals that they are not only historically voiceful, but have also played their part in history. In particular the material of women can create a new image of the past making them more visible in African history, which continues to be written on the basis of European sources and even an African perspective has been lacking until now (Luig 1984: 178). It is not only that a local history is a necessity, but the existing documented history is mostly written from a macro-structural perspective, paying little or no attention to the everyday history of the people. Although, they have experienced, perceived and contributed to it at a local or translocal level.

My narrowed perspective concentrated on the narratives of typical women, which was in my case a suitable method, as the access to it did not pose any problems. However, this cannot be easily extended to other African countries owing to differences in social organization. Ruth Finnegan (1970: 98) assumes that every society is likely to have certain genres that are considered suitable for women, but to discover the "right" method is not always as easy as indicated by the following example from a research project in Somalia. In a context in which written documents are scarce and under circumstances in which women do not consider themselves as important, there emerges the problem of a "lack of sources". At first glance it seemed as if women had nothing to say about themselves and past events. Gradually the researchers discovered that women do have their own special form of oral transmission in the form of poetry, which documents the political resistance of women against colonialism and patriarchy, and reveals the strategies of women's organizations and movements (Hasan/Adan/Worsame 1995: 165-182).

What is meant by Oral History is not clearly theoretically and methodologically defined and the variety of terms given to the method covers "oral literature" (Finnegan 1970) or "oral tradition" (Vansina 1985). The spectrum of forms of orality is multiple and the variety of sources can differ. Apart from personal voices – on which I concentrated – Jan Vansina subsumes other sources such as tales, proverbs, reminiscences, eyewitness accounts, hearsay, poetry and visions (1985: 8). Even the playing of drums or horns can carry special messages depending on their function and have been used in political or religious narratives; something Ruth Finnegan observed during her fieldwork in the Akan region in the 1960s (Finnegan 1970: 79). The interesting and complex method of Oral History is on the one hand the message and on the other hand the instrument of transmission. The form of transmission can change and with the exception of one funeral, drums or horns were never used during my stay. Instead proverbs and stories are often told and nowadays take written form, e.g. schoolbooks. The schoolbooks I used for my Twi-lessons were an additional source of information for the interviews: I came across a story about an old woman, who had been consulted for advice in an emergency. The story of the *aberewa nyansafo* which I did not pay much attention to at first, later became an important issue and is now a point of reference for the construction of identities of the Subqueenmothers and the Queenmothers.

The relationship between the narrator and the researcher is not always an easy one and it can, in particular for local researchers, result in unexpected difficulties, as the Malian researcher Mamadou Diawara experienced in his hometown by conducting a study on local history. It was not possible to ask direct questions or to behave in an ignorant way. The narrators became skeptical, and even feared that he would doubt their competence (Diawara 1985: 10). The problems faced by the researcher do not only lie in accessing the source, but also in the relationship to the narrators. The implicit difficulties for a local researcher can be overcome, as Diawara suggested, by collaborating with non-local/foreign researchers (1985: 16).

Discourse as a research and analytical method is widely used in sociological theories and texts, but the term is a blurred concept, largely because there are so many conflicting and overlapping definitions formulated from various theoretical and disciplinary standpoints (Fairclough 1992: 3)[5]. I have taken the concept of a critical discourse analysis elaborated by Norman Fairclough, which seemed to be useful for the analysis of my material as it combines the analysis of text with social theory. With his notion of critical he differentiates his approach from conversation analysis, which pays more attention to correspondence than production. Critical also hints at the process of production of discourse and its further social implications. In this concept discourse is embedded in three dimensions (1992: 4):

---

5   The traces of discourse analysis are threefold: the English term "discourse" and the French term "discours" mean everyday language; second, the term has become institutionalised in symbolic interactionism and socio-linguistic, which dealt with conversation analysis. And third, in the tradition of structuralism and post-structuralism, the term discourse constitutes the construction of reality (Keller 1997: 310-311).

1. Text analysis in its written or spoken form
2. Analysis of discourse practice such as the process of production, distribution and dissemination of text
3. Analysis of institutional and organizational circumstances

From a constructivist perspective, discourse is constitutive for the construction of reality and the collective level of meaning and symbolic order. The level of analysis focuses on the processes of social order in which discourse is produced and gives meaning to the constructed reality. The structures of lifeworlds in the everyday world is partially constructed by discourse, which is transmitted by discursive practices using the medium of language and expressed in agencies. Gender, identity and subjectivity as social constructs are constituted within discursive practices which shape social spaces and social practices. "Objects" of discourse are not helpless, but can themselves shape and change discursive practices and act as agents by negotiating with the various types of discourses at the same time transforming their "preconstituted object" situation. Subjects here form the interface of enabling and restricting their room of manoeuvre, which in its tension maintains the dynamics of discourse. Because discourse does have to be contextualised as it is already in its social meaning, gender-asymmetries are embedded in the "contradictions, dilemmas, and struggle at the institutional and societal level" (Fairclough 1992: 97). Discourse thus signifies the social world, constituting and constructing it by giving meaning to the construction of social identities, social relationships and the construction of the system of knowledge and belief (Fairclough 1992: 64).

The data upon which the discourse analysis is based emerged from interviews and partly from a few newspaper articles. As a method which is mainly based on communication the limitations of a critical discourse analysis are given for two reasons. First, it requires excellent knowledge of the local language which I definitely did not have. Twi is a highly symbolic language and the meaning of the specific expressions, metaphors and proverbs are extremely complex. Even the English translations needed further explanation. Apart from some expression which I came across during the interviews, I did not pay attention to the wide range of phrases used on a day-to-day basis. While discourse usually extends a duration over a longer time-span, the discourse analysis within my study only represents a detailed part. Reconstruction of the beginning of discourse and the change over years was impossible within such a short time, and need an additional time for research. Even sources of information such as the daily newspaper or past issues of which I could read in the National Archives in Accra, are less informative than expected. This should not mean that the discourse is of less social importance, but it indicates that written information in the media has in this case remained an insignificant source of information.

I obtained written materials such as minutes of meetings at the National and Regional Houses of Chiefs in Sunyani and Kumasi as well as brochures and publications from women's organizations. Another source of obtaining information was the Internet. Before I went to Ghana I conducted a preliminary research on glocal women's organizations. I will call this a way of obtaining data a virtual de-territorialized method, since it would have been possible, to conduct from other parts of the world and is not place bounded.

After this review of methodology and methods, I have come to the conclusion that methods are not isolated techniques which can be easily used like tools, but are highly dependent on the context of situatedness encompassing the situation of the field as well as the positioning of the researcher, which means the situation in the field. With these remarks I will close this chapter and proceed to enter the lifeworlds of Nana Yaa living in Susuanso.

4 KNOWLEDGE TRANSFER OVER GENERATIONS: CONTINUITY AND CHANGE

The transfer of knowledge between the old and the young generation is analyzed in this chapter. Focussing on it reveals the process of knowledge generation and its further transmission. By adapting a temporal perspective, I intend not to reconstruct historical changes in a chronological linear way, but to concentrate on the main changes in structures of communication on the one hand and changes in the symbolic and social order of knowledge and society on the other. This approach of seeing the past in the present clarifies how continuities and discontinuities of knowledge elements and of daily practices came into coexistence. As an initial terminological clarification I would like to distinguish between the transfer of knowledge, which is meant to describe the general process between generations and knowledge transmission, which is the medium of knowledge transfer. Knowledge transmission requires further differentiation as the acquisition of knowledge and the "search" for knowledge.

The medium of orality continues to be the main form of knowledge transmission. The transfer, distribution and memorisation of knowledge in oral cultures require, as indicated by George Elwert (1987: 243), a complex societal organization of knowledge depending on a specific form of institutional environment. The organization of knowledge depends highly on gender, age and social status along with such questions as: who is authorised to transmit knowledge ? Who has special knowledge such as on history or medicine ?. Independent from the degree of the main form of communication as language, written or oral, or body language, the specific social media is inextricably bound with the social organization of knowledge. Artefacts as another symbolic medium of communication can be used for memorising and transferring knowledge. From other parts of Africa recent studies on a microlevel hint at the variety of possibilities of using objects such as those fabricated by blacksmiths in the urban area of Zinder (Niger) to keep knowledge within one endogamous group (Waibel 1998: 149) or paintings on walls by women in rural Zimbabwe to retain their knowledge about seeds (Schäfer 1998: 135). The importance of these examples lies furthermore in their non-confirmation of an assumption in academic discourse of a one-dimensional shift from "orality to literacy" as Walter Ong (1982: 138) has predicted for developing and industrial-technical societies. Oral culture is not opposed to written culture; they can co-exist and do not necessarily have to contradict each other. However, the written form is dependent on standardised writing and a technological apparatus (Elwert 1987: 240). This discussion will turn its focus in the near future on virtual spaces through the emergence of new forms of communication such as the internet, which has spread through Ghana at an enormous speed covering at least the bigger cities and towns. It is only a matter of time before it also reaches the village of Susuanso, and it will definitely be another future research topic. Since it has not yet reached there, I have disregarded this issue for now and turn instead to the discussion of the validity and context relevance of formal education in developing countries and its meaning for everyday knowledge. Literacy rates as indicators of human development in Ghana in 1995 accounted for 49 % of the female and 72.9 % of the male adult population (UNDP 1995: 83). The importance of education in Ghana is of national concern. State expenses, which are almost 50 % of the national budget, invested in improving and expanding primary and secondary education reflecting the overall efforts. To use the term formal education, I use it strictly for education in primary and secondary schools whereas for the process of knowledge acquisition outside the system of education I will use the term informal education.

4.1 The Old Generation: "The young ones will not listen"

The transfer of everyday knowledge has in the past and continous to be largely institutionalised within the family or kinship context. Every person in Susuanso is a member of the mother lineage. The extended family *abusua* comprises of the female and male members of the same lineages, whose matrilinear decent can be traced back to a common ancestor and is symbolised by family stools, so-called *akonua tuntum* (black stools) which are kept within each lineage in the family house. Not all of the members live in the same compound or even in the same village, but it is a common pattern that within the town, their houses are usually close to each other. Within one compound the amount of people constantly varies owing to frequent visits by family members pursuing seasonal work in the cities and who regularly return to Susuanso, e.g. a seamstress who spends half of the year each in Kumasi and Susuanso, taking her sewing machine back and forth as required. Usually three or more generations share the same compound and only a few houses are inhabited by only one or two generations[1]. Old people remain in the compound until they die. Depending on their health and as long as they are able to walk and work, they will go to their farm, even if they can only walk with a stick and even if it takes them one or two hours to reach the farm. A younger person carries the food collected there back to the house. With the food,

---

1 The reasons for this varies: whether it can be that new houses are still under construction and gradually more rooms will be attached or it is done by intention as e.g. the house of my landlord where only he, his wife, and two fostered girls lived in. It could have easily been inhabited by at least six or seven people.

which varies in amount, the old people still contribute to the living situation of the family while being supported by the family members with goods such as soap, Milo[2], sugar or other items. I only observed two elderly women in the town living alone in the rotten parts of a house and who complained about their poor living situation and the carelessness of their family members for not supporting them or providing them with sufficient food or money. These situations were, however, exceptions within the town as a whole. The spatial proximity between generations and everyday communication within the compound appear at first glance contradictory to the expression of the older generation complaining, *"the young ones will not listen"* and if they listen, *"they will not follow"*. The following trajectory of a typical old woman as a constructed case, is not an individual experience, but experiences of individuals and of the historic society within the specific symbolic universe (Berger/Luckmann 1966: 96). It is a reconstruction of how the present older generation was informally educated by their grandparents.

4.2 The Process of Knowledge Generation

Nana Yaa[3] is an old woman aged about 90 years, who lives with her daughter, a granddaughter, two grandsons, four great grandchildren and two fostered girls. Despite her age, she still goes to her farm to work almost every day, something she has always done and she still feels strong enough to do hard work like weeding. One of her farms is close to her house having received the piece of land from her father when she was young and unmarried. Originally from a nearby town called Adroba, her grandmother settled after marriage in Susuanso and also gave her a second piece of land in Adroba. Both farms still belong to her, but she now shares one piece of land with her granddaughter and great grandchildren. All her life Nana Yaa has lived in the compound where she was brought up, and did not move to her husband's house in Susuanso. He died some years ago. During her whole life she never went to school or hospital. As an infant she accompanied her grandmother to the farm who taught her everything about farming. On her first piece of land she established a cocoa farm[4] providing her with a regular income until 1984 when the farm

---

2 Milo is imported cacao-powder, and like many other imported goods, expensive to buy.
3 In the local language Twi, Nana is the title for the elder people. It can be used to address grandmothers, grandfathers as well as respected people such as the Chief, the Queenmother, the Subqueenmothers and the Subchiefs. Yaa is the female name of the weekday Yawoada. Men born on that day are called Yao.
4 Gwendolyn Mikell argues in an empirical study conducted in the region of Sunyani, that in particular between the 1920s and 1940s women were successful farmers working on their "own account" (1985: 17). Only later, after the 1940s did the economic situation change in a negative way towards women, who gra-

was destroyed by a bushfire. She continued farming with food crops some of which she sold at the market. She now organises both farms by a method of mixed farming with crops such as yam, coco-yam, plantain, groundnuts and some maize. She farms seasonally and does not plant everything at one time, which guarantees she always has something to eat. As regards young people, she says that they are not real farmers today, because they plant everything at the same time. And she adds:

"They do not know because they do not listen to the old people. It is because of Christianity and when they go to Church they will not listen. It is the nature of the young ones to blame the old ones. Their life is powerful, the old people are weak. They will not listen so there is no need to tell them. Because of your special request it is that I am talking".

Nana Yaa draws a sharp distinction between her generation and the following one which already includes her own children. Many of the old people have not converted to Christianity, while their children were born into a Christian context, which began in Susuanso with the establishment of the Presbyterian School and Church some 70 years ago in the 1930s and was gradually[5] followed by the Catholic Church with its affiliated school and some smaller churches. For the old people, Christianity was the major reason for changes in the communication structure and for the weakening of the position of old people in the family. While Nana Yaa is now in a weak position, her grandmother experienced a different situation.

Besides farming, her grandmother also taught her how to store crops over a longer period. The crops are put on shelves, which are installed over the fireplace in the compound, high enough that they will not burn while the smoke keeps small animals and insects away and preserves seeds and grains for the next season of cultivation. The shelves are called *pata* and are made of bamboo and still used in many houses today, with some even storing a large amount of maize. This practice has been only partially replaced by new forms of storage such as wooden shelters covered with roofing sheets which demand chemical treatment for preservation. Younger men for storing large portions of maize nowadays prefer this form of storage. Large quantities of crops such as Yam, which can also be stored in an open part of the compound, are covered with special leaves whose smell prevents goats and mice from eating the crop. Her grandmother taught her how to treat herself with herbal medicine, which not only includes knowledge about leaves, roots, and plants, but also how to prepare or apply them properly. The herbs are not planted strategi-

---

gradually, with the shift in land tenure system, faced increasing difficulties in the expansion of their land.

5 The first Christian missionary, the Basle Mission, came in 1828 to Ghana, out of which the Presbyterian Church was later established. In 1834 the Wesley Methodist Church entered Ghana, and in 1880 and 1906 the Catholic Church (Sackey 1996: 84).

cally, but grow wild between the houses and around the town. With their knowledge of the variety of herbs, old people still treat themselves for malaria, skin disease, stomach pains, headache or swelling. None of the old women and men has ever bought medicine at the local drug store, because "*it would not help*". The certainty of their own cure, success of treatment and trust in it has not turned the old people away from their own practices while many younger people in town frequently buy medicine at the drug-store or visit the hospitals in Sunyani or Duayaw-Nkwanta.

Most of the old women and men acquired their practical knowledge from the next but one generation, which would be the grandmother (MoMo) in the case of the women and grandfather (MoFa) for the men. The transmission of knowledge was gendered. "*Men moved with men and women moved with women*", an old man said. Only in cases where the grandmother was absent did another female relative such as the sister of the father or the sister of the grandmother take over. Even when the mother was present, she was of less importance for the transfer of knowledge than the grandmother. The generation and contents of knowledge medical or agricultural was transmitted and exchanged in multiple situations such as within the compound, on the way to the farm or during farm-work, and reflected and copied in many situations of common work during the variety of daily activities. Previous experiences and proved practices were transmitted this way from the past to the future, embedded in the practical process of the presence. While it was shared with other members during the elderly people's lifetimes it is not individually, but "socially derived" (Schütz 1965: 348). It also implies that although it was the grandmother or grandfather and not the mother or father, the knowledge transmitted was based on a longer process of experience and of the solution of problems. The time aspect of the knowledge transferred is therefore of importance, because the long historical duration sedimented not only the content of knowledge, but the meaning of actions in an "experimental depth" (Schütz/ Luckmann 1973: 113).

Nana Yaa explains that her grandmother or so-called *obapanyin* within the family was not only of importance for her own education and that of her sisters, but as the eldest woman within the family, she was also the female head of the family and together with the male head, the *abusua panyin*, who is a formal Subchief, she had the final word as regards disputes within the family or problems between two families. Meyer Fortes observed during his fieldwork in the early 1960s that maternal grandmothers were not only responsible for child-rearing, but also had a certain authority within the family and even in some cases behaved in an autocratic manner (1962: 63). Within each family the eldest female and male person together formed a parallel structure based on the principle of seniority. Beyond the family context, the Subchiefs and Chief of the palace formed the political male structures, while the old women were of importance for assisting and informing the Queenmother in the palace who consulted them for advice. This relationship was referred to as consulting the *aberewa nyansafo*, the wisdom, knowledge and experience of the old women which as we will see in Chapter 5.2 has recently regained importance.

The Complexity of Rites: Bagoro
Both, the Queenmother of the town and the grandmother[6] within the family were responsible for the sexual education of the young women. The Queenmother, especially, was responsible for the moral education of the young generation and exercised great influence over the women in town (Rattray 1969: 84). Mothers were only marginally responsible for the sexual education of their daughters. Elisabeth Grohs who observed nubility rites in East-Tanzania argued that mothers were excluded from the exchange of sexual topics giving the reason that the personal experience of the mother with the father of the child should not influence the child (1980: 166). It is therefore the duty of the grandmother to educate the grandchild.

The institution of what is nowadays called "puberty rites" was aimed at avoiding pregnancy before a young woman marries. The Twi word *bagoro*, which literally means lifedance, was gradually replaced by the Christian name "puberty rites" which is problematic in the sense that the name "puberty" distinguishes between physiological and social puberty, by emphasising the biological maturity over the social maturity. *Bagoro* however is both, an individual and a social transition in the sense of van Genneps liminal rites (1960: Viii). Those rites were performed between the age of 13 and 20 depending on the social maturity of each young woman. It started with a ritual bath at the riverside and the old women of the family introduced her to the spirits of the river. This ritual then transferred from the house to the river accompanied by songs and dances. Nana Yaa explained that after this all her friends came and served her for one week, collected firewood and water, while she was not allowed to leave the house. They would sleep and eat together in one room. During this week she received gifts from neighbours and her parents in the form of food and goods such as cooking items or cloths. For Nana Yaa this meant that from this time on she had to visit the Queenmother regularly who tested the young woman for pregnancy by touching her naked breasts and providing her with further instruction. If she were to have to become pregnant before marriage, she would have had to leave the town with the man in question and could have gone back after delivering. The institution of visiting the Queenmother served both as education of the young women in prevention of pregnancy and thus bearing children out of wedlock as well as a form of control over the young women.

---

6 The same constellation was observed by Elisabeth Grohs in Tanzania. The grandmother was the closest person to the young women in talking and joking as well as in matters of trust (Grohs 1980: 50-51).

Bagoro was also connected with the acquisition of a first piece of land[7] so that girls at a young age could establish their own farms, which they kept after marriage, even if they moved to other towns. Okali (1983: 47) commented that women even began to work as independent cultivators long before men. The acquisition of the first piece of land did not follow any specific pattern. In the case of Nana Yaa the first piece of land came from her father's side, while in other cases girls received land from their brother, mother or even in some few cases from the husband of the grandmother. The inheritance of land is not directly linked to the matrilinear descent unlike titles or goods, but could rather be received from the father's as well as from the mother's lineage. *Bagoro* was therefore also an economic institution with the receiving of gifts and land, which most elderly women still have in their possession. In addition, land was received from the husband after marriage, whereby he cleared a piece of unoccupied land which women could keep after a divorce or after his death. The different "modes of accumulation" (vgl. Geschiere/Koenings 1993) and the access to at least one piece of land, guaranteed the economic security and autonomy of many old women throughout their lives.

Men usually received land from their grandfathers (MoFa) or directly from the father's side as well as from the mother. The plots of farmland for men or women were not regarded as individual pieces of property, but as lineage property which was controlled by the matrikin. If plots became too small or the farmland was not longer fertile, new or larger pieces of land could be obtained from the Chief, who as the keeper of stool land could distribute the land among the people in town. Both women and men could ask for additional land. Land scarcity as such was never a problem in the past, but the destruction of land and cocoa farms through annual bushfires and the introduction of new monocultures such as maize were used as arguments by the old women as the main reasons for changing agricultural and nutritional situations.

The process of knowledge transmission was institutionalised in two ways: in informal education within the matrikin as a processual acquisition of knowledge for both young men and women, and in the social institution of *bagoro* exclusively for women and in the consultation of the Queenmother. The acquisition of knowledge was dependent on the authority of specific persons; for Nana Yaa it was the grandmother within the family and the Queenmother of the town, and for men it was the grandfathers within the family. The matri-

---

7   The issue of kinship and cacao is a prominent topic in research. A clear pattern of research explanation between the influence of the introduction of the cashcrop and the economic situation of women does not exist. Even within the Akan region, researchers such as Fortes (1960) and Hill (1962) have come to different results (Okali 1983: 8). Apart from the methodological perspective, the multiplicity of different and varying constellations makes the reality harder to catch, but reveals the flexibility and variety of inheritance and diversity of female economic situations.

linear descent was the context of knowledge transmission. This formed gendered female and male spaces in the authority to transmit and in the process of acquiring knowledge. This institutionalised form of knowledge transmission based on the principles of age and gender also existed in other African ethnic groups but with differences and specifics in the social organization such as the secret societies of the partilinear Mende in Sierra Leone (Schäfer 1995a: 291) and underwent significant changes in recent times.

The Continuation of Knowledge Exchange

Although transmission was gendered, the same generations of men and women exchanged their knowledge to a certain degree after marriage. "*Both knew the same*", old women and men said. The gendered transmission was complementary on matters of livelihood except that women had a broader knowledge about children's illness and cures. The social stock of knowledge for everyday practices was accessible for both men and women and was routinised in daily practices. Although social distribution was gendered, it was also complementary between genders. Special knowledge was bound with specific work as in the case of the local midwife who had been trained for almost twenty years by her mother and who now trains her own daughter in matters relating to pregnancy, delivery and curing children's illnesses. This form of knowledge is still relevant in the present context, with methods of curing based on herbal and natural medicine and, since she works part-time in a health station in the neighbouring town, Yamfo, she also has access to modern forms of healing, enabling her to expand her own experience without relinquishing the knowledge she had acquired. In order to get away from the status of an untrained midwife, she tried to obtain a license from the Ghana Medical society, which would officially give her the status of a trained midwife. Her primary education and formal occupation as a farmer required the additional support of "a man to stand behind her" in the sense of financial support. He did however not support her efforts at professional acknowledgement. For the recognition of her knowledge and experience, it was therefore not her status as an untrained midwife, but her personal situation which hindered her taking her profession further.

For the old women the matrikin continued during their lifetime to be the main context for the exchange of knowledge and for innovations. The introduction of new crops such as cassava in the 1970s and the new ways of preparing the main food *fufu*, new kinds of herbs such as *acheampong*, and coping with severe situations such as droughts in the 1980s, were challenges within internal and external situations. The practice of sharing among women was upheld among close friends or sisters in particular who also continued to live in the same compound or moved to another house or town. Experience was, and still is, shared by visiting in the same town or travelling to another village or town outside Susuanso. Observation of their own experiences and practices has not changed, not even due to influences of modernisation and Christianity. What has changed however is the specific universe maintenance and specialised sub-universes, which mediated and legitimised their knowledge. By turning to the specific form of mediation and legitimisation of knowledge I will leave the process of knowledge generation.

4.3 The Mediation of Knowledge: Symbolic Spaces and Practices in the Everyday World

The process of knowledge becoming an "objective" fact has been maintained during Nana Yaa's lifetime via processes of legitimation. Legitimation can be defined as a process of giving meaning to the social world. Besides the institutionalised processes of knowledge transmission based on orality, knowledge was symbolically mediated, depending on the capacity of actors to act on and react to the social world and on the transcendence of experience. Both the generation process of knowledge and symbolic mediation constitute the relevant structures of social agency. The construction of symbolic universes (Berger/Luckmann 1966: 92) as another layer of realities outside the everyday world creates a frame of agency and a system of putting order to the lived world. Those symbolic universes are constructions of imagination (Schütz 1962: 407) or in the words of Henri Lefèbvre, "imagined spaces" (1991: 38). Their realities cannot be approached in a cognitive way, but since they are enclosed in an invisible world are made visible through symbolic practices in the everyday world. The process of transcendence beyond the visible world refers to the everyday world and establishes a duality of social and symbolic worlds connected through a specific order. The symbolic order regulates the process of giving meaning to the social world and refers back to signifying society itself (Eder 1988: 64), which means that the social order of knowledge correlates with the symbolic order.

In the further analysis of symbolic spaces I take up the notion of Alfred Schütz's "appresentation" explaining how symbols and their social realities are theoretically grasped. According to Schütz, they are symbols, part of the formation of mutual communication between people. Although they are visible and present in daily reality, they do not refer to themselves, but they function as bridges to another invisible layer of reality. Besides the reality of everyday realities, in which people "live", symbols are only carriers of meanings and are not meanings in themselves, functioning for pairing the realities and are constitutive elements of individual biographies. It is a constitution of the double meaning of symbols as permanently "presented" in lifeworld similarly as "appresented" universes which is of analytical concern. Why are symbols constructed at all? One answer Schütz gives is that symbols are memories of experiences transcended into invisible layers. These layers have been gradually formed out of explanations for the forces of nature and society. Sedimented experiences transformed into symbols have the important social function of assisting in individual or social problematic situations through establishing and giving the power of trust in problem solving (Schütz 1962: 207ff.)

Symbols and their meaning have been the preoccupation of social anthropology since its beginnings. While I do not intend to follow early structuralist, functionalist or symbolic anthropological approaches in my argumentation, which tend to put a dichotomy between the profane and sacred world or claim the relationship of both to sustain the equilibrium of society, I focus instead on the process of transformation of society and less on the reproduction of society. I take up the argumentation that by seeing "the outer world of everyday life as paramount reality" (Schütz 1962: 343), the relationship between these worlds, between different actors, the capacity to act in diverse ways and cope with everyday life reveals insights into the diversity of processes of legitimation.

4.3.1 *"At first there were gods in town"*

Even now many old women and men do not go to church nor have they converted to Christianity. They still believe in the gods *abosom* and in the supreme god *nyankopon* or *nyame*, forming their own religious world. There are hundreds of these *abosom*, who are all descendends of the supreme god (Parrinder 1969: 46) and function as mediators. Their gender differs. Some are male, some are female and some have both sex (Gilbert 1989: 11). They are not located in a specific place, but live everywhere and can come at any time. Nana Yaa explains that:

"Every family has its own gods, some are for the family, some are for the town. They will protect you: When the old people die, the young ones will not do it. They do not obey what you tell them, they do not believe in the gods. Most of them have abandoned the gods".

Each family is protected by two gods, which are given individual names and are approached by worshipping black wooden carved stools *akonua tuntum* with a small hole inside. Usually these stools, which are kept in the house of the male head of the family, lie on their side so that no strange spirit can enter. These rooms have no specific meaning, apart from holding the stool. The door is usually locked and only opened for worshipping, which is by the eldest male and female person of the family every 42 days on a Wednesday called *munukuo*. The stool is also used for pouring libation for ancestors, asking for protection and regarded as the custodians of land and custom (Parrinder 1969: 118). Worshipping the gods and pouring libation for ancestors is done in the same way and at the same time, but differs among gender. Men pour libation by pouring the local alcoholic spirit *akpeteshi* into the little hole in the chair. An old man explained that he had learnt about it when he was young and his uncle *wofa*, his mother's brother, had taught him. Women on the other hand cook some special food, pre-prepared with water from the river

Susuan. Giving food and drinks to the stool does not mean that the ancestors and gods are present in the room: they will however come and take the food and drink offered.

The gods are also consulted in cases of individual problems such as alcohol, infertility, marriage problems or illness. Gods not only have the power to help, but can also punish. For Nana Yaa this is one reason why young people turn away from the gods, because of fear of punishment, which they do not have to expect from the Christian God. With the acceptance of the Christian God by young people, they adopted the name *nyame* of the former God although there is a distinction between the concepts. While the *nyame* God can only be consulted through the gods, the Christian God can be directly approached through prayers. For Middleton (1982: 11) this difference in relationship and the direct form of communication was one reason why people turned to Christianity.

In the past the stool could also be approached indirectly via mediation by a Subchief or in serious cases by one of the four local priests *akomfo*, the gods were asked to help and mediation by the specific person resulted in advice. The priests, two men and two women, who worked as common farmers were not replaced. *"Because of Christianity there is no more fetish priest. And because of this, people do not know what to do with their problems"*. The term fetish is misleading and was first introduced by missionaries, who accused them of believing in the wrong gods (Rattray 1969: 86). Seebode (1998) in a recent study in a village close to Kumasi suggests the term of a ritual expert, as he observed their work concerning child sicknesses, infertility or marriage problems. In contrary to Seebode I prefer the name of a priest since the term expert as such leads to the assumption of theorising rituals. In Susuanso and in the surrounding area, only one female ritual priest is still alive. Although she was a practising Christian she was possessed one day by two *abosom*, who convinced her to become a ritual priest. She abandoned the Church and served as an apprentice to another priest for three years. She now lives in an abandoned and solitary house in the outskirts and explains, that *"[...] many people do not want to be seen when they are visiting me. People are coming from far and near and the Christians are coming at night"*. If she lived in the centre of town, people would not come to consult her. Many people come for personal advice relating to childnessness, money or health problems. With the spirits of the water[8] and the help of her three personal *abosom* she administers advice. Failings are usually not due to her advice, but are attributable to the

---

8   There are three "assistants" in the form of small gods, who help and advise her. Two male and one female with the name "Afia Broni",meant she is born on Friday (Efiada) and has white skin (Obroni). Since she is using water for her mediation, the spirits of it are of special concern. This form of a personified spirit living in the water, is in parts of West Africa a prominent institution called "Mammy Water", while it is believed that a pale women is living in the water. Apart from the name of one god "Afia Broni" which means a white women born on a Friday, no other indication existed to the institution as such.

customers themselves, like the one Chief, who had forgotten to pay for a sheep and after having asked for assistance for his town, many people have since died in lorry accidents. The hidden institution of the ritual priest as mediators to the gods will although marginalised even remain in the future. For the old people the gods are within the family and the town will continue to press on people to become priests.

Apart from the family gods two *abosom* guide the whole town. The two gods are called Takwabena and Kwasibarima, whose names are not specified, and are symbolised in the public with a cemented block which is built along the street-side close to a drinking bar. This block is called *pimasare*, which means "you meet and and you go back" suggest that by going there with your problems, you will be relieved when leaving. This cement block can be approached individually by puttings eggs or fowls on its side or in serious cases by the Chief or Queenmother of the town. In very serious cases they consulted the ritual priests for advice. This was done at times when there was a drought or if severe accidents had happened in the surrounding area, or at times when thieves were in the town.

Both the private and public space, were constructed as symbolic spaces visualised in the form of artefacts as stools or stones. The idea behind it and the meaning attributed to it, was the responsibility of the older men and women in the family and the royal elders such as the Chief and Queenmother for the public. Communication with the world of ancestors and gods was institutionalised to maintain the continuity and authority of individual practices in the everyday world and to act upon the solutions of problems of individuals or the whole town. Whereas the symbolic space in the public has lost its meaning completely and the stone is no longer worshipped, individual worshipping is still practised by old people within the family although the concept behind it is no longer shared intersubjectively, but is individually restricted. The religious world as one form of legitimation of knowledge does not give meaning to the agency of the younger generation, but has been substituted by the concept of Christianity. The "appresented" religious world of the old generation is undergoing a continual process of decline for giving meaning to the social world, bound with the weakening of influence of older people in legitimising their knowledge within the family and of influencing social processes.

4.3.2 *"To drive the sickness out of town"*

Christianity was also of influence for the gradual decline of another public institution protecting the town from disease or epidemics. At times of an increase in deaths such as child mortality in the town, the Queenmother of the town assembled all of the women over the age of thirty years in the palace and informed them of the situation. All of these women went to the bush to collect some special leaves, which had to be pounded. Afterwards, women swept the houses, compounds and streets, collecting all the dust around, mixed it with the pounded leaves and deposited it at the entrance of the town like barriers on the entrances of the streets. The barriers across the street were meant to keep the sickness away after it had been driven out of town, preventing it from re-entering or barring the way for an epidemic raging outside the town, thus preventing the town from crisis and disaster. Movements and cleaning rituals were accompanied by singing and dancing. Although it lost its meaning in the 1960s and is not practised any longer, the old women could remember it well. Two old women demonstrated the movements during an interview: the piece of cloth symbolises the act of sweeping dust and "driving out" of sickness while the other women danced in the same way while carrying the dust out of the town.

Nowadays when a child dies, some old women individually practice it in reduced form by going around the town, collecting eggs and putting them on the perimeter between the town and the bush. Nana Yaa comments on the reaction of the people: *"They laugh at me, they do not believe, they do not take it seriously. If only they believed it would help"*. This expression indicates, that knowledge which is no longer embedded in a social structure, but rather reduced to individual property, and therefore not socially legitimated, fails to have any transformative effect. By using the public space in the past, women mediated between illness and society. It was not illness as such which was of concern, but rather the condition of society. Illness is not considered an individual problem of curing, but is more a social phenomenon involving not only those who are affected, but the whole town (Lachenmann 1982: 146-147; 151). Modern forms of curing individuals should rather include the social and cultural context of the specific person and not only be addressed towards the form of illness.

With the body movements and singing the prevention of disasters is expressed symbolically and display how the wider environment can be influenced. Since this form of practice has been restricted to elderly women the constitution of the interrelatedness between society and the conception was based on adopted experience. A similar situation could have been observed by Ute Luig for the ethnically related Baule in the Ivory Coast, where women used their bodies to defend against illness and prevent disasters (1990: 273). In colonial times those dances were taken up by men who invented other new dances which formally excluded women (Luig 1990: 273). Body movements in the form of dancing and exercising symbolic power are one element of agency with the aim of manipulation and transformation of the environment and the exercise of social competence (vgl. Bourdieu, 1985).

*Figure 3: An old woman performing the ritual
of driving the sickness out of town*

4.3.3 Worshipping at the River Susuan

Meanings were also attributed to nature, in particular towards the river and its connection with the land. These cultural conceptions are social mappings regulating the everyday world. Nana Yaa goes on, *"every river has a special taboo day and on that day you should not go to the farm"*. According to the old people, the river is born on a specific day of the week called *ndjida*, literally translated as "a thing you do not take", and marks the day on which the river Susuan should not be crossed. For Susuanso the river is called *Abena*, a womans' name, indicating that she/it was born on a Tuesday. The river which flows only along one side of the town, not only marks the spatial borderline between the town and farmland. The conception directs that all of the farmland surrounding the town is also included, even those parts of farmland which can be reached without crossing the river. If people go to their farms on that day, which only ever happened in cases of ignorance thereof, bad accidents happen, as Nana Yaa explained:

"One day I gave the land to some labourers who were working on it on the taboo day, because they came from outside and they did not know. And there were nine pythons on the land, and the labourers killed them. After this, they went to tell it to the fetish priest who consulted the gods and they had to give him coco-yam, chickens, and it was put along the banks of the river on the farmland".

The river and the farmland are connected in a symbolic relationship. While the river is a symbolic and spatial barrier, its objective is to protect the land and people in a symbolic manner. The river is also connected with the belief that the fish carry messages to the neighbouring river Tano, which is believed to be the husband of the Susuan river. The river was also a symbol of worship and pouring libation for women, who put eggs or other food along the riverside. The messages which were given to the river were meant to be carried by the fish to the supreme God *nyame*. It was therefore in the past forbidden to catch a specific kind of fish. Nana Yaa remembers that once when she went with some friends to fetch water from the river during the dry season, when there was almost no water in the river, a big fish suddenly appeared in one of the remaining ponds. They stopped fetching water because they were afraid that the fish inside would die and even put some more water in the pond, thinking the death of the fish would bring disaster to the town.

The Chief forbade the women to go to the river, it almost dried up completely and only at times of heavy rain has a slight stream of water. Nowadays the Chiefs go to the riverside and pour libation there by slaughtering sheep. From the old women's point of view, it was the prohibition by the Chiefs which resulted in the river drying up. To make the river flow again, as Nana Yaa suggested, one has to take the sand out of the basin. Men perceive the dried up riverbed differently. They argue that a damn built in the North is keeping the water away, which I could understand. Only there is no dam built in the North.

The river has been a space of transition between the natural and the religious world. Nature has been conceptualised as another "parallel" world (Luig/von Oppen 1995: 6) and personified with a female name and the belief of fish as carriers of messages. The symbolic appropriation of nature, worshipping, the ritual bath and water used for pouring libation, indicates that the river had multiple meanings in the everyday world of women. The river as a source of power became an object of gender-relations by regulating access to it. Concepts of nature and the appropriation of it are cultural constructs which are constituted by men and by women. This argument is of importance since it overcomes the dichotomies of women being close to nature and men to culture. For both the "ritual topography" (Schlee 1990: 1) contributes to the symbolic constitution of social identities. Nature has therefore a cultural meaning, as a "symbol of identity" (Schlee 1990: 13), and even more differentiated is constitutive for gender identities and power-relations. Nowadays the taboo day is still respected by the whole town, the context of its meaning is rather forgotten by the young generation.

During Nana Yaa's lifetime knowledge was mediated in different symbolic spaces connecting the "presented" with the "appresented" world: during *bagoro* young women were introduced to the spirits of the water, by worshipping gods and ancestors through the stool, at the riverside or the cement block, or dancing and singing in public. The artificial products such as the stool or cement block or even the natural scene at the riverside are vehicles of conceptions. These overlapping spaces have one common aspect. With the exception of private worship of the gods/ancestors, the practices are done in public spaces, visible for all the inhabitants of the town. These symbolic practices in their different dimensions were upheld by elderly women and together with or separate from the Queenmother. Older women over the age of thirty had in Susuanso a transformative effect on society: in defence, prevention, education and the solution of problems. They mediated in a space "in - between": between the gods/ancestors and society to maintain continuity, between nature and society, disease and society and between generations. The space "in-between" is not a space of dominance versus suppression, but a space of transforming and regulating social relations. Experiences and the ability to transcend it through diverse forms of communication such as worship, dancing and singing was keeping the "presented" world in line with the "appresented" world. The diversity of forms of communication constituted relevant structures for agency not only for women themselves, but defined an institutionalised form of social agency for all of the inhabitants of the town.

It is the constitution of the space "in -between" which enabled elderly women to have the power to transform social relations based on their experiences. Since there is not a word like power in Twi, the Twi word *tumi* literally means to be able to. The emic concept of power is a prominent topic in recent feminist discourses, e.g. Lenz/Luig (1990) who focus on the multiplicity of power and the different layers towards a more differentiated concept of processes of power, turning away from Max Weber's definition of power, which situates power on the "winner's" side (1990: 46-47). This goes along with the proclamation of analysis and understanding power relation in Africa by referring to emic concepts of power as proposed by Arens/Karpf (1989: XII). Power can be used by one person over another, but the relevant point is that power can also be based on experience, which is indicated by the exclusion of young women from the practices of the older women, and not on a formal structure as for example state relations. This aspect of the transformative power of elderly women is currently in other parts of Ghana and Africa part of local discourses on witchcraft. The power to influence society and the ambiguity of power of transformation and of exclusion, explains why in many parts of Africa especially old women are accused of performing witchcraft and the implementation of disease. This discourse is connected with rapid ongoing socioeconomic changes, insecurity and the dawn of new diseases like AIDS as Luig (1997: 25) and Auslander (1993: 147) have observed in Zambia. Old women, whose huts were burned down or are the objects of witch-finding rituals, were accused of empowering themselves through destruction. The inclusion of localities into a global context and the rapid changes at local level make rituals in the present part of an interwoven web of social change, thereby breaking up the dichotomy of "traditional" versus the "modernity" to a new phenomenon with new definitions of meanings in a glocalised world. As regards research on local knowledge this implies, that the knowledge of the old generation can not necessarily be revitalised, used or applied in the present. Since knowledge is still connected with personal capacities, local discourses and its social meaning as well as translocal connections have also to be taken into consideration.

Changes in the lifetime of Nana Yaa are in particular the conception of symbolic spaces in the public, while individual spaces have been retained by the old people up to the present stage. The ability of transcendence of experience has been reduced to the personal worshipping of gods/ancestors or personal actions against disease. What has accompanied Nana Yaa throughout her lifetime is a constant, latent process of loss of giving meaning of experience to the social world and this is the reason why old women nowadays describe themselves as weak and powerless in the family context. It is the decline in meaning and disappearance of symbolic practices which de-legitimise knowledge of the old generation and are the reasons for the individual loss of control and authority in the family context. Symbolic spaces and the exercise of power are not isolated from other forms of power such as the political power women had through forming a female political space with the Queenmothers. With the gradual process of de-legitimising the power to maintain the social order towards the palace has been cut-off.

With the change of symbolic practices in reference to the loss of giving meaning to the social world the structures of communication within the family and the institutionalised form of knowledge transfer between the generations have shifted and the forms of transmission and in particular oral transmission have gradually blurred. *"They do not listen"*, *"they are not interested"*, *"they do not move with the old people"* are expressions nowadays of the old generation for the blurring of transmission and explanations of the non-acquisition of knowledge by the young generation. The main reason has been the underlying process of Christianisation, which as a competitive universe has resulted in a change in the symbolic world and an accompanying establishment of a new gender-ideology.

4.3.4 Symbolic Spaces in Transition

Christianity as a religious movement started in the early 19th. century in Ghana and spread through the work of missionaries in the 20th. century from the coastland up to the Northern Region, which is in contrary to the southern part which is dominantly Muslim (Assimeng 1989: 84; Klingshirn 1971: 54ff.). Middleton, who analyzed the process of conversion in a village in southern Ghana, concluded that it was linked with the expansion of education, which was in particular attractive for the sons of Chiefs opening new possibilities in the growing of cocoa trade. Slaves were among the first to convert expecting freedom as well as widows and poor women (Gilbert 1989: 10). Apart from the process of active conversion, Christianity entered the lifeworld through schools (Klingshirn 1971: 256) and even today the two primary schools in Susuanso are within the institutional structures of the Presbyterian and Catholic Churches. Education and Christianity were accompanying processes, adapted from within via education as a Christian person, taking up the belief by reading the bible, prayers and singing Christian songs. The changes in symbolic spaces were not enforced by the Christians or through regulations, but rather diminished gradually. *Bagoro* was replaced by the blessings in the church and has completely vanished since the 1970s, without sexual education of young women being substituted by any other institution. As early as the 1960s, the practices of driving the illness out of the town had stopped. Singing traditional songs such as *nnwonkoro*, a female song tradition and group activity of gathering and singing together, only sung by women as an exchange of moral issues has further lost its meaning (Klingshirn 1971: 54-55; Anyidoho 1994: 141ff.).

Both education and Christianity contributed to the construction of a new gender-ideology, which compiled the missionaries' vision of educating girls in school to be good housewives and mothers (Klingshirn 1971: 180). The curricula of French and British schools in other parts of Africa foresaw household training for women (Staudt 1989: 77), and in particular within the context of development projects on nutrition or childcare which are upheld today. Despite the fact that education offered new avenues for women, the Victorian construction of gender-dichotomy of women towards "privacy" and men towards "publicity" has remained in present discourses. As we will see in the next Chapter (5) the dominant image of women as housewives for the kitchen is further maintaining the formation of boundaries with the artificial division of a public and private sphere and only recently has become part of a public negotiation. The "Victorian ideology of dichotomised gender behaviour" (Staudt 1989: 71) is reproduced in the churches and partly internalised by women. In one case, the priests of the Catholic Church advised women not to hide their money, but to show it openly to their husbands who could make further use of it. Women were also instructed on how to dress and behave in the public, e.g. not to wear mini-skirts or to drink alcohol during a funeral. Part of the construction is discursive and reproduced by women themselves: during a discussion in the Pentecoastal Church concerning the question as to who suffers more, men or women, the majority of women proposed that men suffer more on the account of the long journeys they undertake to reach their working places outside Susuanso. In everyday life, however, women are burdened from the early morning hours until the evenings with farm-work, cooking, fetching water and even late in the evenings with washing dishes.

The self-perception of the majority of women following the Christian belief reproduces gender-ideologies and boundaries preventing a challenge to them.

This ideology is used by men to keep women out of political institutions and also in educational institutions, whereas vocational schools in particular (often headed by women) offer training for women in the areas of catering, dressmaking, cooking and nursing while keeping women away from subjects on economy, technology or agriculture. The education system in particular, as we will see in Chapter 6, favours the education of men in terms of access to these institutions as well as inside them. Naked data on enrolment rates for the years 1991-92 indicates, that 45.5 % of enrolment rates into primary school are from women. With the continuation the number drops to 22.2 % who enter form six in secondary school, as well as in the year 1994-1995 25 %[9] of students at the University of Ghana (Legon) were women (vgl. Women in Public Life, 1998). Education as such was, however, of less influence than Christianity in the transmission process of knowledge between the generations. It was more the vehicle for transporting a new belief.

4.4 The Young Generation: *"Nowadays we are Christians"*

The generations following Nana Yaa's distinguish themselves from the old people by claiming to be Christians. *"Nowadays we are Christians and we do not believe what the old people say"*. Christianity is present in the everyday world in the language, e.g. in greetings, in prayers on the farmland before starting to work on it, before eating and in common prayers before and after a meeting. The insides of taxis are often decorated with Christian ornaments, Christian expressions are on signs of shops as well as Christian songs being sung at funerals. Although the Christian belief has entered many aspects of daily life, marriages are still conducted in the "traditional" way, by exchanging a small amount of money and some goods such as a bottle of the local spirit. There is now the tendency, that "traditional" married couples are marrying for "a second time" in Church – such as in one case in Susuanso, where a couple married in Church after more than twenty years of "traditional" marriage. The ceremony of marriage in Church is modest and short. After the exchange of rings between the couple and a common prayer, the marriage is fulfilled.

Almost all of the younger people belong to one of the churches, whereas the boundaries between the churches are fluid: couples can belong to different churches, and members of an extended family often go to different churches. Most people follow other activities within the church apart from the Sunday service, e.g. the church choir, bible lessons, youth groups or one of the women's groups attached to the church. These women's groups further reproduce the self-perception of how to become and behave like a good Chris-

---

9 The percentages differ only slightly among universities. In Cape Coast the percentage of women was 25.4 % and in Kumasi at the University of Science and Technology it was 18.7 % (Women in Public Life 1998: 97-102).

tian. In gatherings with women's groups from other towns or villages, topics such as cooking, reading the bible and singing of songs are central. These groups have an additional social welfare function, providing personal mutual assistance where money is scarce, e.g. paying the children's school fees. These functions are institutionalised within the churches, which have turned them in recent times into social welfare institutions. With the state withdrawing from the social security system in accordance with the conditions of the structural adjustment programme of the IMF and World Bank in the 1980s, a nation-wide "cash and carry" system was introduced in the health sector. Before entering a hospital or seeing a doctor, payment has to be made in advance. In times of accidents, terminal illness or expensive treatments, people can seldom cover the expenses by themselves. The prevention of such cases is seen in the Catholic and Presbyterian Churches of Susuanso in two ways. First, a weekly contribution of Cedis 500[10] by each church member is registered in individual booklets and in cases of emergency the amount required is paid out. Second, when a congregation member falls ill, special collections are added in addition to the common one. This collection is handed over after church, accompanied by a visit by all the church members to the patient's compound. The church is therefore not an institution, which can be separated from the state, but is closely intertwined with some of the functions of the state. The closeness between the churches and the state also offers new resources in the development context where male interests are favoured. After multiple visits to the different churches and the Catholic Church in particular, I wrote a note in my notebook: The church is not just a space of belief, but is a political arena, in which political decisions are made at different levels and from which women are practically excluded. It is a male network (10.2.1999). This was based on observations of interactions between the District Director of Agriculture, the Director of Agriculture of the Catholic Diocese of Sunyani and a local "broker" (Bierschenk 1999: 60), who are all members of the same church and the same political party, which was at that time in opposition to the ruling NDC party. Projects such as bee-keeping, the improvement of seeds and pig-raising are conceptualised and realised by the Catholic Diocese, and are intended to support farmers in the region with tools, money and access to other development organizations. The interconnectedness of the local broker between these institutions was three-fold: to have the further support of the political party, the church and a German development organization. Within these male structures and connections women are absent, which indicates, how these "modern" institutions have a detrimental effect on preventing women from accessing new forms of knowledge while further reinforcing the ideology of privatising women's spaces. To put the abstract concept of state, the church, and development into a local context reveals an institutionalised form of personal networking in development and in access to new forms of knowledge, is channelled along male structures. A local project on improved

---

10 Roughly about 25 Cents.

seeds initiated by a German development organization was implemented and guided by the broker and subsequently completely conducted by men, after receiving incentives such as boots and the possibilities of access to bank loans. The project aimed at improving the soil by planting a special sort of beans. Women were not taken into consideration within the project design as farmers. They were only addressed when it came to the processing of the beans, which can be used for preparing the local food *fufu*. In fact, this development approach is nothing else then a continuation of the reproduction of the Women in Development approach (WID) whereas women are recipients of external knowledge, but not considered as being knowledgeable. In its consequences their ability to critically deal with and negotiate the implementation of new forms of knowledge along the question of sustainability is completely neglected.

Brokers are positioned between local community and development organizations, which have become of growing importance in other African countries. The withdrawal of the state from society has opened new spaces for organizations like farmers' associations, the churches, religious movements or other clubs (Bierschenk 1999: 62)[11]. As a "strategic group" in accordance with Evers/Schiel (1988) they have a common interest in local and national politics. The structural position of the local broker is ambivalent by mobilising and appropriating resources (e.g. knowledge, power, religious aims) on the one hand and being dependent on external donors on the other hand. While the German co-operation had an agreement with the Catholic Church to continue under their auspices and to pay the broker's monthly salary, it failed to fulfil the agreement, which put the local broker into the critical situation of not being able to repay his debts.

The male network of access to resources, the possibilities to influence politics and development – even if it merely seeks to reproduce old concepts of development – is further in a contradictory situation for the transmission process of knowledge. As we will see later, men are of less importance for the generation of knowledge by the young generation. They seldom transmit acquired knowledge, further disseminated or reflect critically in an open discourse on it, but rather, they tend to monopolise and hegemonise it. The institution of the church being engaged in local development favours male interests while it is restricting in a discursive and practical manner the interests and knowledge of women through an exclusion of participation in decision-making processes on Church matters or in the negotiation on development projects. As an institution which has entered and shaped male and female spaces, the Church is not only a social institution as described above, but in its wider consequences of relevance for individual practices and for the individual stock of knowledge, less in its content than internalised in the produc-

---

11 By following the typology of Bierschenk on brokers, he differentiates between religious groups, associations of migrants, ethnic and cultural movements, and leaders of farmers (1999: 66-67).

tion of subjective frames of agencies through the reproduction of gender-ideologies.

Although women in Susuanso are not involved in the multiple official channels of development co-operation and in the distribution of resources, they are in a situation of being the most important source of knowledge generation for the present young generation. For the present generation of young men and women there is not the same clear pattern of knowledge generation and acquisition in comparison to the one of their mothers and grandmothers. Rather, complementary to the knowledge gained from their mothers, they follow different strategies in the "search" for knowledge.

4.4.1 Different Strategies in the Process of Knowledge Generation

With a change in the perspective towards the young generation aged 20-30, the verbal distinction between the old and the young generation becomes less sharp than mentioned before. Though I was methodologically focusing on this age group, it also refers to their mother's and father's generation, so finally all three generations are covered. On the basis of the interviews, it was impossible to find a common institutionalised pattern of knowledge transmission as it had existed in the past. Therefore I constructed three types, the "traditional", the mixed and the educated, to sift out the aspects they have in common and those that differ.

4.4.1.1 The "traditional" type: Afia

Afia was brought up by her mother and is now 25 years old. Her mother gave her a piece of land two years ago as she had worked on it since infancy. After marrying she received a second piece of land from her husband, which she had to relinquish after her divorce. She completed primary school, but she did not go on to secondary school due to financial constrains. She now earns her living as a farmer from the harvest of maize, cassava and oil-palms. She uses the method that her mother showed her for a mixing of crops. The method she learnt at school for planting crops in rows did not seem as practical, since it is more difficult to weed. She therefore follows the *"traditional"* – a term used by Afia – way of planting crops similar to the one her grandmother used. Although she was not directly educated by her grandmother, she listens to the conversations of the old people. Afia explains, that she often listens to the old people but she does not inquire about the meanings as *njida* any deeper and makes up her own mind about it. Tuesday is her day of rest from hard farm work.

Afia got to know about the use of herbal medicine due to a personal sickness and is frequently using it, which does not conflict with being a Christian. One day she had pains in her chest and went to hospital in Duayaw-Nkwanta. The doctors told her she needed an operation, otherwise she would die. She refused. Meanwhile her mother's friend collected some herbs which she started to use and she recovered from her pains. She decided not to go back to hospital again.

Afia is closest to her mother and the Subqueenmother of her family. Both have been of importance for the acquisition of knowledge. She takes the personal relationship for advice especially since her husband is not taking care of the child and generally comments on the Subqueenmothers.

"They are of importance. Sometimes I visit the Subqeenmother to talk with her, but usually when there is a problem I talk to my mother first. They should call all the women and the girls together. Especially the girls, and talk to them. Also the girls who live a bad life and advise them so they would stop. But they did not even organise them. But maybe they do not know that they should do it. I wish that they would do it".

What Afia means by a bad life is the informal sexual relationships between the young men and women in town, which often result in unwanted pregnancies. Many young women already get pregnant under the age of 20 years old, and since fathers are not willing to marry, they seldom take over the financial support of the child. The relationship with the Subqueenmother is complementary in matters of sexual education and personal advice.

Afia's case is typical for many young women in Susuanso. Upon completion of primary school, most of the young women stay in the town and make a living as a farmer. Some start as an apprentice seamstress or begin trading on the street selling food such as porridge, kenkey or fried fish. Usually they start farming at a young age accompanying their mothers to the farm and gradually receive their own piece of land. The method of mixed food crops and the small amount of cash crops is similar to the farming methods of the old people. The most significant change is the fact that the institutionalised form of accessing the first piece of land guaranteed by bagoro has vanished. Just the sexual education of the young women is no longer embedded in a institutionalised social setting, but reduced to individual communication. The acquisition of knowledge concerning farming was directly linked with the mother, who took it over from her own mother. In a similar way she got to know about herbal medicine and its use. Only indirectly through passive listening as opposed to active communication does she have some knowledge from her grandmother, the active communication comes from her mother. The active process of knowledge transfer between the old and the next but one generation has been almost completely cutoff. This leads to the assumption, that the old people would probably retain their knowledge. When I was interviewing another young woman, and she happened to mention that they are not allowed to cross the river without going into further detail, I sent her to ask her grandmother why. The same evening she came to my house explaining what her grandmother had told her and she now knew the idea behind it. Almost all of the young women are aware of the use of herbal medicine, but never address it actively in an attempt to broaden their knowledge from their grandmother. The institutionalised form of knowledge transfer has shifted from the grandmother to the mother. This has evolved to become a problematic situation, whereby an organised form of sexual education of young women is lacking. This explains the rise of unexpected pregnancies, when another woman said that she did not know that she was pregnant until delivering the child. The education provided by the Subqueenmothers of the families is still done on a individual basis such as between two friends, while the social institution similar to bagoro has not been replaced by another one.

4.4.1.2 The "mixed" type: Kofi

Kofi was born in Susuanso and brought up with his younger brother by his mother, who was a farmer and died some few years. He is now 24 years old and lives with his brother in a small house. Having completed secondary school, he is currently waiting for admission to a teacher training college and earning his living as a farmer. His main cash crop is maize. He uses his money to pay for his and his younger brother's education. Kofi explains his childhood as follows: *"It was my mother, who taught me all the time, I went to farm with her. As for my father, he was living here in town and sometimes worked at Kumasi as a worker. However, he has turned to another woman and did not take care of us. It was up to my mother to educate us"*. Kofis mother became the main role model during his childhood. When he was about with her, she was the one who taught him about herbal medicine. *"Normally when we were going to farm, she definitely came to me and showed me, this is for that. It is not a problem to use the herbal medicine, because it does not need the support of the smaller gods. And God has created them, for us to cure ourselves"*. His knowledge of herbal medicine has become an additional source of income at the present in helping people in town to cure themselves. By collecting leaves from the bush and preparing them, he helps to fight against malaria, a cold or headaches. For his age, Kofi is an exception in the knowledge about the various forms of treatment for himself and for other people. In contrast to some other young men who resist this form of treatment with the argument of Christianity, he, for his part, legitimises his practices by referring to Christianity. Whether they do not know about the herbal medicine or they consciously avoid taking it by explaining *"I am a Christian, we are against this kind of treatment. This medicine was brought up by the small gods. So if you are going to take it, than you have to worship them. Obey all their rules. But as Christians we are against such things"*. The religious background is interpreted as a resistance for using herbal medicine. Despite he knows, that other Christians are using it, he for themselves is rejecting it. It is left to the subjective interpretation of each one concerning his attitude towards it. He was also an exception when it came to knowledge of *"lives of the old people"* in terms of the meaning of the river as a protection of nature and society. He got to know the cultural meaning from his mother, "*I was close to her, so anything I do not understand I could ask her*". The interpretation is grounded in individual explanation, that the taboo day is meant for the protection of the land and preserves the destruction of the vegetation.

For financial reasons Kofi has not adopted the method of mixed farming by his mother, who had also given him a piece of land. He plants the maize in lines, which makes it easier for him to weed. He learned this method in agricultural class at secondary school, experimented with it and has finally adopted it, too. When it comes to innovations and the exchange of agricultural knowledge he addresses his friends in town. During harvest time they help each other in working on each other's fields and by joining forces to collect the harvest from each friend's field.

The case of Kofi being informally educated by the mother and in addition having gained a formal education in secondary school, does not make him an exception. Most young men were directly educated by the mother, who is also the main person of their informal education. The interest of Kofi about the conceptions behind the river and the teaching of herbal medicine indicates also, that the generation of his mother knows about it. However it is up to each person, whether they wish to teach it to their sons and daughters or not. Even in those cases in which the fathers were present in town, they were not of the same importance for the education of their sons. Fathers or grandfathers were no longer of concern for the transmission of knowledge. The former gendered space of transmission concentrates on the person of the mother with the continuation of a patri-hegemony of knowledge by the fathers. In a few cases it was the grandmother (MoMo) who educated the young men but these were rare exceptions.

4.4.1.3 The "educated" type: Akosua

Akosua is now 24 years old and attends teacher training college in Sunyani. In the future she would like to teach in Susuanso. Her level of secondary education means that she is almost an exception within the whole town. Akosua's parents are both uneducated, unable to read and write, and live off their farming activities. Akosua has a small piece of land on her mother's plot where she plants some yam, cassava, maize, okra and pepper as well as plantain. The planting and selling of plantain goes towards financing her education. She stays at the training college in Sunyani during the week and comes home to Susuanso at weekends or during vacation. She follows the "traditional" way of farming, which is the same as that pursued by her mother and of her sisters in the form of mixed farming. For Akosua this form of farming is the most efficient one and she did not adopt the farming method she had learned at school. For her, her mother was of special importance for her informal education concerning farming and in the use of herbal medicine in the treatment of malaria. In other cases of illness she combines "modern" and "traditional" ways of curing.

"When I am not feeling well the only thing I do is to go to hospital for some treatment and medicine. At times I have this sickness malaria, my mother used to go to the nearby bush, collect some leaves, cook some and I drank some and I bathed too. Even last time when I got malaria I went to the bush to collect the leaves, like my mother showed me, but as for the other sicknesses I do not know".

Knowledge about the variety of herbs is reduced however to one type of treatment. For Akosua the Subqueenmother of her family is a close reference person apart from her mother "[...] *if anybody has a problem they will contact them, if they need any advice. She is very close to me, and if I have a problem I contact her and she will tell me*". Akosua reflects on the situation of young women in connection with the Subqueenmothers and Queenmother in town. In her personal very close relationship with the Subqueenmother of her family she explains.

"They have to advise the young women, nowadays nobody tells them how they have to go with men. It caused so many problems. Girls nowadays do not know anything, they go for sex without being taught. They need sex education and they need to contact the Queenmothers. But nowadays, they have put it aside and because of Christianity the young women feel shy to go there. Because of Christianity we do not do that".

For Akosua the Subqueenmothers and Queenmother of the town should take responsibility for the younger female generation. Akosua's high level of education has not taken over a discourse on "modernity" in the sense of establishing a dichotomy between the less educated people in the Susuanso and herself as an urban educated teacher. Rather she integrates the different forms in a manner of reflection on "traditional" practices, their change as well as the dilemma situation between the young women and the Subqueenmother and Queenmothers of the town.

Out of the construction of those three types, within one generation a mixture of different forms of knowledge exists. For the young generation the acquisition of knowledge is on a first stage dependent on the knowledge of the mother, who is the main source of informal education for coping with everyday life. Especially the young women have adopted the mixed farming method of their mothers, and indirectly of their grandmother, whereas young men tend to use the farming method of monocultures similar to their fathers. What has mainly changed in comparison to the past, is the transmission along the gendered form of knowledge, concentrating now on the knowledge of the mothers. The practical knowledge e.g. about herbal medicine or farming is still based on the medium of orality and the copying of practices, even in some cases from their grandparents. Indirectly many practices of the old people as the mixing of crops, women mainly follow, or the use of herbal medicine, however not to the same extent, are still valid. In particular the storing of a small portion of crops is still done in the same way, apart from the storing of large amounts of crops as maize which men often prefer to keep in large wooden shelters. Despite some elements of knowledge being still valid, it is not socially legitimated and mediated any longer, but de-contextualised from former "imagined spaces" (Lefèbvre 1991: 38). The use of herbal medicine indicates, that the use of it depends on subjective trust and interpretations towards it, and on the experience in using it for oneself and in assisting others. The individualisation and fragmentation of knowledge refers to individual experiences and depends on the personal success or failures as well as on the individual reference to Christianity. I would therefore suggest to talk of "personalised" knowledge among the young generation, which should indicate that knowledge is not structurally embedded any longer, socially legitimated and secured, but personalised depending on individual orientation of mixing and strategising.

It should also be stated that the radio has become an important and new source for the individual stock of knowledge in particular for the young generation. There have been two radio stations broadcasting for the past two years: the state Radio Brong-Ahafo (B.A.R.) station and the private radio station Sky Radio. At the beginning of fieldwork the radio was underestimated although it is a common form of media. I first learned that the radio is more than a mere form of entertainment when I got into an informal discussion with my landlady. She suddenly interrupted me and said *"Wait, I want to listen to the radio, it is about typhus"*. After half an hour of a doctor explaining about the disease, how to recognise and treat, people could call and ask questions. He immediately answered on the spot. He not only recommended going to hospital, but also contacting the local herbalist. I realised that the significance of the radio is more than mere entertainment with people listening to it intensively in the morning, taking it to the field and in the afternoon while preparing food and supper for the evening. Topics cover a wide range such as agriculture, special youth programs, AIDS or alcohol problems. Those programs are mostly held by experts, doctors and extension-officers. When I asked a group of young women sitting on a corner about what they listened to, one answered *"Family-Planning, at Radio B.A.R. It is very interesting, because they can teach us more about how to take good care of yourself. The programme is on every week"*. Family planning is an issue for young women. But it is also a problem for young women to talk with their mother about it. When I asked a young woman how she got to know, it took her some time until she hesitantly answered "my auntie". This passive form of information is substituting to a certain degree for the active knowledge transfer which in the past had been institutionalised between the grandmothers and the grandchildren. Yet, the young generation discusses a wide rang of issues among themselves.

In the introductory chapter I have given a first example of two young men discussing the right form of maize to be planted. The exchange among peers is further a strategy of insurance towards ones own decisions. Not only of knowledge gained, but the constant process of knowledge innovation is to a high degree still internalised and not externalised to societal institution.

4.4.2 The Meaning of Formal Education

Formal education in schools in its relevance on the process of knowledge generation is of less influence than I had previously estimated. The contents of the curriculum involving agricultural subjects in particular are oriented towards Western innovations and modernisation, which can hardly be combined with local practices. As one young man drastically commented, "*I did agric. The school method is very difficult for you, because they taught as, that those people are using irrigation systems or machines. But in Ghana here, we do not have those things*". Apart from the financial implication, the adaption of foreign methods and the transfer of technology can hardly be realized in the local context, since they are not available at all, expensive to buy and to maintain[12]. The refusal to adapt to a foreign method turns the perspective towards the continuation of traditional methods. "*I am doing it the way my grandmother did it. The one I have learnt at school takes some money to do*". Implicitly, since foreign methods have been taught, the relevance of local valid knowledge has decreased in value, since it is not confirmed, emphasised or discussed in its validity. Owing to active neglect valid local knowledge is in a contradictory situation between its existence outside the school and its competition with promoted external knowledge within school. The contradictory situation is at least reflected by the pupils and students in Susuanso. Sabine Speiser, who worked in Andean Countries in Latin-America, commented on the relationship between teachers and pupils, that those pupils in their everyday reality and in coping with everyday situations know more than their teachers (1996: 318), however the hierarchical relationship prevents an active acquisition of this knowledge by teachers within the school context. The structures of integrating local knowledge within the schooling context need the openness of curricula towards it. Since curricula are designed at national level, the diversities of local specific knowledge can hardly be achieved in every textbook. The integration of local diversities can however be integrated through an interactive form of communication within the classrooms. This would dissolve at least the tension between foreign knowledge and local knowledge towards a critical discourse on the local valid kind of knowledge.

---

12 Steve Tonah, who wrote his thesis on the interaction between the state and agropastoralis households in Northern Ghana concluded that projects implemented to improve the agricultural situation by introducing modern farm machinery, improve seeds and herbicides failed due to mismanagement, high operational and maintenance costs and failed state politics (1994: 119-127).

As an initiation of "decolonisation" of knowledge[13] in schools the variety of local valid knowledge should be part of the curriculum. Because knowledge itself is constantly changing and adapting to new situations, the interactive form of teaching should avoid the prediction or teaching of the right form of knowledge. The relevance of the specific kind of knowledge should therefore be part of an interactive curriculum in accordance with present changing situations, e.g. in agriculture, nutrition or in health matters and in reflection on finding out solutions towards it. Through this the school curricula can become another space of creating new elements of knowledge, leading to an independence of external knowledge.

4.5 The Emergence of Ambivalences in Gender Relations

The 20th century was a continuous process of the social and political marginalisation of female spaces and a shift from the public to the private sphere. Women were not able to transcend their experiences and knowledge in public or exercise social and political power. Power is meant here as a defined and socially approved part of social structure within the family and the town. With the gradual de-legitimisation of knowledge the socially defined and, within the social structure embedded roles of elderly men and women as mainly responsible for knowledge transmission was not substituted or newly defined to other actors. The major discontinuity towards the present situation is that no clearly defined social apparatus for transmitting exists or has been substituted either by the Churches or by forms of development cooperation. With Christianisation and modernization a plurality of options of knowledge elements for one's own strategies came up. Although former knowledge elements are now in a competitive situation, many elements of the past have continued to be valid. It is, however, not only this plurality which is of sociological concern. More important is the fact, that through the change in social structure, the subjective stock of knowledge for individual agencies gained weight in comparison to the social stock of knowledge. Problems of individuals were solved in the past on the basis of the social stock of knowledge. It was part of a common socially approved experience, whereas problem solving is now a matter of one's self-relying experiences. This shift implies a major burden of problem solving and decision-making of the individual, although the relation among peer groups is used for discussing and securing one's decisions as well as dealing with major issues within the family. Although women have become the main source for knowledge acquisition for the young generation and take over the responsibilities of future generations they neither have a defined role for this nor does it correspond with power in the public or political space

---

13 Here I paraphrase the title of Gudrun Lachenmann's study "Dekolonialisierung der Gesundheit" (1982) towards a de-colonialisation of knowledge.

for social regulation, legitimation and transformation. This leads to the next chapter, in which the discourse, its emergence and the connections women have translocally established, will be described and explained. The focus will be on the Subqueenmothers, who can be characterized as the successors of the *obapanyin*, the old women within the extended family.

5 "Traditional" Institutions as Arenas of Knowledge Struggle

"Traditional" institutions have become, at present, ever more important by regulating private or public matters. Since Ivor Wilks (1975), T.C. McCaskie (1995) and others have explored in-depth on the historical formation of the institution, I take up an analysis of the present time with a slightly historical review, avoiding discussion about political plurality in today's Ghana, which has been described by Ray et al. (1995). Instead, I take the double interface between "traditional" institutions and the new form of organization emerging out of it such as the Queenmothers' association, as well as the interactions between this new form with other women's organizations into consideration.

The organization within "traditional" institutions is gendered in so-called "parallel political structures" or "dual-sex systems" (Kaplan 1997: XXXI; Okonjo 1976: 45). Within these structures women occupy certain positions parallel to those of men. In a comparative survey article Annie Lebeuf (1963) exemplifies this by using twenty different patri- and matrilineal ethnic groups located in diverse parts of west-, east- and southern Africa that these "parallel or dual structures", with their differences and similarities (e.g. in formal social organizations, in the process of election, the distribution of power, responsibilities and accountability) have underwent significant changes in the past due to different processes such as colonisation or modernisation of the postcolonial state, women within those institutions have lost their position completely or in parts[1]. The formation of "parallel" or "dual" structures in its epistemic meaning does not indicate sameness or competition, but should indicate an idealistic complementarity relationship between female and male structures (Stoeltje 1997: 44) and a certain autonomy within each structure among women and among men (Lebeuf 1963: 112).

The relations between the actors within these structures are thereof of interest, in the anticipation that "traditional" institutions are not static models, but are nowadays the objects of glocalised discourses on gender-relations.

---

1 Okonjo has given a detailed description of this process for traditional political institutions among the Igbo in Nigeria, in which the female *omu* as the head of all the women in a community had her own cabinet, her own courts and regulated market affairs. When colonial rules established local governments they recognized only the male counterpart *obi*, also through financial support. In addition through the influence of modernization especially through development cooperation and market change the *omu* has lost her social and political functions (Okonjo 1976: 45-65).

While I have conceptualised "traditional" institutions as arenas, I follow a dynamic approach, which should reflect the importance of its constitution in regards to knowledge and to those women, who are formally within – but in their context of agency – outside those institutions. "Tradition" has a twofold meaning: it refers to local institutions which had already existed before colonisation and structure the social order along kinship affiliation. The second meaning is the definition of tradition as a contested term used for legitimation and definition of social relations particularly the exclusion and inclusion of women from and in these institutions established in postcolonial Ghana. The term "tradition" is hereby open to a "metaphorical analysis" (Moore 1986: 10), an approach Sally F. Moore used to analyze the transformation of "customary law" on Kilimanjaro (Tansania) between 1880 and 1980. "Custom" in the case of Sally F. Moore or "tradition" as in my case are not mere social facts, but as cultural constructs form the focal point of a wider analysis of social change by taking their making into consideration.

5.1 Asymmetries within "Traditional" Institutions

Female structures are headed in Susuanso by a Queenmother and male ones by a Chief. The focus in research and literature such as the works of Beverly Stoeltje (1994; 1995; 1997) is often on the Queenmother as a single, isolated institution, while constructing her as a heroine and a prominent exception of an "African Power or Elite Woman" and neglecting her in the relationship to the Chiefs, Subchiefs, Subqueenmothers and the non-royal people in town. As regards the origins of the institution of Queenmothers, there is a wide range of descriptions often based on rather hypothetical statements and less on empirical analysis which describe her functions as ceremonial, mystical or as a "moral authority" (Fortes 1962: 65) or integrate her in the discussion about the assumption of an ancient matriarch (Farrar 1997: 579-580)[2]. Other, particularly evolutionary-oriented studies such as those by Meyerowitz (1958) or Busia (1966) explore the historical development of the institution of the Queenmothers and mystifies their essentialist functions as mothers who as the original and sole bearers of the clan, only gradually gave power to the men. The upraise of these empirical and theoretically questionable studies in the 1950s/60s is much more surprising, as R.S. Rattray, who had conducted intensive field research in the early 20th century in different regions of Ghana, had already hinted at the political importance of Queenmothers in local government and jurisdiction, while also pointing out the gradual undermining of

---

2   Farrar highly criticises studies, which confuse the institution of matrilinearity with matriarchy as well as other studies which focus on women as a monolithic category (1997: 582-583).

her position (1923: 82-84). Self-critically[3] he stated that Queenmothers are neglected by researchers and politicians and the male bias has contributed to the construction of her "invisibility" and towards the actual marginalisation in real life, especially in the process of colonial and in post-colonial Ghana. A few recent studies such as that by Kaplan et al. on the institution of Queenmothers and other powerful women like priestesses in the past and present African context, have developed a more differentiated methodological perspective of African gender and power, no longer tending to see her as the "superwoman among the victims" (Kaplan 1997: XXX).

Both the Queenmother and the Chief belong to the royal family of the town. According to oral history of the Queenmother and the people in town, the members of the royal family came from heaven and were the first ones to settle in Susuanso. People who do not belong to the royal family came as migrants having successively settled in Susuanso, and gradually through exogamous marriages were integrated into the structures of "traditional" institutions. Susuanso was founded by Kwasi Dankye, who left the original place where all the royal ancestors first gathered, and from where they gradually dispersed into different directions. The legitimation of the social hierarchy is given through occupation of the royal black stools, which are carved wooden chairs and are kept in the rooms of the Chief and Queenmother. Regularly pouring libations to the ancestors using the local alcoholic spirit or feeding the stool both commemorate deceased Queenmothers and Chiefs. Members of the royal family are the custodians of stool-lands, which belongs to the ancestors. Each member of the community has a right to receive some land from the Chief. In the past Chiefs were not personally wealthy (Rattray 1965: 116) and not the possessors of land. Despite having the right of occupation, but not of property, in recent times stool-land, which is close to bigger cities, is sold to individuals. To date, this has not happened in Susuanso.

The origin of the parallel structure is explained by the Queenmother of Susuanso as the need of both men and women to articulate their interests and concerns through this institution and the need for incidents between men and women (e.g. marriage problems) to be settled together.

The term Queenmother is misleading although the English version is commonly used in spoken Twi and is preferred to the Twi term *ohemma*, which literary means female Chief corresponding to male Chief *ohene*. How the English term was introduced in Ghana is uncertain. Early publications of Ramseyer and Kuhne in 1875 used the English term and R.S. Rattray, a British civil servant and anthropologist conducted his studies from 1907 to the 1920s in the Ashanti region in particular, continued to use the term (Stoeltje 1995: 1). Queenmothers are, in rare cases, the biological "mothers" of the Chiefs. Their relationship is constituted through the lineage system based on matrilinear descent, whereas the Chief of Susuanso is the brother *wofa* of the

---

3 "The white men never asked this; you have dealings with and only recognize the men; we suppose the Europeans consider women of no account and we know you do not recognize them as we have always done" (Rattray 1923: 84).

Queenmother's mother[4]. He was born in Susuanso and used to make his living as a cocoa farmer. Now 80 years old, he was elected Chief in 1979. The Queenmother is formally involved in the election and selection of the Chief, which has meanwhile become a highly political issue often involving the whole town. The Queenmother has to select up to three men from the royal family, whose nominations are discussed further within the royal family and separately by the elders. They send their decision back to her and in the case of disagreement discussion will continue. During this procedure, which can take weeks, bribery and manipulation of the elders and other people involved in the decision-making process are common. The election process also involves the whole town, by "hearing out the voices of the people" concerning the reputation of the selected candidates.

In the neighbouring town of Susuanso, Abesim, after the election of one Chief, quarrels within the town broke out which led to fights, and the police intervening to calm down the situation. The self-nomination of one man as Chief who was preferred by the people in town and the official nomination of another man by the Queenmother and the elders confused the whole procedure and both men claimed to be the chosen Chief. The election process as such reflects the importance of Chiefs in current local political affairs, and the critical and crucial role of Queenmothers within the process. The formal election process is not dependent on the sole decision of the Queenmother, but is a complex situation of different actors, in which public opinion to a certain degree counterbalances exclusion from the formal process. Even in cases of an important higher-ranking Chief such as a Paramount Chief or a Chief of a large area, representatives of the National and Regional Houses are involved. The election processes of Queenmothers are awarded less public attention and have not been a political issue within the institution as yet.

The formal organization in parallel structures goes beyond royal kinship through being connected with non-royal families. On the male side it encompasses the Chief, eleven Subchiefs and one linguist, and on the female side the Queenmother and six Subqueenmothers, to which I will refer closer to in 5.2. Of the eleven Subchiefs, five are directly related through exogamous marriages with the Chief, e.g. one Subchief whose grandmother once married the father of the Chief, or in the case of another Subchief whose grandmother married the Chief "*a long time ago*". The direct matrilateral relationship which regulates the succession of the Subchiefs explains the number of Subqueenmothers. Those five Subchiefs who are directly related to the Chief usually consult the Queenmother as regards family matters, whereas those six Subchiefs, who are not related to the Chief have the Subqueenmothers within their family as their female counterpart.

The Subchiefs are selected within their family and inherit the position when a brother or another matrilateral related person dies, while personal criteria such as good behaviour, good habits, character or personal maturity

---

4   Other relationships can be brother-sister, aunt-nephew (Stoeltje 1998: 177).

count for the election. Subchiefs can also be appointed by the Chief if they are good friends. Most of the Subchiefs were elected at an comparatively old age. At the time of the research the majority of them were in their 70s and had been elected in the last ten years. Only one Subchief was elected eight years ago and is now 44 years old. With only one exception, all of the Subchiefs live in Susuanso and earn their living as farmers or butchers selling meat at the local market, or through the production and sale of handmade baskets. The only educated one works as a civil servant at the district assembly in Bechem and frequently comes to Susuanso at the weekends. The Subchiefs stand in a specific order to the Chief, which is a relic from military times during the 19th. century (Busia 1966: 5-6). Depending on their position during times of war, each Subchief was given a special name[5]. As none of the eleven had a military position, additional positions and a new definition of the function were added and one is now the treasurer, another the secretary or door opener at meetings or responsible for calling meetings. For important or weekly meetings the Chief and all of the Subchiefs gather, dressed in traditional clothes and sandals. For less important meetings the Chief, his linguist, his brother or another Subchief are also present.

The formal organization of male and female structures gathers royals and non-royals within one institution. The formal organization does not however represent a complementarity in the relationship between the different actors in reality, but rather there is a triple asymmetry. The central point of struggle is the actual power constellation in local politics. For meetings at the palace only the Chief, the Queenmother and the Subchiefs are allowed to attend, while the Subqueenmothers are excluded. The first form of asymmetry is between the Subqueenmothers and the Subchiefs. The Chief verbally constructs equal participation between men and women by stating *"both are taking decisions together and are joining together"* which in reality has never been the case in Susuanso. A second form is between the Queenmother and the Subqueenmothers. The Queenmother of Susuanso is absent from the town most of the time and is not replaced by another woman. Compared to the political influence of the Chief, the actual power of the Queenmothers as the sole representative of women is less influential as we will see later.

5.1.1 The Queenmother's Dilemma

Nana Boahena was elected as the Queenmother of Susuanso in 1978 succeeding a Queenmother who had resigned. The selection was made within the royal family with the agreement of the elders. Her personal features such as school qualifications with a secondary-school education favoured her over her illiterate sisters. Her tender age of 28 years, was an additional privilege. As one Subchief argued, *"we did not want to have the old ones back"*, indicating

---

5   As the one who was walking on the left side of the Chief is called Nifa (left) ohene and the one at the right is called Benkum (right) ohene.

that age had become a reason for the selection of the Queenmother. Age and the educational background of Queenmothers have also become in other parts of Ghana important factors for the selection and nomination (Stoeltje 1995: 15). At the time of her election Nana Boahena was living in Sunyani, working as a secretary at the Ministry of Food and Agriculture. Later she established her own business and now trades cooking utensils and electronic goods. Her election as the Queenmother of Susuanso was not a reason for her to go back and live there. She explains her absence by the lack of jobs in the village and the lack of a regular income. Queenmothers do not get the support of the government the way Chiefs do with an allowance of an average of 100,000 Cedis[6] per month. Formally, the Chiefs should share the money with the Queenmothers, something they only do in rare cases and if they do the portion of money is small. In addition money is received from visitors, gifts, by selling trees to be cut by timber companies or the contract with gold-mining companies to mine for gold on stool-land. This money is mostly kept by themselves or shared with the Subchiefs.

Nana Boahena lives in a small room on a conventional compound near the centre of Sunyani with no outside indication that a Queenmother lives there. While some young women trade for her, she is usually busy going to Kumasi to buy items. Her appearance in Sunyani is in a modern style, dressed in Western clothes and uncovered hair. But when she visits Susuanso, she wears the traditional clothes of the Queenmothers, traditional shoes and a scarf around her head, completely covering her hair. The change from one appearance to another is situational and taken up by many Queenmothers, while I also met some who only wore the traditional clothes of the Queenmother.

When Nana Boahena was in Susuanso, she spent most of her time sitting alone in front of her family house and even when she called people to come and see her, they refused. On the other hand, she once mentioned, that "*I can control the whole town*" clearly overestimating her own position there, constructing herself within an ideology of a powerful woman, which in reality, she is not. Her absence from Susuanso was perceived as a problem for the women in town, especially the young women, complaining about her lack of motivation for organising together with them. Most of them have never talked to her and they do not even know where she is living.

Once in 1983, she tried to organise the women in town into the 31st December Women's movement which was at that time a two-year old organization and as an organ of the NDC party represented state politics. The movement and organization of women in Susuanso did not last. When I looked for women belonging to the movement, people could remember that there had once been something going on in that women were organised to clean the town, but nobody knew anyone who might be a member. "*It died*", as one woman in Susuanso said, "*and it was even once or twice during election time*". The refusal and resistance to be captured by the 31st December

---

6   Roughly about 50 Euro.

Women's movement can only be explained by speculative reasons: one reason may be the resistance towards a political movement which represents the interests of the government and its ruling party, the National Democratic Convention (NDC) in the name of women and is less a channel for self-articulation of the interests of women. In other towns of Ghana the movement which used to have branches or cells even in the remoter parts, has also weak support or does not exist for the given reason, that it imposes politics on women without transforming those social institutions and politics, which are detrimental to women's lives (Woodford-Berger 1997: 47). A second reason may be that the opposition party, the National Peoples Party (NPP), has a strong backing in Susuanso where its members constitute a majority. And it may also be due to personal reasons as regards the Queenmother, whose presence only once or twice a month, makes a permanent organization rather impossible.

In other towns or villages such as those observed by Brydon (1994: 232) in the Volta Region the movement was represented by Queenmothers who took up the WID discourse by realising income-generating projects such as gari-processing or tree nursery. Even when I asked the Queenmother if she was still a member of the movement, she denied this adding that she had only been involved at the beginning when she was expecting some economic resources but had stopped long ago. She is now a member of the Sunyani Ladies Club, a welfare organization which discusses issues regarding working opportunities and self-help aspects. This organization meets once a month and was established in 1978. Furthermore she is the treasurer of the Queenmothers' association of the Tano-District but was obliged to quit due to illness.

The constellation of an absentee Queenmother is a common feature in the region and in particular in some rural areas, where the possibilities of an income for educated women are limited. Queenmothers are to a certain degree put into a dilemma as, although they have avail of a comparably high level of education, they work in the bigger towns for financial matters and have a loose contact to the villages.

Financial capabilities are not the only reasons for the dilemma of Queenmothers. Queenmothers residing in their villages or towns, complain about being an additional voice at meetings in the palace. Nana Nyarko, who has been the Paramount Queenmother of the traditional area which also encompasses Susuanso since 1984, explains that with her position as a Paramount Queenmother it is compulsory for her to receive a monthly allowance from the Paramount Chief. For a couple of years now, the Subqueenmothers within the town have been putting pressure on her to change the financial disadvantage and to make an equal allowance between Subchiefs and Subqueenmothers compulsory. Although bringing up this topic a couple of times at meetings, the situation did not bring about any change. Her position there is less of transforming politics, or articulating and integrating women's politics, but more of contributing to an established agenda. During a meeting at the

Chief's Palace which I attended once, she commented on the cases brought to the palace such as about projects in the town, cases of fraud or cases of land disputes. Her position is a mediator between the palace and the women in town is of importance for the exchange of information towards the women in town. In daily morning meetings she has organised the Subqueenmothers to discuss issues, ongoing cases and the mutual exchange of information. Even in her formal duty as the advisor to the Chief, in practice her voice only has a limited influence and she explained *"they do not follow"*. When comparing an absentee and a present Queenmother, it becomes obvious that on the local level, the political influence of Queenmothers is limited. The structure in a parallel system does not represent a complementary between the political power of a Queenmother and the one of Chiefs. The complementary is reduced to the formal aspects with limited possibilities for integrating the issues of women.

The Queenmothers' current de facto powerlessness has not always been the case. One Queenmother in retrospective commented, *"they have taken the power after independence"* (Daily Graphic, 27.01.1994). Both the loss of symbolic space such as *bagoro* and their marginalisation within the political space were processes which make the present dilemma understandable. From stories of old women and men in Susuanso it can be ascertained that in the past time both the Chief and the Queenmother, organised separately or in public cases together.

5.1.2 Loss within the Political Spaces: From "Complementarity" to Asymmetry

"Both ruled, but this changed" was a common comment by older men and women. This short statement hints at two processes which have since changed the relationship between the Queenmother and the Chief, but also the relationship between them and the people in town. *"It is not like in the olden days. At first, when something happened, the Chief and the Queenmother were beating Gong-Gong for people to meet and they will come. In anything at all, he and she will be involved, but because of independence, everybody is free to do what he or she likes. So that has created the difference"*. Not only was the whole town involved in accidents or incidents, but both the Chief and the Queenmother settled cases together, organised communal labour – with the Chiefs organising the men and the Queenmother the women – including cleaning the town, weeding around the town or the establishment of a building. Independence as a given factor is not only defined in a political and personal sense, but independence also implies the diminishing ability of people to control the Chiefs and Queenmothers. Those complex political shifts affected "traditional" institutions as a whole during the 20th century, of which I only wish to outline those aspects which are of importance for present discourses.

The Period of Colonialism
The time of colonialism (1874-1957) did not destroy the structures of "traditional" institutions. When the British colonisers captured Ghana in 1874[7], declaring it their colony and naming it the Gold Coast, the judicial and legal administration especially in rural areas remained in the hands of "traditional" institutions. An old man explained that in Susuanso "as for the past it was the Chief and his elders and the Queenmother who have been making laws, do everything, wherever there was anything, whether they were going to communal labour or there was anything serious in town. They used to make their own laws". The establishment of indirect rule, however, diminished the legislative power of higher ranking Chiefs through the involvement of the British Administration, e.g. in the cases of punishment. What changed and mostly influenced the relationship between the Chiefs and the people in town was the regulation of revenues of the Chiefs and Queenmothers and the collection of taxes which the British Administration introduced in 1939 (Ray 1995: 56). Up to that time, Chiefs and Queenmothers had managed thei own financial matters as payments collected through renting land or money received as gifts or through tributes by lower-ranking Chiefs.

With the collection of taxes the Chiefs and Queenmothers gained power and a certain autonomy from the people in town, which was strengthened through collaboration with the British Administration (Ray 1995: 56). The establishment of Native Councils in 1939 brought a major structural change since the British Administration regulated political affairs together with the Chiefs, and by directly supporting them, it diminished the control of Chiefs by their townspeople (Ray 1995: 54; Göring 1979: 132). With the exceptional exclusion of Queenmothers from the Native Councils, the institution of Queenmothers became politically marginalised within the local and overall political system. At local level this meant, that the lineage system as such continued to be the main political context, but it was not isolated any longer from colonial administration. It marked the beginning of "divided sovereignty" (Ray 1995: 48) between "modern" administrative political institutions and "traditional" institutions personified by the institution of Chiefs.

The Transitional Period
What effected "traditional" institutions as a whole were political changes within the transitional period from 1951-57 and the postcolonial period following independence in 1957. Newly emerging political groups whose founders and supporters formed a small mainly foreign-educated elite claiming political participation and a change towards a "modern" political system oriented towards Western political systems. Those groups brought in the ideas of a national identity (Göring 1979: 125) and the ideology of modernisation. How fast those movements spread in Ghana even into the rural parts, indi-

---

7 In 1874 the British started the process of colonisation, which encompassed the coastal region, and until 1901 the Ashanti and gradually the northern territories (Ray 1995: 55).

cated the appearance of the United Gold Coast Convention (UGCC), founded in 1947 which opened its first party branch in Susuanso in 1948 and attracted "so many people".

The first president of independent Ghana, Dr. Kwame Nkrumah, restructured the UGCC as the Conventions Peoples Party (CPP) and within a short time established branches all over the country. Nkrumah's socialist vision and his concept of modernisation and development tended to abolish the "traditional" institutions which he declared a despotic and feudal thing of the past (Göring 1979: 168). Chiefs all over Ghana who did not belong to the CPP, were "destooled". Even before independence in 1956 the Chief of Susuanso, who belonged to a third existing party called the oppositional United Party was destooled, losing his legitimacy to rule and was substituted by the chairman of the local CPP party branch. The United Party emerged out of a National Liberation Movement, in which especially the Chiefs organised themselves in opposition to the politics of the CPP, and stood for the defence and continuation of the "traditional" institutions.

The changes in the political environment did not affect the Queenmother in Susuanso directly, who was able to stay in office, and *"because she was an old woman, nobody paid attention to her"*. Nkrumah further abolished the Native Councils and established in every town and village local councils or so called Village Development Committees, comprising of elected members, who were attracted by the new political system. Those new institutions were part of an administrative body connected with, supported by and strengthened by the CPP. At local level they became the most important political bodies and within Susuanso they took over the management of political affairs such as the organization of communal labour. Members of the local councils were mostly men, rich cocoa farmers and some educated young men. Chiefs were not allowed to participate in these institutions, and were excluded from membership. With the transfer of stool-land royalties and revenues to state- centred and local councils, Chiefs and Queenmothers lost their financial basis (Göring 1979: 196). The possibilities of political opposition were limited as, since 1964 a one-party system had monopolised politics and reacted with severe punishment against every form of opposition. Many people in Susuanso remembered that period as a time of timidity and fear of saying a wrong word to the neighbour in case they would be punished.

A few Chiefs, especially the ones of big areas, also gained power by political collaboration.

"The late Dormahene and some others, they made up their mind, that they are not to serve at Kumasi again. They started making organization, they were making organization to withdraw against the Ashantis, to withdraw and have our own. And Kwame Nkrumah also gave them the promise that if they are able to win the elections, the CP wins the election than they will give him the Brong-Ahafo Region. They will get Brong-Region and after the election Nkrumah got 20 of 22 seats, he created the Brong-Ahafo region".

The incorporation into one nation state was used by some "big" Chiefs such as the Dormahene to separate from the hierarchical system of Chieftaincy which was strongly dependent on the highest Chief, the Asantehene, residing in Kumasi. The newly created regions were a form of independence within the system of Chieftaincy, but at the same time Chiefs remained dependent on and restricted by the government. Even those Chiefs who were not in opposition and supported by Nkrumah were not allowed to enter government politics. Rather, they came, with the 1961 established Regional Houses of Chiefs (RHoC), under further government control which continued as a system of dependence. In 1966 with the fall of Nkrumahs regime *"all the Chiefs who were destooled were brought back"*. The de-powered situation did not change again or restore the old situations. The political influence of the Chiefs remained weak while the town development committees as intermediaries of the dominant discourse of development politics towards modernisation and an improvement in infrastructure kept abreast with centralised party politics. Due to multiple political changes in the following years, the members of those town developments committees frequently changed. Projects once started were stopped, others started but were never finished. The centralised government which dictated politics and predefined development projects realised their politics in a top-down manner, trapping it through the party structure down to the local level.

As a government-imposed institution the National House of Chiefs (NHoC) founded in 1971 had the status of controlling the Chiefs and regulating Chieftaincy on a national level. Both the Regional and the National Houses of Chiefs were established political institutions through which Chiefs were first controlled, but with the gradual management of their own affairs in 1979, gained some autonomy (Ray 1995: 60).

Period towards the Present

This process of regaining autonomy was supported in the "Fourth Republic" since 1992 by the examination of a new constitution and the decentralisation of political power relations in "modern" and "traditional" political institutions towards the regional and local level. This shift away from a centralised state, was accompanied by restructuring the Regional and National Houses of Chiefs. Both Houses became the political centre for regulating juridical, financial and political matters within the Chieftaincy system[8]. The importance of those Houses lies now in their autonomy of not being controlled by Parliament any longer. Politics on a national level is constituted in a collaborative–and tense – relationship. The Parliament has still the power to decide

---

8   The Chieftaincy system is composed of following organs (Nana Odeneho Oduro Numapau II 2000: 55):
    1. Traditional Councils
    2. Regional Houses of Chiefs
    3. National House of Chiefs
    4. A Chieftaincy Committee of any of the above mentioned

about the numerical constitution of the National House of Chiefs. This aspect is of importance for the present discourse on inclusion/exclusion of women within structures of "traditional" institutions. To get into the NHoC means whether to address the NHoC directly or indirectly through Parliament. The Parliament is further allowed to make laws such as adding functions to the institution of Chieftaincy, or for an organ of the Chieftaincy institution which regulates the enstoolment of Chiefs.

The restructuring of political power relations focused almost exclusively on the personification of "traditional" institutions towards the Chiefs. The institution of Queenmothers was not further taken into consideration, neither in the regulation of financial matters nor in integration into the Regional and National Houses of Chiefs.

To summaries it can be said, that "traditional" institutions underwent significant changes during the 20th. century, and have regained social and political recognition after a period of disempowerment. The present dilemma of the Queenmothers and their restriction of formal duties, but not the actual power for transformation, can be explained by the processes described above. On the basis of historical and recent political changes, they have not been included on important political bodies, the Regional and the National Houses of Chiefs. By being restricted through constitutional and customary rights, they have however created their own new spaces for challenging and transforming exactly these political institutions. But first, I want to draw attention to the other two asymmetries: the one between the Subchiefs and the Subqueenmothers and the one between the Queenmother and the Subqueenmothers. The contextual description will explain the upcoming of the new form of social organization and its pragmatic approach towards changing gender relation.

5.2 Challenging of Spaces: The Subqueenmothers

The present situation of asymmetry within "traditional" institutions is challenged by the six Subqueenmothers of Susuanso. The institution of Subqueenmothers is a new phenomenon and I had not read about it before I came to Ghana. Subqueenmothers are selected by female and male family members and are "enstooled" via a ceremonial act whereby they receive their own wooden carved stool. This ceremonial act takes place in the Chief's palace, where all the elders and people from the town gather. In correspondence with the specific Subchief's name, a stool name will be given to her: if he is the Nifahene, her name will be Nifaohemma[9].

The criteria for nomination and selection are personal, such as the way they talk to people, their openness, patience, behaviour in public and even the

---

9 Nifa means left. So the Nifaohene is the Subchief, who sits on the left side of the Chief.

way they walk. With the enstoolment of a Subqueenmother, appearance also changes: hair is shortened and shaved in a special rounded form around the head. Usually they wear a scarf around their head in public. For special occasions they dress in the "traditional" style and wear special shoes. With the enstoolment some other changes can also occur, which vary depending on the locality: Subqueenmothers in Duayaw-Nkwanta are not allowed to cook or eat in the public. Even their meals must be taken in their rooms, sitting at a small table invisible to the public. If they go to their farms, they are not allowed to carry things on their heads. For the Subqueenmothers of Susuanso there were no additional restrictions. All of them continued to make their own income by going to their farms almost every day. Apart from one Subqueenmother, who is a teacher, all of them live off their farming activities.

With this new habitus (Bourdieu 1976: 170) they clearly distinguish themselves from other women through clothing, behaviour and name. The notion of habitus in the way Bourdieu uses it, indicates that the body becomes a repository of dispositions: predefined institutional structures and acting upon themselves in the sense of a appropriated "body politics". This habitus, and here Bourdieu is clearly right, is an embodiment of symbolic appropriation and a disposition to new forms of practices and of representation (1976: 165) which draws the line of distinction.

Subqueenmothers are enstooled to settle cases within the family, to advise and assist people in town and to be present at funerals by sitting besides the Subchiefs. The codifying of their position opens a new frame of action within the family context by deciding on cases such as the maintenance of children, marriage issues and financial quarrels. Minor cases are usually settled by the Subqueenmothers alone, while in serious matters, both the Subqueenmother and Subchief decide upon it. They also join together for the pouring of libation to the family stool in memory of their ancestors. The enstoolment of a Subqueenmother also depends on the will and financial situation of the Subchief, who has to support the enstoolment with presents such as clothes, the stool, shoes and some additional expensive items like food and drinks for the people taking part in the ceremony itself.

Just how the phenomenon of Subqueenmothers occurred can not be clearly answered despite the fact that I followed this question and discussed it with people at the "traditional" council, the various Chiefs and Queenmothers. When I asked why there are now Subqueenmothers, the general answers from both men and women were that *"every Subchief needs a Subqueenmother"* and concerned *"customs"*. The first Subqueenmother in Susuanso was enstooled in 1985, and then successively in the last ten years. In comparison to the Subchiefs, almost all of the Subqueenmothers were young at the time of their enstoolment, with ages ranging from 29 to 40. It can however be explained that they replace the *obapanyin*, the eldest woman, within the family. One Subqueenmother argued that she had to wait to become a Subqueenmother until the *obapanyin* within her family died. What can be observed is a shift within the family context whereby the eldest women who were the female head of their families, are now being formally replaced by younger Subqueenmothers. This shift can be summarised as a shift from seniority status to symbolic habitus.

The capacity within the family for political (settling cases) and symbolic (worshipping ancestors, funerals) practices is two-fold: with its radius limited to the family context and on the other hand it enables them to extend the boundaries beyond it and to challenge old spaces. For some time now, the Subqueenmothers of Susuanso have been putting pressure on the Queenmother and the Subchiefs to obtain permission to attend meetings at the Chief's palace. Despite exerting pressure for several years, they have not succeeded. Dissatisfied with the restriction of their spaces to the family context and taking the absence of the Queenmother as well as their own exclusion as a problem, they struggle towards extending their rights. Interaction with the Queenmother reveals the tension between them and the Queenmother claims to be the only woman in town who has the permission to attend meetings, "*I am the only Queenmother, they are for the houses, not for the town*". Restriction to the family by setting boundaries and the ongoing struggle for power follows a gender hierarchies. Gender in the "traditional" institution is in this context not a basis for solidarity and common interests among women. The division between royal and non-royal kinship establishes and manifests the hierarchical arrangement. Ann Whitehead (1984) came to similar conclusions in Asia, where kinship sets boundaries, hinders common mobilisation and is one reason for the demobilisation of a common movement within "traditional" institutions.

Through networking across kinship structures the Subqueenmothers have established a common ground for self-empowerment. In the form of informal gatherings they discuss issues which go beyond the family context as well as strategies of how to participate in political institutions and how to input innovative ideas. Topical discussions are addressed to solve social problems within the town. Some issues they have taken up, are about the increase in teenage pregnancies in recent times, employment issues among young people, the stream drying up as well as the high expenses during funerals, which usually put people in debt for a lifetime. Discussions are linked with deliberations on strategies which can be taken up. Within these discussions old and new elements are reflected upon and negotiated in order to solve pressing problems. The Subqueenmothers demand an revitalisation of *bagoro* in a redefined way to be compulsory for all the young women in town. At individual level within their own families they started to practice it by talking with young women about sexual education, as well as connecting it with aspects of HIV/AIDS and the meaning of formal education. In reference to the young women one Subqueenmother argued "[...] *they can become something better, than just farmers*". The new definition of "puberty rites" should help the young women to earn their own income before establishing a family or preventing them from becoming mothers out of wedlock. The logic of the redefined form of *bagoro* is less on exercising control over young women, the way it has been in the past, and more to advise on, support and enhance financial and individual autonomy. The Subqueenmothers realised that the social institutionalisation of *bagoro* in including young women of these families where no Subqueenmother exists, can only be possible by having the political power to bring it into realisation. Since they have failed to enter the palace by lobbying, the Subqueenmothers have joined the newly established Unit Committee Council, established in the context of decentralisation and a political body aiming at including elected town members from outside the "traditional" institutions. The elected members, however, did not attend the regular meetings that took place. "*It is not working*" complained one Subqueenmother and it became an artefact of state policies, but not an arena for political issues concerning the town. Aware of its failure, they were turning their strategies back again towards the Chiefs Palace. In a similar way of integrating old and new elements of knowledge, Subqueenmothers are pushing on revitalising the dried out stream. They argue on a cleaning of the river and a planting of trees along the stream-side to keep the flowing of water. However, this topic is even more delicate than the one on *bagoro*. Since *bagoro* is quite an isolated institution, the revitalising of the river which is still a source of power, is a public affair turning around the prohibition of Chiefs for women to go to the stream to an active appropriation by the Subqueenmothers. The ecological discourse of the Subqueenmothers, which seems from an outside perspective as a "best practice" in environmental aspects, has a much deeper political connotation as being part of a self-empowerment process and an open confrontation with the persistent knowledge order.

The two sides of the struggle within "traditional" institution and outside are part of an analysis and of strategising self-empowerment. While observing and analysing their lifeworlds, they have taken up a discourse to change power hierarchies and social realities to integrate their knowledge into the political setting. It is a process of critical analysis, close to a sociological analysis, which is a form of exploring and strategising the (long) way of getting into the palace which aims at social transformation.

5.2.1 *"We are not too shy"*: The Long Way to the Palace...

The struggle of boundaries and the exclusion of Subqueenmothers from the palace is embedded in a local and, as we will see later, in a translocal discourse around the notion of "tradition" and on vanished spaces, which as a cultural construct is used for the demarcation of spaces and for the definition of social relations. The following small excerpt highlights the dynamics of the local discourse between Subchiefs and Subqueenmothers. The argumentation of the Subchief's side is, that they would invite the Subqueenmothers to the meeting, but they would de facto never come, because they are too shy. This argumentation came out of the interviews I had with the Subchiefs. When I confronted the Subqueenmothers during a common meeting with the argument of shyness, they started laughing. "*At the family meetings, we meet each other and discuss things with them so we are not shy*", explained one Subqueenmother as the reason for the laughing. Shyness can not be the reason, because they also talk with the Subchiefs within the family, settle cases with them and attend public funerals. It is not shyness which keeps them away from the meetings, but a lack of information and deliberation, because the Subchiefs never invite them. If they did they would go. Shyness as female attribute defines gender boundaries in restricting the Subqueenmothers to the family level and thus establishing boundaries to the public. The Subqueenmothers see the real reason for the lack of information as the fact that the Subchiefs do not want to share the money with them and want to monopolise the political sphere. Being isolated from the meetings, they never hear the topics of discussion or only hear parts of them and sometimes only through other people but never through the Subchiefs who keep the information and do not channel it to the public. The legitimation of Subqueenmothers for challenging the "doxa" (Bourdieu 1991: 242) the taken for granted world, is based on two moments:

First, with their self-definition of being the direct link between the people in town and the palace:

"We want to go to the meetings to get information to listen what has been said and to influence the decisions. We can send the decision-making to the people in town. We can also suggest things, we can help the men, especially when it comes to the women's side".

They claim to fulfil the procedure of sharing information between the palace and the people in town and in addition they want to influence politics.

Second, by referring to the *aberewa nyansafo,* the knowledge and wisdom of the old women, who used to be the advisors to the Queenmother, the Subqueenmothers claim to keep this knowledge. The social construction of the *aberewa nyansafo* is legitimising the strategic actions of entering the palace and reacting to social issues. The appropriation of political space should furthermore open the gate to the redefined symbolic spaces, filled with new elements of knowledge.

5.2.2 ... and how to get into the Palace

The discussion about the attendance of Subqueenmothers finally became a topic in the Chief's palace.

The Palace

The palace of Susuanso ahemfie literally means the house (fie) of the Chief and is located directly on the main road in the centre of the town. Only the Chief and members of his family live in the house, while the Queenmother's palace ohemmafie is almost opposite on the other side of the road. This form of arrangement differs from town to town and there is no specific settlement type as such either for each palace or for the location between both houses. The buildings as such do not differ from the other houses in the town, except big wooden entrance doors replace gates. The size and external architecture are alike. Only the Chief's palace is painted more often than other houses. The inside of the Chief's palace distinguishes it from other houses. The rectangular inside of the Chiefs palace has an exceptional setting. Going through the main door, which is usually open and only closed when the Chief is not present, one stands at the entrance side on a small flat platform which is used for minor meetings. To the right and left of the open interior compound are storage and bedrooms for the Chief and his family. Opposite the entrance side, another bigger platform, with the Chief's stool in the middle directly located under a fan, is used for the spatial arrangement of meetings. To the left and right of the Chief's stool, the Subchiefs sit in a specific order. If the Queenmother is present she sits on the Chief's left. Apart from this special arrangement of the two platforms, the uncovered middle part of the palace is used for daily work such as the drying of cocoa or laundry. Chickens, dogs and cats move freely throughout the compound. The Queenmother's palace is built in a standard fashion without any platforms and only used for small personal meetings. From the outside neither palace has any special exterior representation hinting at its political importance. The doors are usually open enabling people to go inside and talk to the Chief or Queenmother. The empty spaces between the cemented stone buildings even let people see, what is going on inside. The palaces have no special taboos or restrictions and apart from special harvest meetings, anybody is allowed to go there at practically any time.

Since the new constitution and political restructuring, the palace has become the major location for meetings. It has become a place for juridical cases, e.g. in cases between two brothers or between two villages, and a political place. Every local initiative, government initiative or development project must pass through the Chief's palace. Before decentralisation, the government could directly implement its politics on the village without having consulted the Chief and elders. With a direct link between the Chief and the district assembly man, who represents the town at the regional district assembly meetings in Bechem, the connection to "modern" institutions is established which decide upon development in the region.

Apart from the importance of the palace as a political space, it is a financial place where money changes hands from visitors from the nearby gold-mining company, for example, or the sale of trees by the Chief. The palace is also a place of representation where public events take place or the Member of Parliament meets the people of the town. The meaning of the palace is manifold: political, judicial, representational and financial.

The Palace and the Meeting: Changing Spaces

In a meeting between the Chief, the Queenmother, the Subchiefs, the Subqueenmother and the district assembly man, the discussion entered another stage[10]. The Subqueenmothers brought forward the notion of being the aberewa nyansafo which was defined differently by the Chief and Subchiefs in a rather metaphorical expression: if there is a meeting and no agreement can be found, the members disperse and withdraw into small groups in a quiet corner. This withdrawal and discussion in small groups is called the "consultation of the wise women". The meaning attributed to it by the Subchiefs and Chiefs differs from that of the Subqueenmothers.

On the contrary the Subqueenmothers argued against the exceptional symbolic meaning by referring to their social importance in the family and their increasing responsibilities in society. As female heads of their families they are capable of solving family problems. They can do the same for the town. The Subqueenmothers' defence continued that women constitute more than half of the population in Susuanso. Not only is the number important, but also that they as female heads can mediate the issues of women much better with the palace, and through this mutuality can contribute to solving issues affecting the town especially as regards education. Even with an increase the number of people in the traditional setting, the weight of the decision of the palace would nevertheless increase. The reactions of the Subchiefs and Chief differed: some were rather skeptical, others even favoured the idea. As one Subchief said *"There were no Subqueenmothers in the olden days, so it were the Chief, the Subchiefs and the Queenmother who were attending meetings. But now we have to modernize it, so we should not stick to the custom. We can also make some change"*. Even the Queenmother who was at first adhered to the argument of tradition changed her mind. When she is not present, the Subqueenmothers can represent and replace her. The final decision which took place some weeks later gave the Subqueenmothers permission to attend on the condition that they are not allowed to talk openly in the palace. One Subqueenmother commented on this, *"then we whisper into the ears of the Subchiefs"*.

The Subqueenmothers have used self-organization to create a new space for discussing and analysing the social world. This has created a constant process of reflection and examination of perspectives to overcome the restrictions of their agencies. Their aim was not to alter the structures of "traditional" institutions as such, but rather they had to be changed in order to react to social or environmental issues. By altering the structured space they would gain the authority to speak for themselves and the power to speak for others. Through the transformation of a long established social institution new definitions among and between gender and of the social order have taken place. It is also a process of legitimating their intended actions at societal level. The struggle of the Subqueenmothers can be broadly defined as a movement from

---

10 In Chapter 2 I have already discussed how it came to the meeting.

the private to the public sphere by self-organization in a informal way across kinship relations. Articulation was motivated by their common habitus and common identity as being knowledgeable women. This form of act can be described as a "microcosm" of a social movement. In accordance with Neidhardt's definition of a network as the basis of a social movement, it is characterised by a lack of a clear organizational structure or a defined programme (1985: 196). However, the moment of solidarity is objectifying the subjective situation and as such an additional factor for networking. To form a network was less the strategy as such, as it was a medium to re-define meanings attributed to symbolic spaces. In its social consequences, the network is a vehicle of transforming social relations and the social structure. It is therefore not a social movement in the sense of further increasing mobilisation, but of transforming symbolic, political and social spaces based on the factor of their historical knowledge and gained new experiences. This way can be characterised as a discursive struggle for symbolic spaces with a political outcome. The outcome is a complete new scenario and not a replicate of the past version of the *aberewa nyansafo*. Whereas in the past the day-to-day experiences and knowledge of the *aberewa nyansafo* was used as a source in political decision-making processes at the palace in the form of frequent consultation, now the logic of practice is the other way around: continuing presence in the decision-making processes serves for legitimating knowledge and innovative practices. History in the form of historical knowledge becomes in real time even more important, contributing towards the shaping of identity and for the formation of knowledge repertoires. The instructive past and intended future mark the turning points of social marginalisation and the social order of knowledge. "The negotiation of social memory is in fact history in the making" as Heike Schmidt (2002: 203) in reference to Elizabeth Tonkin's book *Narrating our Past* (1992) has pointed out on the core of the issue.

The network is the basis of a broader social movement since the discourse at local level does not emerge out of a vacuum, but is connected with translocal discourses on gender relations in "traditional" institutions, which has been going on in Ghana for some years. Two moments have to be seen together: first of all the network of the Subqueenmothers is not an exception in the region, but is embedded in a wider discourse and part of further networking processes. Second, the strategies they have taken up on the local level are unique in the sense, that no agenda or programme are fixed which have somehow predicted their strategising. It is a specific local manoeuvring connected with a translocal dynamic movement.

5.3 Discourse about Political Spaces: *"Due to Beijing"*

The discourse on the challenge of the "traditional" order at local level also takes place at a higher level and is part of a wider transformative process. As I have described the process of losing political spaces by the Queenmothers during this century and the present situation of dilemma, they have become active in entering the Regional and National Houses of Chiefs. Already during the elaboration of the new constitution, which was finally passed in 1992, some Queenmothers, who were loosely connected at that time, have put pressure on the Consultative Assembly responsible for working out the constitution, about being admitted to the Regional and National Houses of Chiefs. They have elaborated and formulated a proposal which has however been turned down (Stoeltje 1995: 16). The new constitution created a paradoxical situation by defining a Queenmother as a Chiefs: *"Chief means a person, who, hailing from the appropriate family and lineage, has been validly nominated, elected or selected and enstooled, enskinned or installed as a Chief or Queenmother in accordance with the relevant customary law and usage"* (Constitution of Ghana, 1992). Chiefs and Queenmothers are therefore politically and judicially put into the same category, although this does not correspond with actual participation in political institutions, from which Queenmothers were still excluded. Since I have already hinted at the importance of those Houses, it should be added that Chieftaincy affairs further encompass the conduction of studies and re-evaluations in customary law, jurisdiction, evaluation, the interpretation and codification of traditional customs and laws affecting Chieftaincy (Constitution of Ghana, 1992). Both, the Regional Houses and the National House are hierarchically organised and structured. The Regional House of Chiefs comprises of the Paramount Chief of the specific region. Out of every Regional House, five Chiefs are elected to the National House of Chiefs (Kumasi) which encompasses 50 Chiefs headed by an elected President. The meetings usually take place once a month. The National House of Chiefs constantly interacts with Parliament on ongoing political issues.

The struggle of the Queenmothers to enter the Regional and National Houses of Chiefs, was taken up again in 1994, by the acting President of the National House of Chiefs, Nana Odeneho Oduro Numapau II. His motivation in starting the discussion within the Houses came out of the public debate on gender-issues in Ghana, in the wake of the fourth World Women's Conference in Beijing "[...] *and when this Beijing thing came then it is a topic for women, making their proper role*" by explaining that "*gender balance has been very topical these days*". Beijing entered Ghana through the media, issues on gender were taken up in national and regional conferences, and public discussions on gender was sustained by the multiple women's organizations. His specific aim as a male "lobbyist" was to strengthen the "traditional" institutions with the active presence of Queenmothers whose position he legitimated as being the founders of the institution of Chieftaincy. With the clear notion on defining and inventing Queenmothers as "mothers" of the institution, he is essentialising and further moralising the importance of a possible admission. His "revolutionary step" was realised in a concrete proposal for the integration of the Queenmothers as well as the magadjias[11] from the two northern parts of Ghana: Within every region five Paramount Queenmothers should join the Regional House. One of those five, should be elected for the National House of Chiefs, which would bring the number of Queenmothers to 10.

Finally, each Regional House of Chief decided upon the proposal in 1994. Out of the ten Regional Houses, only the Volta and Western Region supported the idea. Each of the other eight regions rejected the proposal. The answers from the different Houses were multiple. The Regional House of Chiefs of Brong-Ahafo (Sunyani) explained the decision as follows:

1. In some areas the institution of Queenmothers is unknown; those regions would be of disavantage like the Northern Regions, who do not have Queenmothers or the Central Region, where Queenmothers are only ceremonial.
2. Queenmothers and Chiefs form a unity and do not stand in competition with each other. If she is with the Chief in the same House and they dispute, they will carry it back to the villages and endanger the peace. By custom, they do not stand in competition, and can not be represented at the same forum.
3. The meaning of the *aberewa nyansafo* should not be exposed.

A closer look at the first reason on the differences between the regions shows that the proposal of the President of the National Houses of Chiefs to define *magadjias* as Queenmothers was not seen as a possibility of balancing the differences between the regions. While Chiefs have an undoubted political position in each region, the position of Queenmothers is controversial and some even reduced to playing a ceremonial role. The argumentation however in its negative formulation did not foresee the possibilities to adjusting the ceremonial position of Queenmothers or adjusting the ones of the *magadjias*. The second reason constructing unity as harmony is an idealistic explanation for maintaining the hegemonic position. Queenmothers joining the same forum like the Chiefs in the palace is definitely a constellation at local level which can be easily extended to the upper level. Through the restriction of expansion, the dilemma of Queenmothers was prevented from being changed although at regional and national level, they would have had at least a chance and option to change laws or to redefine customs.

Although the denial closed the doors to the Queenmothers, it remained a public discourse. Since then, Queenmothers have taken up the discourse

---

11 The institution of *magadjias* only exists in the Northern Part of Ghana. They are women leaders on the village level and act as representatives of all women in the village. They used to be elderly, wealthy women whose symbolic role has recently been extended towards involvement for organising women's groups and in the negotiation of interests with NGO's and local Chiefs (Padmanabhan 2002: 93-94)

again, which has also opened the gate for a deeper scientific analysis. Gender-relations in "traditional" institutions became a subject for research studies and workshops. A co-project[12] conducted with qualitative research methods at the University of Ghana (Legon), has been made public as "Women in Public Life in Ghana"[13] in the media such as newspapers and TV. One outcome of the study was that Queenmothers and *magadjias* should form parallel institutions to those of men (1998: 56) which currently appears impossible to achieve due to economic reasons and as such has not been discussed by the Queenmothers themselves. Their own separate institution would also be questionable in its effect on changing other institutions. The research study resulted in slight changes. During a "Women in Public Life Seminar" organised by the National Council of Women and Development in 1998 in Kumasi, thirty Queenmothers and thirty Chiefs discussed the results of the study, which demanded altered behaviour by the Chiefs to customs and tradition. The Queenmothers furthermore repeated their claim for admission and equal monthly allowances of 100,000 Cedis in correspondence with the Chiefs. Although the Chiefs continue to reject this, they have at least recognised the existence of *magadjias* in the northern part of Ghana as Queenmothers (Daily Graphic, 20.8.1998), which means that their existence within "traditional" institutions is formally recognised.

At a national level of discourse, the National Council of Women and Development is supporting the Queenmothers' aims, by organising seminars and publishing its results in the most popular newspaper of Ghana, the Daily Graphic. It is not only the information towards the public sphere which is of assistance to the Queenmothers. Academic knowledge becomes integrated into their argumentation and thus an important asset for their claim of transforming social institutions. Research results as such become politicised by being integrated into political negotiations and an asset in the knowledge repertoire of women's organizations.

5.3.1 The Negotiation of Tradition: *"They want us to live like in the ancient times"*

Tradition has become part and parcel of the discourse on transforming "traditional" institutions. A metaphorical analysis of who defines tradition and how it is defined refers to the level of language, which as a spoken form consti-

---

12 The study has been a collaborative project between the Institute of Statistical, Social, Economic Research (ISSER) of the University of Ghana and the Development and Project Planning Centre (DPPC) of the University of Bradford, United Kingdom.
13 A summary of the study which up to now could not have been published in complete due to financial constrains, encompasses the chapters on "Women in Institutions of Governance", "Women in Service Organizations", "Women in Politics and Leadership in Civil Society Institutions", "Women in Security and Law Enforcement Agencies" (ISSER/DPPC Research Team, 1998).

tutes the meaning of the social order. The negotiation of tradition emerges out of the gender asymmetry and on the competitive situation of a new definition of reality and of social relations. Definition refers to the social level, while negotiation indicates the interactions between the subjects. Tradition in its semantic meaning frames agency at institutional level and is a point of reference for both genders. It is a human product which is not codified, similarly making it the object of definitions and interpretations. Tradition in the context of the discourse described above is defined by the Register of the Regional House of Chiefs as "[...] *it is the established way of doing things in the community*". Established and maintained, as implied by his further explanation as something that can hardly be changed, that has lasted a long time and will remain as such. Tradition means the fixing of institutional structures which – I just want to remind – had been established in postcolonial Ghana as the Regional House of Chiefs in 1961 and the National House of Chiefs in 1971. But it is also a negative definition of the spaces of Queenmothers of exclusion. "*The position of the Queenmother had been that of a mother, who will report to the Chief. She will stay at home. As it is now the duty of the Queenmothers, they are mothers and they must stay at home*". While in the past some old Queenmothers did stay at home most of the time due to age, the image of a Queenmother still moving around in her home has not been overcome, and nowadays denies her moving around in public and thus participation at this institutional level. The term mother is used here in an essentialising manner, by drawing its biological meaning and not its political relevance. The deep image of a Queenmother living in her home not only maintains the image of them as being immobile outside the home, but as the following quote indicates, also encompasses the image of young women and girls as future housewives which similarly restricts their further education. "*We are expecting them to live in the house, as household people, they are for the kitchen. You see, you sent your female child to school and after all she will go and marry. So we are ignoring that women are fighting*", as another employee at the Traditional Council in Duayaw-Nkwanta explained. The quote hints at the ongoing construction of women belonging in the household, which indirectly favours the formal education of boys. By using the word "kitchen" and "housewives" it is still the Christian construct of femininity and of closed female spaces. Kitchens as closed or separated rooms do not however exist as such. Cooking usually takes place in the open part of the compound, e.g. when preparing crops such as yam or cassava, pounding of *fufu* or preparing soup. For the Queenmothers in particular this image constructs the restriction of entering the Houses, while for women in general it continues as a legitimisation for not supporting the education of women. The construct of a fixed closed space similarly is a form of exclusion from political and educational institutions. This image of the "kitchen-bound" Queenmother did not go unanswered by the Queenmothers. In a paper submitted by a Queenmother to the National House of Chiefs, she draws attention to tradition by designing tradition as a dynamic concept, which needs to be connected with social changes. *"Times are changing and we have also been re-examining our roles and responsibilities"*. The time aspect has a double meaning. First of all, tradition is used to legitimise the position of Queenmothers as a social institution. By referring to their tasks as advisors to the Chiefs, settling disputes and formal duties of the Queenmothers, she defines Queenmothers as the repositories of tradition and custom. This line of argumentation maintains and legitimises the institution as such. It is therefore an argument of legitimising its existence. And second, the dynamics comes in by bridging the legitimisation of an old institution with a perspective of its relevance for the present and for the future in which women should be a part of.

The discourse on tradition is a discourse on both opening and fixing of boundaries. The crucial difference in the interpretation of tradition between gender is the inherent time aspect. For the male side, tradition is in this context a tool for preserving and conserving conceptions of gender-relations and for keeping women out of social institutions such as schools and political institutions. Women on the other hand draw the attention of tradition towards a re-examination of the past, integration of the present, the need to change and look towards the future. Tradition in a re-examined form should open the political space for women. Two different temporal frames of tradition exist between gender: the male ones by referring to the past and cementising the present structures, and the female ones by referring to the past as a form of legitimising the institution and changing it towards the future.

The time aspect in the discourse on tradition is therefore of methodological importance, because time is another form of framing spaces in the sense of inclusion and exclusion. The struggle at the discursive level reveals how language works in practice and despite its flexibility is a medium which contributes to the fixing of gender-constructs and gender-relations.

5.3.2 Creation of New Spaces: The Queenmothers' association

In 1987 Nana Ama Serwaa, a Subqueenmother of Duayaw-Nkwanta, came out with the idea of founding a Queenmothers' association. Dissatisfied with the current development of the political meaning of the institution of Queenmothers, her aim was to bring the Queenmothers and Subqueenmothers together on a platform and in a common body. The motives for formation came out of the diffuse relationship between Queenmothers and Chiefs. A common platform was seen as a chance for identifying the problems of political relations and searching for solutions especially concerning their dilemma. A third motive was to discuss the past, present and future social relevance of Queenmothers in a changing society. To legitimise her activities, Nana Ama Serwaa constituted the Queenmothers as being the custodians of customs and as the *"mothers"* of all the inhabitants in the villages and towns. *"Mothers"* became a collective political identity which should be the basis of solidarity and for further mobilisation.

From the time of the idea until its inauguration seven years passed before it finally came into office in 1994. During this time Nana Ama Serwaa travelled throughout the country, using her own money to drive around and talk to the Queenmothers by explaining the advantages of an association. She rented the halls of the District Assemblies where the Queenmothers from the villages and towns gathered. Gradually in every region a nucleus of Queenmothers was established and which now covers all regions of Ghana with the exception of the northern parts of Ghana, whose *magadjias* have not developed their own branches, but join the Queenmothers' association at the annual national meeting in Kumasi. Nana Ama Serwaa describes the result of mobilisation as *"I have been trying to bring them up. And I can say that through the efforts I have been making, I have been able to make other Queenmothers also spring up"*. The way of mobilisation can be explained as starting with a personal movement transforming into an almost national organization, which is even more astonishing from a logistical point of view considering the country still has a relatively unstable infrastructure.

The Queenmothers' association is formally organised at district and regional level. At district level Queenmothers and Subqueenmothers meet regularly four times a year at the hall of the District Assembly. At regional level, they meet three times a year in the Regional Houses of Chiefs. The procedure of election forsees one Queenmother from each traditional area being elected to regional meetings. This procedure guarantees the permanent link between the smallest organizational unit and the regional level and simultaneously prevents the exclusion of some traditional areas. The ten elected Queenmothers/Subqueenmothers occupy specific functions: as President of the region, Vice-President, Organiser, Executive Member, Patron, Auditor, Assistant Secretary and Treasurer, while two of them have no specific function. Despite the formal organization, it does not yet have a permanent office or program.

At both levels they discuss topics such as the decentralisation process, education, the environment or economic development. Recently they started a campaign on health aspects focusing on breast feeding in particular. The campaign focused on the importance of breast feeding for the health of the mother and her baby. There was also a critical discussion on the use of imported artificial baby food which not only endangers the health of the child; such expensive products also put pressure on the mother's finances and these costly imported products are thus of concern for the national economy. As a result, they demand a ban on advertising artificial milk products in public. The campaign indicates that the discussion went a long way towards emphasising the own knowledgeability and represents a counter-discourse against Western products and Western modernisation. Western products should not replace the knowledge of individuals and have a negative implication on health to boot. Furthermore, they have taken up the concerns of teenage pregnancy, which is part of a broader discourse on population politics. The perspective is to prevent young women from early pregnancies. Queenmothers have came out with their own concept of bagoro – which I have already mentioned – for avoiding early pregnancies and the implications that young unmarried women, who become pregnant usually leave school and do not receive financial support from the fathers. A revitalisation of bagoro should make young women aware of this. At the same time aspects of modern forms of family planning and aspects of AIDS should be integrated into the communication process between the Queenmothers and the young women. In some villages Queenmothers started to take up this form of communication and enabled a larger number of girls to gain secondary education. *"There is a logic in the cultural practice"*, as the Paramount Queenmother of Duayaw-Nkwanta proudly commented on the efforts. The Queenmothers even went as far as to urge the parliament to draw up a national law, which would extend not only to a few individual women, but to the young female generation as a whole. This law is still being discussed and is not yet passed.

The Queenmothers' association addresses its meetings towards acting on social issues at local and national level. The discussions pursue the goal of combining experienced knowledge with modern elements of knowledge. As part of this discussion the Subqueenmothers of Susuanso regularly take part in the regional meetings and in meetings at district level. Access to new forms of knowledge is given due to topical collaboration with other women's organizations in the region. For example, they have exchanged ideas in common meetings about bagoro as well as in another case environmental aspects concerning the river and the planting of trees. This aspect has been taken up by the Subqueenmothers in Susuanso, hinting at the dried out river Susuan.

The organization in common meetings is not the only form of the exchange of knowledge. Some Queenmothers work in the offices of other women's organizations such as the 31st DWM or the NCWD. Among the Queenmothers and Subqueenmothers the flow of communication is guaranteed through formal meetings, but apart from these less formal activities exists besides such as funerals are used as an occasion for discussing their affairs. In one case the Subqueenmothers of Susuanso used the funeral of a deceased Queenmother to meet and to discuss current topics with other Queenmother. Funerals are separate from the formal meetings and used as another way of informal knowledge exchange. The Queenmothers' association has established a common ground outside the "traditional" institutions and is now a form of organization which dissolves gender-hierarchies among women within the traditional setting. Concerning the creation of knowledge, the platform functions to discuss everyday knowledge, new elements of knowledge such as scientific knowledge or knowledge generated by other women's organizations as well as historical knowledge. All these different forms of knowledge are connected with an analysis of social situations and multiple strategies for acting on social issues.

5.3.3 Moving in Different Spaces: Nana Ama Serwaa

New elements of knowledge are also integrated, further channelled and distributed by individuals within the Queenmothers' association. The founder of the Queenmothers' association, Nana Ama Serwaa moves as a Subqueenmother within and outside Ghana, taking up and discussing ongoing and new topics. She is now over sixty years old and calls herself a farmer, a hotelier, a midwife and a Queenmother. Born in Duayaw-Nkwanta, she trained as a professional midwife, opened her own clinic in Sunyani, and meanwhile has been elected as the Krontiohemma[14] of Duayaw Nkwanta. After retiring she turned the clinic into a hotel. Her own educational background has given her the opportunities to be part of different associations. When working as a midwife, she involved herself in politics, and is now a member of different forums such as the National Commission on Culture, acting as Vice-President of "Parents of Students in Cuba" and is the President of the Ghana Hotel Association.

She defines her activities as "service for mankind". As a member of the Ghana Commission on AIDS, she travels to other African countries such as Namibia, Kenya, Senegal or Ivory Coast and overseas to Mexico. Experiences gathered during her journeys are shared with other Queenmothers by informing them and discussing them, whether within the framework of meetings or separately by calling some of them together in her hotel in Sunyani or in her hometown. Having the possibilities to travel abroad, definitely make her an exception. The interesting thing is that she works as a mediator by gathering information, bringing it back into the meetings and distributing it again. Furthermore within Ghana, she attends seminars and workshops as well as the New Year School[15], which is specific to Ghana. Global, national and local issues are discussed among academics, politicians and practitioners. For Nana Ama Serwaa it is a forum for broadening her knowledge, taking up discourses and discussions with the other Queenmothers. Moving in different social spaces at local and national level and belonging to various sources of knowledge, does not make her an exception. Stoeltje also refers to the case of

---

14 The Krontiohemma is in the second position of the hierarchical structure of the Queenmothers.
15 The New Year School takes place every year at the University of Legon in the form of a one week seminar between Christmas and New Year. Originally it was founded by students as a work camp in 1949 and gradually established itself as a well known school. The discussions are around issues of national and international topics and are combined with development on the community level. The participants joining the NYS come from people working for local NGO's, academics, of the public sector. A selection of themes form the past 50 years: 1956: Knowledge and Independence, 1975: Man's Habitat-Cities, Towns, Villages and Houses, 1991: Multi-Party Democracy and Ghana, Challenges and Prospects. The NYS the special function of a public forum, being a political neutral refugium. "It is often said that the New Year School is the only place where one can speak one's mind without fear of any politically induced reprisal" (Appiah-Donyina 1992).

a Queenmother from the Volta region, who is a member of the Commission of Civic Education (1994: 2). Both examples show, that the Queenmothers are not necessarily restricted to "traditional" spaces, but are actually broadening the horizon of their worlds towards "modern" spaces.

5.3.4 Self-Organization: Female Economy, Social Security and Public Sphere

Within the Queenmothers' association income-generating projects have become central for economic self-organization. Economic empowerment has been considered a major starting point for reacting to the so-called dilemma situation on the one hand and for opening up spaces for other activities on the other. *"If you have economic freedom, you can do something"* Nana Ama Serwaa said. It is also a reaction to the harsh economic situation and the increasing costs of water or electricity due to privatisation of companies. Some Subqueenmothers argue that the additional income is needed nowadays to feed themselves and the children within the family. It is therefore not only an opening of spaces, but also a form of suspension of the ongoing economic crisis. During meetings at the initial stage and in collaboration with the 31st December Women's Movement, Queenmothers started with small projects such as the production of the local soap, gari-processing, snail and beekeeping as well as the production of "tie and dye", which is a special techniques for dyeing material. Within every district they canvass the district assemblies for starting capital which averaged 300,000 Cedis[16] for each group. This money was shared between the different projects so every projects got a small amount of capital. To avoid risks, they concentrated on a few projects, which did not cover every town or village. Every group could decide upon their own project. The loan received was handed over in a certain autonomy out of the annual budget of the district assembly, and was not from any national or regional program. This had the advantage, that the usual bureaucratic procedure of lending money through the banks, which also means repayment at high rates, could be avoided as well as predefined programs or the levying of state interests. One project I was able to observe was the production of local soap in Duayaw-Nkwanta, as the Subqueenmothers in Susuanso had not yet started with such a project. Local soap is made out of dried banana leaves, soda powder and some perfumed ingredients. The round formed pieces are wrapped in small plastic bags and sold for 200 Cedis. One piece usually lasts for a week. Production is done by the Subqueenmothers themselves, while the product is sold by young girls of the family at the market or by carrying it in a basket on their head through the town. The income is shared between the Subqueenmother and the young women. Part of the money is also put aside for the monthly repayment of the loan, the accumulation of own capital within the organizations, and the procurement of new ingredients. The production of soap is seen by the Subqueenmothers of Duayaw-Nkwanta as a successful

---

16 Which is roughly about 75 Euro.

project, with some additional money coming in and is of benefit for the young women. Up to now, the production of another type of soap is already being taken into consideration, and once the loan has been paid off, they will apply for a higher one, which could be used for diversifying production by adding gari-processing.

The economic activities constitute through their social and cultural embeddedness a "women's economy" (Lachenmann 1995: 9). This term indicates that women have formed new creative ways of solidarity to bridge the economic situation and to guarantee the survival of family members by way of assisting each other. Its embeddedness follows an own rationality. In many parts of Africa such as Senegal or Zimbabwe, women have organised themselves into savings clubs, in church groups, funeral associations or in the formation of a cereal bank (vgl. Lachenmann 1993; vgl. Schneider 1999). Gudrun Lachenmann states that this form is a creative reaction against state policies imposed policies of social security. This gender specific form is building up a "capacity of solidarity" (Lachenmann 1993: 5) and of connecting the productive with the reproductive space. This connection and the social importance of it is however overseen in mainstream development politics or in state policies. The basis of the formation is new in the way that old forms of solidarity such as within the family are further developed and extended across kinship structures. The initiative of establishing own economic structures is not isolated outside the market, but "embedded" (Polany 1978: 75) in a new formation of social relations, addressed to support themselves and other family members[17]. This form of economic orientation of women is addressed on securing and maintaining the production of subsistence and follows in its logic of action a "moral economy" (Elwert/Evers/Willkens 1983: 286) by assisting each other in coping with daily insecurities and uncertainties.

Eva Maria Bruchhaus (1988) has observed similar phenomena of women's self-help initiatives in other parts of West Africa, especially the process of how women are active in securing their livelihoods in times of economic breakdowns by establishing associations dealing with the production of vegetables, fruits, flour-mills and oil. The transfer of technological knowledge in regards to mills, as in Burkina-Faso, is based on a South-South relationship and exchange. By travelling abroad and mutual visits among women from neighbouring countries, an adopted and innovative technology was developed which seemed to be in comparison to external initiatives more sustainable (1988: 54).

The form of economic and social assistance is also expressed in symbolic forms. *"We assist each other"*, *"we help each other"*, *"there is union"*, *"each ones welfare is the welfare of the other"* are comments often heard from the Subqueenmothers. Nana Ama Serwaa added the aspect of public sphere on the importance of self-organization. *"So you see, you have to let yourself be*

---

17 Recent empirical studies conducted in Asia, Africa and Latin-America have concentrated on the gendered structure of economy and its embeddedness (vgl. Lachenmann/Dannecker 2001).

seen or your voices been heard. When you are always in your shell and you are always in your house or in your room. Nobody will hear you". The quote hints at the public effect of forming an organization. The generalised expression of Nana Ama Serwaa on the initial movements of women described as *"coming out of our shells"* refers to its metaphorical meaning of transition from the private sphere to the public sphere on the infrastructure of self-organising. To put this metaphor into an context of a theory of agency, would mean that the coming out is a form of newly structuring social spaces by the creating of new forms of social ties and is the initiative of turning around negative processes of social marginalisation and of knowledge order.

5.4 The Knowledge Pillars

At local level self-organization in the form of informal gatherings has started a process which Bourdieu described as a collective action to change the world in the form of a knowledge effect (Bourdieu 1991: 127). It is not self-organization per se, which has a knowledge effect, but the process of examination of one's own situation and of the consconsinants as part thereof. This process will be summarised and discussed as a process of doing "reflexive modernisation" according to the definition of Scott Lash (1994: 113-115). Reflexivity means the setting free of constraints of social structure and the change of rules and resources and giving an altered meaning to the social order. By building up a critique on past and ongoing processes, by reflecting on historical knowledge and building up capacities for integrating new elements of knowledge, knowledge is made explicit and becomes a structuring element of society. Less in is content, but at a meta-level through having knowledge of knowledge. It is this form of second order knowledge of communicability and explication which is a new structural moment signifying social change. The knowledge effect is emphasised in two ways:

1. With the construction of the *aberewa nyansafo* the Subqueenmother have created a common symbolic identity which is aimed at opening new spaces such as entering the palace.
2. In referring to the past and through opening a political space the aim is to re-define symbolic spaces which have disappeared by integrating new elements of knowledge.

The legitimation of the symbolic order is achieved through a transformation of the institutional order. With the common symbolic identity and the expansion of spaces, boundaries among and between gender are shifted. The partial collapse of representation (Bourdieu 1991: 126) takes place by changing social relations and by signifying the world with new symbolic meanings and the act of naming. The effect is that the mechanisms of the construction of knowledge "becoming" reality (vgl. Berger/Luckmann 1966) through the change of gender-relations and the transformation of social institutions. The new production of meaning is embedded in the notion of reflexivity. This process of "reflexive modernisation" as Lash (1994: 111) argued contains the increasing power of social actors in regard to social structures. As a process it is a self-definition on development and in comparison to mainstream development politics, an alternative form of "doing development" by reacting and acting on the real. This kind of "sub-politics" (Beck 1994: 34) is also a partial counter-discourse to Western imposed forms of modernisation.

By building up a new knowledge repertoire between old and new elements of knowledge, the self-organization of the Subqueenmothers can be metaphorically described as the formation of pillars. Those local pillars are connected through translocal interactions such as face-to-face and discursive with other forms of organizations. Appadurai was clearly right in defining a locality as a relational and not as an absolute space (1998: 178). In a similar way the Queenmothers' association is also a new pillar. The difference to the local level lies in the knowledge repertoire. Here, scientific knowledge has become integrated into the knowledge repertoire. Research studies have succeeded in *magadjias* from the northern part of Ghana being recognised as Queenmothers, for example. The Queenmothers' association bridges ethnic boundaries and the long constructed dichotomy of the economic and political important southern part of Ghana in comparison to the northern part Ghana. Because of its decentralised organizational structure it covers the whole country linking in its extension distant localities, and through seeing the localities together its effect is a knowledge change. Both pillars are new forms of organizations across kinship structures. The horizontal crossing indicates that in present Ghana kinship structures are emphasised and are gaining political importance. As a new space of interaction it is referring to and changing the "traditional" structures out of which it originally emerged. Emerging out of it and referring back to it has a double form of de-hierarchising "traditional" power structures on one hand and on the other by the parallel establishment of a horizontal network on aspects such as on social security. For the generation process of knowledge this means, that everyday knowledge, scientific knowledge and translocal knowledge elements are integrated and translated. New elements are also discussed and translated through the collaboration with other women's organizations and through movements of individuals. Towards the aspect of collaboration among women's organizations I will turn to the next Chapter and discuss the form of interaction under the topic of networking.

6 SOCIAL NETWORKING BETWEEN WOMEN'S ORGANIZATIONS

The central focus of this Chapter is the networking between women's organizations, where I leave Susuanso and move to the locations of Sunyani and the distant Accra. By using the term networking as a derivative from network, which has gained a "new popularisation" (Latour 1999: 15) in social theory and in particular in the sociology of economics[1] since Granovetter's approach to the embeddedness of social relations in economic interactions, I refer to theoretical direction. Clyde Mitchell[2], the founder of network analysis in social anthropology is using the term network as a metaphor for interrelations in a social system and social network for specific linkages among a defined set of persons which further explains their agency (vgl. Schweizer 1988: 5). The term social networking has a double meaning: agency can result in networking and new forms of contexts of agencies can emerge through networking. Up to this stage and beyond I do not take the "classical" topics of sociology and social anthropology such as ethnicity, trade, migration, moral economy and social security into consideration, social networking remains on a metaphorical level without any meaning. It can take place between everybody and everywhere, whereas my aim is to investigate in the context of knowledge.

First of all, social networking is a new form of organising social relations along the interfaces of women's organizations. These interfaces are institutionalised in "nodes" such as the Women's forum on the one hand and at a personal level on the other. Secondly, within the institutional and personal level, networking is a medium for the circulation of knowledge over distances and for hybridising local and global discourses. And third, while knowledge is articulated and politicised, networking offers new opportunities for ways of transformations. With these three features of form, medium and practice, networking creates new spaces as well as shaping social spaces across distances within a processual continuity, which brings the metaphorical meaning down to a stable level.

---

1   See also Powell/Smith-Dwelt on economic agency in Smelser, Neil J./Swedberg, Richard (1994).
2   Clyde Mitchell was director of the Rhodes-Livingstone-Institute in Zambia, which had its focal point on ethnicity, urbanism and migration. In the succession of Max Gluckman, Elisabeth Colson and Godfrey Wilson. Mitchells merit was to take up Gluckmans' situational analysis and to develop it into a qualitative network analysis.

While each women's organization[3] is a network of individuals in itself, I will only refer to an institutional analysis of the National Council of Women and Development (NCWD) as the national umbrella organization of all women's organizations in Ghana and of Women in Law and Development Africa (WiLDAF) as a pan-african organization. The organizational structure reflects the internal translation process and the flow of discourses and politics.

6.1 The Women's Forum at Sunyani: A Platform for Change

The regional Women's forum functions as a central platform for all the women's organizations in the Brong-Ahafo Region and takes place on the first Thursday of every month in Sunyani. It is organised and financed by the National Council of Women and Development[4]. Women from various women's organizations attend the meeting coming from religious organizations such as the Christian-based Catholic, Methodist, Presbyterian and Pentecost Churches, the Muslim Ahmadyya and Gonja association, professional organizations representing hairdressers, nurses, policewomen, the national chemical sellers association, the traditional birth attendants, the market women as well as representatives of the Traditional Court, the District Assembly, the Queenmothers' association and the 31st December Women's Movement. The number of participants, who are aged around forty, attending the forum ranges from 60 to about 100. Usually two women from the same organization go to the meeting together. Many women belong to more than one organization at the same time, with the majority combining membership of a Church and a professional/job-based association. The diverse forms of organizations are part of the daily lives of women and offer services for each other as self-help or mutual financial assistance while a gender or political perspective is in most cases absent (vgl. Schäfer 1995).

The Women's forum was established in November 1998 and is the only platform for assembling women's organizations on a regular basis, preceded only by loosely connected organizations. All the organizations are registered at the Brong Ahafo Network of NGOs, BANGO, which was set up by the representative of the NCWD. During this initial phase, women from the urban area of Sunyani and the nearby towns were present. The concept, however, foresees the invitation of women from the surrounding villages in future. This was a prevalent discussion topic among the participants, these suggestions of the Queenmothers of the surrounding villages and towns to attend the meet-

---

3 Rita Schäfer (1995) has analysed the broad range of women's organizations in African context in particular from a perspective of development cooperation. Also Gudrun Lachenmann has frequently pointed out the social and political relevance of women's organizations in Cameroun and Senegal (1995).

4 The expenses for one forum cover rent, minerals and small snacks up to more than 100, 000 Cedis.

ings. The representative of NCWD hesitated to extend the forum until acceptance was ensured.

The forum takes place in a hall near the district assembly and is designed as an open forum. The participants are informed some days before the meeting occurs via an invitation letter which is distributed by a "messager", a young man riding around the town on his bicycle and giving the letters directly to the specific person, who is usually the president or head of the organization. The forum starts at around 11.00 a.m. with Christian and Muslim prayers followed by a talk by the invited representative of the NCWD. It continues with the presentations of the different topics which takes on average a half an hour. Each topic is presented by a locally invited person, dealing with the specific issue. The presentations are followed by discussions between the women and the presenters or among the women only. Many women contributed towards the discussions, which were lively and active. At the end, announcements were made about current issues related to women in other African countries, new institutions or meetings in the region or about the politics of the National Council of Women and Development at Headquarters in Accra. These were concluded with Muslim and Christian closing prayers. The duration of one session is about two to three hours and the local language Twi is spoken[5] with only partial switches to English for some expressions. The discussion topics are selected by the representative of the NCWD and selection is oriented towards issues discussed at global and at local level.: "The civic rights of Ghanaian Women", "Reproductive Health" "The UN-Conference: Women's Health Facing the 21st century", "Old Age in Ghana", "Women and Mental Health", "Violence against Women", "Inheritance Law", "Women's Rights", "Women in Vocational Schools". I would now like to describe some of these discussion topics.

Violence against Women

The topic of violence against women was introduced in a detailed report by a policewoman working at the police station in Sunyani. She first presented figures about the number of violent acts against women in the Sunyani district indicating that the figures had drastically increased between 1997 and 1998. The different forms of violence encompassed rape, killings and beating up of women in public and in the domestic sphere. She also made it clear that those figures did not represent the actual reality because many women still do not dare to go to the police station. Violence is not only prevalent between men and women, but also between women against foster children or daughters-in-law. Violent acts are committed in different forms and settings, e.g. physical, psychological, economic, domestic, cultural and gender-based. With this differentiation the multiplicities and complexities of violent acts make it clear, that it can effect women in one or several ways. To defend oneself

---

5   Here I especially want to thank Janet Asantewaa, a hairdresser, who worked in Germany as a medical assistant for about twenty years, and helped in the translation from Twi to German.

against it she recommends different strategies such as self-protection through self-organization, mutual control and support, as well as through using the media, talking and discussing it in public.

The participating women contributed with comments, telling of personal experiences or of cases known to them. One woman mentioned that religion is also a reason for men to forbid women in general to go to the police, with the argument that a Christian should not go to the police. There is therefore a religious-based reason for woman being restricted in availing of external help or being too timid to leave or divorce their violent husbands. Another woman stated that women have to go into politics to introduce new laws and to intervene in government politics so as to abolish those forms of economic violence as the exclusion of women from membership as some trade unions like the Transport Union of Ghana (TUG). Furthermore, cultural constructs must be questioned. Many women still believe that husbands beating their wives is a sign of love. Those constructs must be discussed in the public, convincing women that it negatively impairs their psychological and physiological health.

The topical range not only encompasses the personal lifeworld. Diverse women hinted of forms of violence in other parts of Ghana like the practice of *Trokosi* in the Volta-Region, where widows are forced to sleep in the same room as their dead husband for three days or the practice of circumcision, which is done in other parts of Africa.

The different strategies women came up with and recommended to each other were broad. Some encouraged others to organise themselves as a form of protection and shelter, as well as to take up judicial and political strategies or using the public sphere to draw attention to the problem.

The discourse on violence against women and the different forms it takes is not an exclusive local discourse, but a glocal discourse. As a national one-year campaign, it was taken up in 1998 by the National Council of Women and Development and realised through the media, workshops, political actions or direct interactions with women at local level. Ghana is not an exception. Since the early 1990s, women's organizations world-wide have started a campaign on the different forms of discrimination against women. The CEDAW (Convention on the Elimination of all forms of Discrimination against Women) was accepted by the UN in 1979 and in 1986 was ratified in Ghana. At the World Conference on Human Rights in 1993 in Vienna, women's rights were accepted as human rights (Holthaus/Klingebiel 1998: 34ff.). The importance of the manifestation is the tutoring of women on subjects such as the dynamics of rights (civil, political, economic, social), which makes rights part of their daily lives. The discourse on violence against women has been especially taken up in Southern Africa by women's organizations. In Zimbabwe, women's organizations have put pressure on the government to integrate women's rights into the constitution, while collaborating with women in rural areas and formulating new laws on inheritance, family and land rights (Schäfer 1999: 300). The focus of those organizations is addressed towards changing the lives of women at all societal levels. The

Women and Law in Southern African Research Trust (WLSA) with its Head Office in Harare (Zimbabwe) comprises of legal professionals, sociologists, psychologists and political scientists. Through intensive research in rural and urban Zimbabwe, they identified the life situation of women and established a common process of reflection between the organization and the women. To emphasis the rights the organization has put up demands such as political lobbying, has intensified an actor-oriented research on laws, amendments and published brochures in the local language (Schäfer 1999: 309). Its efforts in establishing a public discourse about a study on inheritance has resulted in measures taken up by companies to guarantee the security of widows (Schneider 2000: 146).

The discourse on violence against women, which has declined from an international level to the local level, is articulated as a matter of social and political context, and bridges the perspective of the individual situation with the wider structural context. The discussion at the forum made clear that to act against the forms of violence, multiple strategies must be taken up, starting from the realities of women up to the political level. Self-defined strategies such as self-organization or going into politics reflect that women identify and analyze their own situation turning themselves into subjects of agencies as well as reflecting on their own agencies through being themselves actors of violence.

Health
Health issues were discussed at almost every forum. On the topic of "Old age and traditional knowledge" a male doctor, who was educated in the United States and now works in a private clinic in Sunyani, gave a talk. By referring to the ancient knowledge of the people in Greece, he exemplified medical practice as preventive and not curative as is the case nowadays in the "modern" health system of Ghana. The science of nature in theory and practice has revealed that the application of natural medicine is important and a good way of treatment. He explained that the knowledge of the old people should not be forgotten, but is of importance when reacting to illness and it is more important than the knowledge written in many books, although it is underestimated. He argued that they should not follow the way old people are treated in industrial societies, living in isolation and neglected in old-people's homes. Rather, old people should be treated with respect and should be kept within the family context until they die.

The women reacted critically to the presentation. One raised the question that traditional knowledge is often associated with the accusation of witchcraft. The use of herbal medicine should therefore not only be described in a one-sided manner. Others contributed to the positive aspects of traditional knowledge, and discussed it by comparing the present with the past. Women used to give birth to more children than nowadays, were stronger and lived longer. Nowadays people die at a fairly young age.

One woman blamed the use of chemicals and fertilisers in agricultural production for the change in the health and nutritional situation and for the increase of illness. A final comment was made by a women saying that the negative effects of the economic situation leads to overburdening of women with work, who under the conditions of economic uncertainty and financial pressure (e.g. paying school fees) lack the time for rest. This situation has caused an increase in death due to hypertension. The issue of health was discussed during the forum by including the changes towards the present and actual structural, economic and environmental situation. The interesting feature is, that the Western-trained medical doctor did not follow the paradigms of modernisation, but was pointing out the use of "traditional" knowledge, which has been proved as valid by long-lasting experiences. He takes a critical position as regards the "belief of modernisation" and emphasised a "re-embeddedness" of traditional knowledge. For the women's part, traditional knowledge was critically reviewed. Despite the efforts of development, they questioned the consequences of economic and environmental development. Their own health situation has become an object of development. Sudden deaths such as on the way to the farm, permanent headaches, an unhealthy diet etc. have led to a negative "embodiment" of the present situation. Regular visits to a doctor or to hospital have become a luxury since it is impossible to pay immediately. Health from their point of view must take knowledge, environment, social and economic context into consideration.

Education in Vocational Schools

The topic was introduced by an assistant working at the District Education Office. She began her talk with the question of why the number of boys exceeds the number of girls at school. She partly gave the answers by pointing out that the education of girls is attributed less importance than that of boys. Girls are still kept at home to help wash the clothes, to work on the farm, prepare of food or gather firewood. A second reason is given by early teenage pregnancies which keeps the girls away from school. Thirdly, it is due to continuation of gender-constructs and the attribution of "femininity", that girls will later become housewives. And the last reason addressed the economic situation, in which girls are more likely to be kept out of school than boys. In a second part, she explained, that education in Vocational Schools is gendered. Women continue instruction in catering or dress-making while only a few take up the chance to take up "male" jobs and become carpenters, builders or technical engineers. Women are however strong enough to take up male jobs which would widen their job opportunities instead of only taking up "soft" jobs. The review of gender-constructs and cultural-constructs is one chance of opening up better job opportunities for young women and of overcoming traditional perceptions of female and male spaces. Finally she finished her talk with the well-known sentence that to educate a man, you only educate an individual, to educate a woman you educate a whole nation.

Figue 4 and 5: Conducting "Critical Theory" at the Women's Forum in Sunyani

The women clearly responded to this talk by pointing out the difficulties of the present situation. It has become a matter of finance for the payment of school-fees, food, the uniforms and school books. This issue of finance should not only be left up to them but also borne by men, who often fail to pay enough money for their children, even those who could financially afford it. The responsibility is often left to women alone. Education is therefore of concern not only for the mothers, but also for the fathers. Women were also concerned about "mixing" men and women in Vocational Schools, although they did comment positively on opening up of further possibilities of education for their daughters and identified their own behaviour as a way of changing gender-perceptions.

Conducting "Critical Theory"

The forum, which was initially conceptualised as a sharing of experiences, turned out to be a space for conducting "critical theory" (Habermas 1981: 549). Critical in the sense that the personal lifeworld becomes a methodological object of analysis by pointing out the negative influences of current processes. The confidence of the lifeworld is not taken for granted any longer. The identification and explanation of the "pathologies of modernity" (Habermas 1981: 554) such as violence and illness are made explicit and are an object of reflexivity. It is not explicitly knowledge in its different dimensions as "traditional" or "modern" as such which is articulated, but the processes of the constitution of the social world. The plurality of lifeworlds in the presence and the increase of risks have led to a "Homeless Mind" (Berger et al. 1977) with the accompanying negative consequences in the living conditions of women or by directly affecting them. Social institutions such as law, religion, economy and education need to be transformed. The development of outlines for agencies such as organising themselves, going into politics and using the public sphere was articulated by the women themselves. Transformation goes along the politicisation of the interface between private and public lives.

The multiplicity of outlines articulated for agencies did not result in a common agenda, but towards opening up options of taking up different ways. This leaves the opportunities for each women's organization open and does not turn into a prescribed dogma for change. What has not been taken up during all the forums to date is a technically oriented discourse on development in general and in particular on Women in Development. This is astonishing in as so far as the NCWD was originally established as a "national machinery" with the aim of enhancing the status of women. However, by taking up global feminist discourses in connection with local lifeworlds, the forum initiates a process of a self-defined and self-initiated concept on development through the medium of exchange between women's organizations. Through this form of networking the forum is located, as a social political institution, on a "middle level" (Lachenmann 1989: 4) with an articulation, an initiation and opening of self-defined ways and not of an implementation of an innovation through the administrative procedures of planning from above.

The interactions which took place during the forum are conceptualised as a process of learning from each other through a sharing of experience. The relationship between the representative of the NCWD and the experts on the one hand and the audience on the other hand is based on a "motivational approach" (Butegwa/Nduna 1995: 17) with the answers and comments given by the audience which also has the power to give the direction. As an open-ended learning process it is carried out through dialogue, leaving the answers open to the audience. This concept, which is used in adult education, has its roots in the ideas of Paulo Freire's theory and methods of popular education following the principle of "learning through sharing and education for social change" (Butegwa/Nduna 1995: 59). Learning is meant in this context as a process of reflection, analysis and action and as such conceptualised as a process of common discovery in order to initiate social change. The role of a trainer is to create a motivational learning environment, facilitate the participatory process, support the dialogue, but leaves the answers and solutions to the groups (vgl. Butegwa/Nduna 1995). Popular education lead to a critical awareness of the law and use it as a tool for social change. Its theoretical roots refer back to Paolo Freire, whose literature has been extensively studied by members of WiLDAF and whose ideas and inspirations have been further adopted. Women should define the ways and strategies for further independent action. One training aspect is the building and strengthening of women's organizations through a process of self-reflection, by taking hierarchical structures, the thematic focus as the aim of the organization, the past objectives and the future image into consideration. The traces of this learning method has been brought to Sunyani as a result of long personal networking between the representative of the NCWD and WiLDAF-Ghana. By attending regular workshops of WiLDAF in different parts of Ghana she has taken over and introduced this method of adult education. The politics of WiLDAF follows networking as one strategy and is focusing on the process of building and strengthening organizations, offers training for transformation and special courses in leadership, which is defined as motivational, stimulating and a sharing of roles (Butegwa/Nduna 1995: 17). The exchange between women's organizations is not only topic centred, but is also on didactics such as learning methods and tools for transformation.

6.1.1 Organising Development: The National Council of Women and Development

The office of the NCWD is located within the block of the regional ministries and the attached administrative offices. The office is equipped with tables, some chairs, a telephone, a typewriter, the daily newspaper and a few brochures on Women and Development. It is headed by the regional representative, who is assisted by a part- time secretary and a young woman or man doing their civil service. As the only representative for the Brong-Ahafo Region she is responsible for 13 districts. In her old car she frequently drives to rural areas outside Sunyani, using her own salary for her fuel expenses and accommodation. Moving around in the region, enables her to maintain personal contact with women's organizations in the rural parts. With her personal commitment on a permanent basis, she channels information and obtains information on the activities and concerns of women. Out of her own experience, she has established these form of interactions, which was initially different when she started working at the NCWD where she was supposed to hold only workshops in the villages. She realised that they were only addressing the attendance and interests of men, who hoped to obtain access to resources, while at the same time their wives worked on their farms. Realising that planning ahead had its consequences in addressing the wrong recipients, she changed her policy to establish direct and permanent contact to women, even across long distances. Working with intermediaries also failed to get her into contact with women and women's organizations. She also tried to establish a Women's forum in another district capital, but this failed due to logistic problems with the local district assembly, which did not invite the local women's organizations, but the female schoolchildren of the secondary schools.

The distance of urban-rural networking can only partly be bridged by the use the local Radio-Station, Sky FM, which has established a special women's hour once a week where she discusses women related issues. For her, the personal contacts are however the main ways of building up capacities. A lack of money, the problematic relationship with government departments, and efforts which go unrecognised by foreign NGO's are major factors hindering the extension and intensification of her work. Despite the fact that she works within the complex of regional ministries, she is not part of the political decision-making process. Rather, her opinion is asked for and incorporated. For example in the design of a project. The interests of women are added to concepts, but they are never part of the whole planning process from the very beginning.

Her personal mobility is also the only way of keeping up with the politics of Head Office in Accra, where she attends the meetings of all representatives at least once a month. The information she receives, she distributes in the Women's forums, as for example the announcement of the start of the World Women's and African Women's Bank in Ghana. Infra-structural problems restrict her efforts to be more effective in the processes of networking in mobilising other women and in lobbying mechanisms at the political level. Financial reasons and a lack of support from the political bodies have restricted her work in the capacity building of networks and advisory functions. Her rural situation excludes her from appealing for fund and support from international donor-agencies. All attempts in the past at fund-raising have not succeeded based on the argument of the donor-agencies of supporting only the urban organizations, namely those in Accra. Out of a desperate financial situation, she began to form a self-carrying informal system of money lending. In Chapter 6. I will describe how she started, even outside the institutional structures of the NCWD, with establishing a form of *Susu*, which are "traditional" forms of money lending.

At this level, the work of the National Council of Women and Development is practically left in the hands of one woman, her own personal mobility and her contacts to other women's organizations. Within the institutional structures she has freedom and space to network on the realities of women, to address their issues to the public, and to react on it through opening up processes of self-defined development. This process opens up a perspective to challenge structures, to debate between issues under the recognition of diversities. For DAWN this form of interaction seem to be much more fruitful for empowerment, than the dogmatic assertion of "true" feminism (Sen/Grown 1987: 80). The strength of networking lies in the building of alliances as a medium for further strategies in their plurality. It is the establishment of communicative "nodes" linking the local with the regional and national level, which leads to a new situation of expanding one's own cognitive horizon. The underlying structure of information and communication serves not only to expand the "communicative accessibility", but to form new social ties and social coherence.

6.1.2 The Women's Forum at Accra: Another Platform for Change

The Women's forum in Accra only slightly differs from the one in Sunyani. It started up back in 1996. With its office located near the national ministries, as well as close to national and international NGO's. The meetings take place in a nearby hall of a media centre, in the heart of Accra. The program in its succession starts with the opening prayers, followed by reading and confirming the minutes and a general introduction of a representative of the NCWD announcing news or comments on pressing issues. Only the number of topics differ, with an average of six or more during one meeting, which are chaired by the President of the NCWD or by the director, both women. The only man attending the meeting is the minute-taker, who works as an employee at the office of the NCWD. Minutes are transcribed in the form of summaries and distributed at the beginning of the following meeting, attached with a list of participants including the name of the organization, its address and – if available – a telephone number to maintain contact among women. Continuity of regular attendance is usually assured by two women from the same organization. Women get to know each other in a rather friendly, familiar way. They gather in front of the meeting room, already expecting each other, chatting and talking in a familiar way. Some even use the opportunity to sell beads or other handicrafts.

Usually about 100 to 140 women attend the meeting. As I have already characterised in the introductory chapter, women come from different organizations. In addition, participants come from educational institutions such as the Ghana National Union of Poly Students and the University of Ghana (Legon). The clear difference in comparison to the Women's forum in Sunyani lies in the attendance of women working at research institutes such as the Women in Development and Research Centre or the Gender Awareness Foundation, as well as representatives from national NGO's like CEDEP (Centre for the Development of People) and from international organizations like UNFPA (United Nations Population Fund).

The major topics were not only discussed once, but over a longer time span in subsequent sections resulting in the establishment of standing-committees dealing with one topic in depth or organizing events such as International Women's Day, the Women's World March, campaigns such as Violence against Women or workshops on the concern of prostitutes and AIDS. During each forum a member of each committee gives a short talk to inform the other participants. Participants are not only involved in this process, but channel issues to their origin organization and vice versa report on activities and experiences assembled within their organization. Through the division of tasks, a constant process of interaction and information sharing is given between the forum and the participating organizations.

Apart from the standing-committees, ad-hoc groups for urgent matters are also set up. In one case they concerned the increased abuse of drugs in schools and the distribution of drug-contaminated stickers, supposed to make schoolchildren addicted.

The forum takes global and local issues into consideration. An example of a local issue is the often discussed sanitation situation at market-places in Accra and the difficulties of interacting with the municipality, who are supposed to be responsible for the cleaning. In a similar way global issues like the Beijing Platform for Action (1995) and its agenda to change, out of which the NCWD has chosen poverty, girl-child education, human rights, health and Violence against Women. Attention is also drawn to other "gender activities" in Africa as making aware of a women's conference in Zanzibar, which dealt with topics as the use of children as soldiers or the sale of arms to African Countries. The dynamics of glocal knowledge exchange is also supported having the access to information on "hard facts" as statistics on the situation of women and gender in Africa through access to research institutes, whether conducting their own studies or referring to international UN studies (as the Human Development Report), which are presented during the forum. At this level scientific knowledge in the form of a reliable and accurate gender-dissegregated database serves as an asset for formulating policies.

The bridging of urban and rural connections is integrated through the individual mobility outside the institutional structures of the NCWD. One woman who attended a workshop on Renewable Energies Development System in Kumasi, pointed out the use of one specific Solar Cooker constructed for the drying of local pepper. This prototype was constructed by a women, coming from the rural area, experimenting with solar cookers for the drying of pepper, and used the workshop for a demonstration. Knowledge is not only distributed from the urban to the rural areas, but through personal connections circulating in the other direction and submitted to the respective organizations localted in urban or peri-urban settings.

The public actions taken up by the women attending the forum varied and were partly done in collaboration with the National Council of Women and Development as the sole initiator or were taken up with the various organizations. Apart from a strong collaboration with the media, the public was addressed through a common march to the residence of President Rawlings. The orientation and intervention towards national political institutions did not only encompass a constant process of lobbying. The NCWD set up a demand to the President to establish gender-desks (called Gender and Development Desks) in all Ministries and departments. Out of past experience with only having one gender-desk in the overall political system and its almost complete marginalisation in policy processes, they expected to have an influence in every political department as the basis of building up a strong coherence between policies of each department.

The perspective of action is in particular on the local level, however, the global perspective is working as a back-screen. In comparison to the forum in Sunyani, the actions are already more professionalised and organized, being assisted by media and scientific research institutes. Although the underlying aim of the forum is to improve the living conditions of women, it is less critical in its articulation of negative consequences of past modernization. This is not surprising, since the women represent an urban literate strata, used to a "modern" life-style. This was illustrated by the intention of creating an own NCWD-piece of cloth to celebrate the 25 years of the NCWD, which costs six months of the budget of the office in Sunyani. However, the focus of a politicization of issues concerning women is strongly present at both forums.

6.1.3 The Organizational Structure of the NCWD

The National Council of Women and Development was established in 1975 by the Government of Ghana as the "official women's machinery" for promoting the advancement of women. Before, "women's issues" were part of the social welfare department or the community development department (Awumbila 2001: 54). A step outside those institutions did not result in an active transformative policy having its main function as an advisory body to the government and formulating policies within the Women and Development framework, by taking women's worlds isolated from the broader context. To enhance the status of women income-generating projects, consciousness-raising, education and training programs were implemented aiming at integrating women into development at first hand. Those efforts remained weak whether they were addressed at the concerns of women and did not reflect the real every-day policies of women. The major changes had been in legal policy as the change of the Intestate Succession Law in 1985 or the ratification of the CEDAW in 1986 by the government of Ghana. After its dissolution in 1986, it was restructured in 1991 and has since then gained national and international importance. Mariama Awumbila states, that within the political system of national state politics, the NCWD has in theory a clear mandate, but in reality it is limited in its effectiveness at influencing and changing government policies (2001: 55) which makes the current shift towards a building up own capacities of development even more understandable.

In its current programmatic politics, the NCWD has reacted at the lack of support by the government by attracting international donors and by its orientation towards being a platform of scientific knowledge generation. Early approaches were given up as being primarily an advisory body to the government by changing towards training programs for women to go into politics as its own methodological perspective towards gender and not on women's issues. The turn implicitly goes away from a reaction on structures to an active acting on structures and institutions. Its changing focus can be characterised in short as from "implementing" politics on women from above to a "channelling" from below. This change is partly due to the reflection on women's paradigms on the international level and the insight that steps of durable transformations need the connections with the local organizations in the urban and rural areas. Glocalization is therefore not only a flow of discourses and of knowledge, but institutions are reacting on it by changing their organizational structure, their content and the methodological perspective on society. The formation of the Women's forum was one example of a mutual connection between the diversities of local women's policies in connection with global discourse.

With a well established infrastructure the NCWD is – apart from the 31st DWM – the umbrella women's organization with offices in all regions of Ghana. The organizational structure is separated into three parts: a management council consisting of fifteen members, representing the Ministries as of Finance, Agriculture, Industry, Science and Technology, and Health and Education. Furthermore, a Queenmother, as well as a dentist and a female banker are joining the Council. The Council regularly discusses the direction of politics, financial matters, administrative issues. The major work is done by the thirty employees working in the Head Office, which is divided into five units: Plans and Policy Analysis, Research and Statistics, Aid and Project Coordination, Human Resource Department, Finance and Administration. The executive secretary represents the official politics of the NCWD and is responsible for the common meetings with all representative from the regional offices.

In recent times the emphasis had been on research as well as on the establishment of a documentation centre. Studies were already of concern at the beginning of the NCWD. The former methodology taking factor and quantitative analysis on a macro-level into consideration, gradually shifting their empirical focus on gender-relations in social institutions, which are nowadays conducted with qualitative research methods such as biographical interviews and semi-structured interviews. Larger research studies are still highly dependent on external aid and even the study on "Women in Public Life in Ghana" was co-financed by the Development and Project Planning Centre, University of Bradford, U.K. The empirical results could only be published in a summarised book, due to a shortage of money for publishing the extended version. It is not only the process of knowledge production which is financially dependent on external donors, but also the publishing and dissemination of the product. The importance of the results for political argumentation I have mentioned in Chapter 5.

The National Council of Women and Development has turned its original mandate as a "national machinery" to an organization bridging the different existing realities of women in the urban and rural parts of Ghana. The integration into the global discourse on gender has brought in new forms of collaboration and of politicising. This new form of networking is not the only strategy the NCWD takes upon. Workshops, seminars, the support of projects initiated by women's organizations are some of the "classical" of development. Networking as such can be defined as a new form of doing developments in its plurality within one institutional structure.

6.2 The Pan-African Network Women in Law and Development Africa (WiLDAF)

WiLDAF was established as a non-governmental and non-profit organization in 1990 and is in its extension exceptional on the African continent. In the following I will describe first the origin of WiLDAF, which has its roots also in Ghana, and its objective. I have recorded data on the organizational structure out of the constitution and by joining a three day general meeting of more than 100 WiLDAF representatives, which was taking place in Accra in July 1999 under the topic "Women's rights into the next millenium". The interesting feature here is the upheld of the dynamics of institutional structures trying to avoid becoming encrusted in a growing network. Second, I will focus on the process of transnational networking in connecting localities, as well as the agenda building and the translation process into local contexts. The local activism of WiLDAF Ghana can be distinguished by the establishment of its own offices, which have been opened in two regions in Ghana, and the personal networking which makes the work of WiLDAF in other regions invisible and hidden for the researcher.

6.2.1 Initiating WiLDAF: From Local Realities to Transnational Networking...

The idea of creating a pan-African network came up at the end of the 1980s in the aftermath of the World Women's Conference 1985 in Nairobi, where already during the Women, Law and Development forum and on the background of a world-wide women's rights movement the first thoughts about it were articulated (Schuler 1994: 1). Examples of organising along the transnational level were given by the South-American Women's rights network CLADEM (1987) and by the Asian network APWLD (1986)[6]. Six women from Kenia, Uganda, Ghana, Zimbabwe, Botswana and Senegal took up on the idea and worked on the foundation and establishment of WiLDAF. Their

---

6 All three organizations are nowadays in permanent interactions with the OEF/ WLD Network in Washington working on an international agenda (Schuler 1990: 1ff.).

aim was to build up a formal network organization based on decentralised structures and on the principle of networking between individuals and organizations at all societal levels. The networking was meant as a medium and a space for political action.

The establishment of an own network spread through country workshops to other African Countries and in 1990 the formal founding assembly took place in Harare (Zimbabwe) where already 65 delegates from 16 African countries met. The topic of the assembly was "Women, Law and Development: Networking for Empowerment in Africa". The taking up of law (formal and customary) is defined as initiating a transformative process through one common tool. The aim is not only to change laws in a legal sense, but to use it in a wider societal meaning as a catalyst for transforming women's lives. Dorothy Thomas defined transformation in her keynote address to the second general assembly in 1994, as "add women and alter" and not "add women and stir" (Thomas 1994: 12). What supposed to be avoided by focusing on the diversities of laws as social and legal constructs, is the over-generalising, homogenising and equalisation of women's lives (Thomas 1994: 10). The maintaining of the diversity and complexity of women's lives is reflected in the organizational power structure with its emphasis on a decentralised decision-making process. During the first conference the regulations of WiLDAF and the programmatic objectives were passed. The main objectives of WiLDAF are:

- to link law and development to empower women
- to promote the effective use of legal strategies; to strengthen legal rights programs for women at local, national and regional level
- to provide assistance and training to groups; to produce simple legal education materials; lobbying; mobilisation and networking strategies
- to respond to violence against women's rights nationally, regionally and internationally through an electronic Emergency Response System
- to exchange and co-ordinate activities with other African and international human rights and women's rights networks
- to compile and exchange case studies and research

The membership of WiLDAF is opened to the wide range of women's activists, who work in the different fields of development, encompassing academics, community development workers or lawyers. Furthermore individuals as well as organizations can become members of WiLDAF[7]. Right from the beginning WiLDAF set up programs to achieve its objectives as: 1. Training of members and non-members in legal programs 2. Advocacy Programs 3. The setting-up of a WiLDAF-Newsletter. The programs were up to now, added

---

7 The agenda of WiLDAF is clearly separate from FIDA, which is exclusively open to female lawyers and is in its political aims concentrated on the law. Both organizations work closely together, and members of WiLDAF are also members of FIDA.

with campaigning, monitoring, evaluation and documentation. The setting-up of an Internet-Homepage and the use of the Internet for passing information and to facilitate communication. E-Mail appeals are used for pressuring or lobbying governments, development organizations or international organizations. WiLDAF Mauritius started a global campaign against the deregulation and liberalisation of trade in 1999 and tried to intervene in collaboration with WIDE (Women in Development Europe) on EU-Politics concerning the Lomé trade arrangement. With the Green Paper which regulates the EU-ACP relations released by the European Commission in 1996, women of WilDAF-Mauritius feared a new area of competition, of exploitation and of disempowerment contradicting the Beijing Declaration and Platform of Actions. Together with ENDA, an environmental organization from Senegal, they lobbied during a discussion day with the European Commission Delegate in Dakar, Senegal. The permanent lobbying of EU-Politics through WIDE is still going on, trying to engender it by integrating women's social and political rights.

The Internet as a new cyber-space becomes politicised by acting on international politics and turns into a space of "shared politics" (Youngs 1999: 67). Through virtual voices, local realities are defended and transcended on a global level. WiLDAF is only one example of the use of the Internet by women's organizations. Abantu, a network of African women in Britain, has conducted workshops and Internet training for African women and organizations in different African Countries (1999: 144ff.) or TAMWA, the Tanzania Media Women's Organization, as one of the "first e-mail nodes" (Alloo 1999: 157) in Tanzania has addressed its policies on link between the women's movements on issues such as Violence against Women, reproductive health and empowerment. Out of those few examples from Africa the importance of the new Information, Communication and Technology (ICT) system as an appropriated space for the linking of the women's movement in connecting distant relations becomes part of a new glocal networking, not based any longer on face-to-face, but also on multiple "face-to-screen" interactions (Knorr-Cetina/ Bruegger 2002: 923). Arturo Escobar has described in short that through electronic media, women's organizations transform their real physical and social lives into "the cultural politics of cyberspace" (1999: 32). In his argument social movements as the women's, indigenous, environmental or ethnic ones are new political actors, that resist, transform or present alternatives through the dominant virtual and real world[8]. The Internet is forming new modes of operation for contesting policies, whether one of development organizations or one a large network or small groups. The effect of the everyday physical world and culture is represented in a global extent, but the core force underlying the global agency still permits the defence of their localities.

---

8   His argument is based on observation on social movements in Columbia, which have used the Internet in having access to information on biodiversity and have integrated it into their resistance against the destruction of environment (1999: 32).

The electronic form of interaction has only recently facilitated the connections within WiLDAF and has not substituted personal interactions. The extension of it has been, and is still, based on personal contacts. In its quantitative extension up to 1999 the network had grown to include 26 African countries[9] with about 500 organizational and 1500 individual members.

6.2.2 The Organizational Structure: Struggling for Power on the Ground

WiLDAF is structured along geographical and organizational principles. The Headquarters comprises of the secretariat which is located in Harare (Zimbabwe), where a co-ordinator and a financial assistant are employed. Both are responsible for transnational and international collaboration and for the organization of fundraising and the representation of WiLDAF at international conferences. Geographically WiLDAF is divided into four parts: Northern Africa, West Africa, Southern Africa and East Africa. Each part forms a sub-region headed by a sub-regional committee. Every sub-region has one specific common policy such as West Africa with the implication of structural adjustment programs, Southern Africa focusing on violence against women and East Africa on women in armed conflicts. However, autonomy is given to formulating its own national policy and to defining its focal points. So, for example, Zimbabwe works on women and landrights/inheritance rights or Mauritius deals with the policies of Worldbank/IMF, which has lead to a breaking apart of a well organised public service system. In other countries such as Nigeria the issue of HIV/Aids has become prominent within its programme.

Women's rights are therefore a construct of a common framework. In its diversities it is split into social, economic, political rights and the amendment of constitutions. The very broadly defined thematical framework is open and flexible for integrating of new issues such as globalization and regionalisation, the environment, information and media, trade and deregulation, which were discussed in depth during the 1999 meeting.

The most powerful organ is the general assembly which meets every five years and is constituted by all registered members of WiLDAF, de facto by national delegations who have been elected by the national members. Out of the general assembly the board is elected. Up to the third general meeting in 1999 the board has been the most powerful organ in giving the direction of the policy and deciding about the distribution of funds. During the three-day meeting the general assembly changed the constitution by turning the General Assembly into the major power organ. *"How can we teach what democracy*

---

9 The 26 countries are: Kenia, Uganda, Sudan Tansania, Malawi, Mauritius, Zimbabwe, Zambia, Botswana, Namibia, Swaziland, Mosambique, Angola, South-Africa, Lesotho, Cameroon, Nigeria, Togo, Ghana, Mali, Senegal, Benin, Burkina Faso, Ivory Coast, Niger, Malawi.

is, when we are not moving in a democratic system" was one argument for putting pressure on the need to changing structures and the break of being organised in a hierarchical top-down way.

In a similar manner the suggestion of the head-office co-ordinator to be assisted by a deputy-co-ordinator was turned down. The cynical argument of one member that the establishment of supra-supra structures is "born" in Africa, does not mean that the same bureaucratic procedures must be replicated. The decision-making process should follow the direction as being channeled from the country offices towards the head office and not the other way around. This has happened in the past and resulted in unequal financial regulations and in an unequal distribution of funds by the head office. Out of the general assembly the board is elected and composes 15 members of the general assembly for five years. Its composition reflects the regional and language balance. 5 members are from Southern Africa, 3 from East-Africa, 2 from English speaking West-Africa, 2 from French speaking West-Africa and 3 from Northern Africa The problem of languages was constantly articulated during the third meeting. The French speaking delegations criticised the domination of English during the conference, in publications and in the internal communication. Every board member can only be elected once. The board meets once a year and discusses the administration and appoints the regional co-ordinators. Out of the board a small standing committee is appointed, which supervises the secretariat.

The structuration of WiLDAF across the horizontal and the vertical level has despite its extension, left the space for flexibility open. The decentralised structures and the channelling of decisions from the ground guarantees a permanent process of the transcendence and exchange of local experiences and the pooling of information as well as on acting and reacting on local, national, sub-regional and global policies.

6.2.3 WiLDAF 1999: Backwards and Forwards

Ten years after the foundation of WiLDAF, the 1999 general meeting gave space to reflect on successes, failures and on future tasks. One positive aspect has been the rising number of people being active in the network, which is strengthening the link between localities across nations. Despite the use of modern forms of communication, the flow of information between countries and between countries and the Head-Office is not as constant as expected. The equal distribution of information and the mutual support through information is a further challenge. Expansion and information have already contributed to the creation of a *"culture of women's rights"* on the national level by lobbying governments and on the regional and sub-regional level at UN Meetings. Human rights and in particular women's rights are nowadays known in the political contexts and has sensitised institutions and organizations towards a critical dealing with it in accordance with local conditions as customs. On the other hand a backlash can be noticed, paradoxically in the aftermath of the fourth World Conference on Women in Beijing (1995), which in many countries became a "joke" for gender discussions, as well as through a burnout effect of many women through the limitations affecting their lives such as growing poverty, wars and conflict situations. They had to admit that *"African women's movement came to a stay"*. The worsening of living conditions, the volunteer work of many women, restricting them to concentrate on one's own survival. Individual poverty directly affecting them, was revealed by the majority of representatives as the major burden for taking up activities and its alleviation is defined as one of the major future challenges. Economic constraints even put risks on the upkeep of WiLDAF activities. Being financially supported by donors and membership fees, the dependency of external money could not be overcome[10]. The opening of offices such as the one in Mozambique, the regular publishing of the Newsletter and of manuals, travel expenses to conferences, the financial support of workshops and training's has not yet corresponded with an increase of funds.

The challenges beyond the political agenda lies in the continuation of fund-raising, the information gathering and distribution through the Internet, as well as the continuing of networking as the most efficient form of advocacy. The overall topic of women's rights was confirmed, but it was also considered that new emerging issues such as globalization, neo-liberalisation as well as processes with a negative influence on women should be analyzed in depth, research data collected and strategies developing from it. It is less the extension of the network, than the intensifying and upkeep of activities towards a high degree of financial autonomy which are at stake.

6.2.4 ... and from Transnational Networking back to Local Reality

How does the programmatic agenda constituted at transnational level becomes reality on the local level ? WiLDAF-Ghana started in 1992. Two lawyers, Dokas Coker-Appiah and Akua Kuenheyia, who is the Dean of the Faculty of Law at the University of Ghana (Legon), are the initiators and maintainers of WiLDAF-Ghana. Both have already worked together in FIDA, the international association of women's lawyers, which is exceptionally open to the issue of law and its membership for lawyers. Dokas Coker-Appiah, who is the head of WiLDAF-Ghana works in a little office in Accra, which is a part of the Gender and Human Rights Documentation Centre. The small GHRDC has two rooms stuffed with books, computers and documents. Despite financial constraints of maintaining an office and of the infrastructure of working, WiLDAF-Ghana has set up a programme for action. The self-definition of being a "networking organization" as a form and as a strategy has resulted in permanent collaboration with women and women's organizations in the urban and rural parts of Ghana. This covers the umbrella organization NCWD, the Queenmothers, church groups, agricultural extension workers, market

---

10 Some donors are: UNDP, CIDA, Ford-Foundation, UNIFEM.

women, social welfare officers, teachers, nurses, community development workers, people working in NGO's or women belonging to a women's union. Through this form of networking WiLDAF has built up a pool of individuals and organizations for the promotion of a culture of women's rights.

A selection of those laws, which are of concern for women in Ghana, has been done on the basis of a long working experience, since both heads of WiLDAF have been involved in these matters as lawyers, researchers and within their own living context. The first law of concern was the Intestate Law which regulates the system of inheritance. In 1985 the government of Ghana codified the system of inheritance as the Intestate Succession Law (PNDC 111) under pressure from the 31st December Women's Movement and of the NCWD. Before the change of law, wives were not considered as being a member of the husband's family and could not inherit any property, which meant, that many women, who contributed to the establishment of a house for example, had to leave it after the death of the husband. The new law regulated that 3/4 of the property will go to the wife and the children, while 1/4 will go to the family of the husband. The change of law has not only been a formal advantage for wives, but has put many of them into difficulties as struggles between family members, which broke out about the acquiring properties. Many women were not aware of the change of laws at all or have been too timid to consult the police or a lawyer. WiLDAF in collaboration with the different women's organizations has set up a programmatic approach for making women in their districts aware of their rights and offering legal assistance. Even in Susuanso women told me that they know where they can address the issue if the solution of it could not be solved within the family. My landlady explained,

"Nowadays the men cannot cheat us. If my husband dies, I know that I can live in this house, even I am his second wife. Everything we have in the room and in the kitchen belongs to me. They will come to take it, but I know my rights, now we are educated and we know how to get our rights. It is not like in the olden days, when they drive you away and his family is taking over. I can go to my family house, but I know the things here belong to me".

When I was further asking her how she got to know it, she told me, *"we talk all over here, you hear it at the radio, we talk on the market, at my shop, you will go to Sunyani at a certain office, they will help you"*. The channelling of the information about the law had been in the past through the form of networking between the representative of the NCWD in Sunyani, a volunteer, and has regularly participated in workshops of WiLDAF. She took up the inheritance law as part of her own program and also established a close relationship with a female lawyer in Sunyani as well as the local office of FIDA. Even nowadays she regularly takes it up as a topic in the Women's forum, talks on it at the radio or directly discusses it with women in the rural areas.

The above example reveals that the focusing on law cannot be extracted from its social context. The change of law and knowledge about it is not sufficient. To act upon it, to get its rights, does not only turn women into subjects, but points to a way with multiple aspects taken into consideration. The WiLDAF definition of laws encompasses three components: 1. the structure of a law (courts, procedures for exercising the rights) 2. substance (culture of law, customary law) and 3. culture (attitudes and behaviour). To know, to defend, to act on are the principles of the programmatic and transformative approach.

The maintenance of children is another law which in recent times has become more important as many divorced husbands are not willing to support their children after divorce. A young woman in Susuanso, who has divorced from a well-off taxi-driver, has to support her seven year old son Kwasi by herself since her former husband refused to do so. After all the family help and the intervention of some Church members had failed to put pressure on him, she went to a lawyer at Sunyani to settle the case there and succeeded insofar as the former husband pays a monthly fee for food and for the school. The channelling of laws of concern at the WiLDAF office through the NCWD has reached the local level also in the aftermath of Beijing, which has opened up discussions on women's rights in the public, media and in politics. For Dokas Coker-Appiah, Beijing was also a matter of seeing things differently than before. In particular through the integration of a gender perspective, she turned away from focusing on women alone and to continue defining situations as "natural". In particular violence against women, she realised that these forms are not only private, but are a form of discrimination of both the private and public space of women. It is the most recently discussed topic in the public addressing both genders, which WiLDAF-Ghana took upon in 1997. The program of WiLDAF-Ghana plans the adding of a new law every year. Up to 1999 this had been, the inheritance law, the maintenance of children, the marriage law and on violence against women. The inheritance and marriage law are of specific interest, since through the expansion of privatisation and the self-acquired property, women are often excluded from inheritance if the marriage is not registered. About 80 % of marriage is still conducted as customary marriage. Without registration wives have no rights to obtain any property after the husband has deceased. The registration of the marriage is a prerequisite to the inheritance law PNDC 1111 (Awusabo-Asare, 1990: 1-17).

The representative of the NCWD has been one of many other women, who as volunteers have attended training and workshops of WiLDAF, which are conducted in all regions of Ghana. During these workshops women are informed about the specific laws or methods for training which can be used by the volunteers themselves. The training methods are based on concepts of adult education, which have been developed between the main organisers of WiLDAF from different African countries in a mutual process of exchange and published in a training manual. The method of training is substituting a top-down teaching, an approach of mutual participation between the trainer and the trained. In a situation between a trainer and a women's organization, participation is conceptualised and realised as a mutual learning process, embedded in an equal sharing of power and the mutual creation and acquisition of knowledge and skills for both trainer and organization. The emphasis of the interaction is that knowledge is not implemented in a top-down manner, likewise between an expert and a group creating a social and cultural distance. Instead knowledge of the group which is acquired from experience or formal learning is at the centre[11]. The control of knowledge remains within the group. Networking also becomes a method of training, by a sharing of information, joint and collaborative actions, and mobilisation (Butegwa/Nduna 1995: 105). After an evaluation in 1995 of the training and workshops, which was positively felt the volunteers, the strengthening of legal programs was decided upon by having a permanent office as a pilot programme in the Volta Region and since 1997 in the West Coast of Ghana. In both offices female lawyers are available for counselling individuals, volunteers, and for conducting legal awareness programs at the community level, which also involves men and local authorities. The financial support for both offices as well as for the above described training programs has been funded by donor agencies such as SNV (Netherlands), the United States Embassy and the Human Rights Fund (USA).

Experiences in local contexts are transmitted by regular letters and in publications to the office of WiLDAF in Harare as well as both the heads of WiLDAF-Ghana are permanently in interaction with ongoing research studies into gender and law, national and international. The process of knowledge distribution is channelled from the transnational level to the local level and from the local to the international level through the above described form of collaborations.

6.3 Networking as a Knowledge Bridge

Since I have defined organizations as pillars, networking is the new form of interaction between them and can also metaphorically be characterised as a bridge between different locations. As a bridge it structures the everyday world by extending the horizon of world within its reach, which makes the experience of others integrated into one's own context of living. On the local level the networking takes place in the medium of the women's forum and the long-distance networking through the Internet. Both function as nodes of translations. The women's forum through the new hybridising of experts, scientific, everyday knowledge as well as local events and global discourses. Both nodes of translations are distributing knowledge and therefore gain the relevance of creating own stocks of knowledge. Translation also means the

---

11 See also sub-section conducting critical theory.

breaking up of the dimensions of lifeworld into different reaches. Since in the village of Susuanso the "world outside" as the women's organizations is reached in a direct way through the radio, face-to-face interactions and personal contacts, the knowledge of the global is experienced in a already translated form in the Women's forum in Sunyani. They have the knowledge about violence against women as a national campaign, but not of a global women's movement. They are not part of a global movement, but the global discourse becomes part of a local movement. The horizon of the agency of women on the local level is within their immediate reach. The dimensions of reach is however different in the forum in Accra. Here, global affairs such as the World Women's March (Canada) are discussed and reflected upon. Networking in its spatial dimensions has different reaches of knowledge or information. Development is embedded now in processes of mutual learning and mutual strategising with the common aspect of the integration of diversities. The monolith of a semantic development should be substituted by multiplicities of developments and multiple options as well as through new paradigms for changing gender-relations and social institutions through networking coherence. These "meta" paradigms, which are trying to avoid the manifestation of hierarchical structures is best exemplified by the polystructured network WiLDAF, based on decentralised power structures.

7 The Migrating Knowledge

In the following I want to personify the abstract picture of the women's movement along the intersection between the private and the political life of two women engaged in women's organizations. By analysing the personal movements of women, the dynamics, the flow of knowledge and the potential of innovation, I show how personal experience and experiments result in a process of "doing development". I define "doing development" as a pragmatic form of practice based on personal experience and knowledge without working within a predefined agenda or program. I make use of the term development to indicate that innovations are not only made within the institutional frame of development organizations. Experiences other than these are fed back into the frame. Integrating personal experience and innovation into the social stock of knowledge and through acting on social structure in its consequences means to be motors of social change.

7.1 Becoming a 31st December Woman

The first time I met Elisabeth was in the office of the German Development Cooperation (GTZ). She was then 51 years old and employed to organise farmers in the region to form co-operatives. Gradually we became friends and talked about the different living situations in Germany and Ghana. Her career path followed the different stages of her life and her future prospective.

Growing up in Northern Ghana
　　Elizabeth was born in 1957 in a small rural town in the Northern Region of Ghana in the East Mamprussi District. She belongs to the Konkombas, an ethnic group which settled on the land of the Mamprussi years ago and due to fighting over Chieftaincy has led to continuous inter-ethnic conflicts. Her father was a rich farmer, with plenty of land for cultivating crops such as yam, guinea corn, millet, sweet potatoes, groundnuts and pepper. Especially in times of droughts and hunger, strangers from outside came to their farm and asked for food and for a place to stay. In return, they had to work in the fields of Elizabeth's father. Elizabeth was her father's second wife. Both, the father and the mother were not formally educated, however supported the Zion mission, who came to the village in the early 1960s and financed the building of a Church with an attached school. For Elizabeth this was a first step towards education. *"The time when they came I was about four years old. And my fa-*

ther gave me to the pastor. So I was visiting school like that". Elizabeth was not an exception in that she attended school. All her sisters and brothers were also able to attend school, which was free of charge then. The contact with the pastor who came from the Southern Region of Ghana was of special importance, while he took care of her and financed her uniform and school items. The only problematic relationship emerged when her brothers tried to keep her away by pulling her out of school and forced her to go back home.

"My brothers were saying that I would not go to school any longer. Because in our custom we exchange. Your brother would give you to another friend of his and he would collect the sister. So when you go to marry there, the sister will marry your brother. So my brothers were pulling me out of school back to the house. And I would run back. At times it was dark and I run all the night and I run to that place. And I continued like that. I was all the time determining, that I will complete my school".

For Elizabeth, education was the major reason for resisting forces of her brothers and against the ethnic custom of marriage exchange, which comprises of the engagement of young girls during childhood. Despite this passive form of protest against ethnic customs, she describes herself as an outstanding girl, who attracted other people with her appearance and calmness. "*I was extremely quiet, I never talked, I never quarrelled. I never said anything. I never had a confrontation with friends. So people liked me for that nature. I was reserved and at that time, I was pretty and quiet*". The continuation of Elizabeth's education towards higher degrees was not guaranteed at that point of time. On the contrary, she was an exception among other girls in her progress as most of them left school shortly after graduation from primary school.

"There were (in middle school, C.M.) a lot of girls in the school. And even in my village, we were many, but some were growing and withdrawing. So gradually I was the one who forced ahead. I was so much interested in my education and when I finished middle form, I took the exams, and I passed. So I went to Training College".

The completion of school education at 18 gave her the opportunity to leave the rural parts and to go to Tamale, the largest town in Northern Ghana. Becoming a teacher is still a popular decision taken by several women since it provides regular payment in a government, private or religious based school. At Tamale friends influenced her to become a Christian. In bible classes she met her future husband, whom she married at 19. She still regrets marrying that early today, since she wanted to copy her mother, who married after she has known her future husband for a couple of years, in her late 20s. After Elizabeth had finished training college, she taught in Primary School and Preparatory Schools. Teaching made her aware, that education has a broader meaning and it is not sufficient for herself only to educate young people. She started teaching outside Tamale in small communities and taught literacy classes and English. Her commitment towards education was extended across other ethnic groups and based on religious motives.

"I took over the managing"

Within a short time between 1977 and 1984, Elizabeth gave birth to four children, continued working as a teacher even with the evening classes in the villages outside Tamale. Directly after the birth of her fourth child, her husband left to go to Nigeria without any major reason. Up to that time he worked in the hospital of Tamale as a technician.

"He was working and he had his job in Tamale As for this point, I will never understand him. I actually struggled with him, I argued, but he refused and went. So he took our car, a caravan I got from my father for our wedding, and he said, he is going to sell it in Nigeria and with the money he will buy a better one in Ghana. But what he aimed at he did not succeeded and I suffered with the children, I really suffered. He just left without a pesewa in the house".

To date his reasons for leaving are still unknown. During his twelve years of absence, he never sent any message and after his return he never talked about it. He came back home sick and cannot start working today. For Elizabeth her husband's disappearance forced her to take over the sole responsibility for the children and her livelihood. In order to cope with the situation, she went back to her parent's village and worked there as a teacher. With the help of her mother and friends, who took care of the children during her absence, she managed the situation. At the same time she started to help in the villages to organize the building up of schools and health stations. Education, in particular of the young people, was intended to create awareness."[...] *to educate the Youth and to give them awareness to make them know that they can help themselves in many ways. Both men and women"*. The organization of the Youth for development turned her away from organizing infrastructure to organizing people in a movement. Similarly she turned from charitable commitment to political engagement.

"I just felt like organizing. I just wanted to help my people. My whole mind was just to help them come up. I saw that they were being suppressed by other people like the Mamprussi. They are suppressed. So they are always suppressing us. Forcing our people to do what they are not supposed to do. And gain their rights. I realised, I can do something, to educate my people, to organize them, so they will know their rights".

Youth associations of the Konkombas had a major influence in the political arena in Northern Ghana, as a cultural, migrant and development organization at the same time. Moreover, apart from being a catalyst for self-help, they functioned as a highly political active group to form resistance against being political dominated by other ethnic groups which had been in existence for several centuries. The initiators of the groups were educated elite locals, local chiefs, migrants and educated people. It was not purely an association of young people, political activists were in fact attempting to gain political liberation by demanding their own Paramount Chief (Lentz 1999: 310ff.)[1]. Especially the Konkomba Youth Association was a major actor in the uprising of the ethnic war in 1994.

Resistance against Suppression
The organization within Elizabeth's ethnic group increased its awareness towards gender. *"I felt suppressed, because at times when you are at a place and you want to bring out ideas, people do not want to accept it, because they feel, especially a woman, what are your ideas?"*. Becoming critically aware that her gender was taken as a reason for silencing women's voices, she experienced both, ethnic and gender restrictions. However, these did not keep her away from organizing groups in the district. Both reasons rather motivated her to use her own money for travel expenses or to cycle.

"I always asked myself why do I do that. I always had positive aspects. I always felt very deep with my people. When I see them doing things out of ignorance. I felt sick for myself. I did not care for myself really. I did not know what was in my mind. I never thought about myself. But I was so much caring about my people".

In 1986, Elizabeth was asked by the District Director of Education to organize the 31st December Women's movement, which she was aware of, but had never done any active work for. She accepted the offer but did not become a party member of the related NDC. After two years of work in the district, she took another offer of the 31st DWM to go to Cuba for one year with twenty other women engaged in the movement to further her formal education, meanwhile leaving her children at her parents' place.

Cuba as a Catalyst of Gender awareness
The formal education in Cuba deepened her historical and political knowledge. *"And I went there for one year. I did not learn Spanish, we talked in English. We went to study Government Politics. We stayed in the centres. We stayed for real studies. We worked until midnight. We had exams the following day"*. The exchange with women coming from different parts of the world, was an addition to the studies Elizabeth conducted and further motivated her commitment to political organization.

"We stayed in Havanna, at the FMC, the Federation of Women. There were also women from other countries as the Caribbean, Uganda, Zambia, Gambia. They all came. We met different, different people, who came and we learned about political

---

1 For a detailed description of the political development and on ethnicity in Northern Ghana see Carola Lentz (1998).

issues. They all came there. It was very nice. I knew why I studied. I wanted to become better in the future and you must know your historical background. How to be colonised and about the people. And why there are Cubans speaking Spanish. And we went to all the important places. And everything about Fidel. How Fidel became Fidel. And in 1989 he was very strong. He talked and talked and talked. And the people in Cuba are hard working. Men and women are working. And I realised that a woman was to do something better. I saw the Cuban women working. Women still working at nights like this. They work 24 hours. They will work and they are never resting. They are hard working. So within 3-4 months they have finished any comply project. So in fact, that was a great experience for me. Those people [...]".

The efforts of women in a local context and meanwhile as part of a global movement were a catalyst for shaping Elizabeth's awareness and commitment in the 31st December Women's Movement once she was back in Ghana "*I was organising the villages again. Only the women*". From the transnational experience, development became a matter of gender.

Organising Environmental Programs: Examples from India
Within the diversities of projects and programs of the 31st DWM, environmental programs such as the raising of seedlings and the consciousness rising of the importance of trees came to the fore. Elizabeth went around the villages on a motorbike and informed communities, "*I realised that they did not understand the importance of growing trees. So I met the elders and the whole community and talked to them about the importance of growing trees*". The realisation of the projects have however been exclusively for women, while adding nutritional aspects in the choice and selection of seedlings as Mango trees, as well as following the interests of women for fast growing trees which they use for firewood[2]. Together with the women, Elizabeth began to nurse and raise trees along the street sides by choosing a specific tree planting method, which was taken from India. This technical method, "pourswift", consists of digging a hole and transplantation of the seedlings into black soil. Water is put into an additional hole next to it and seeps bit by bit into the other hole. Due to this method the seedlings are constantly watered and water has to be poured in only once a week. This form of labour reductive care, was taken over from the exchange of experience between women from the 31st DWM and women from India. Elizabeth further established a reforestation station and laid the grounds for a demonstration plot. In order to get it better known by the wider public and in institutions she invited all the agricultural officers and the politicians of the Ministry of Food and Agriculture for information and demonstration. The development within an approach of self-help and achieved using technology way did not have a transformative component as such. Aspects such as the transformation of inheritance of land

---

2 Trees in Northern Ghana can be used for multiple purposes as Padmanabhan has shown in her thesis for the Dawadawa, a tree which fruits are further processed into for instance into soup cubes (2000).

rights were not included. In the northern part of Ghana, women only have access to land in conjunction with a male person: their father, their brother or their husband (Becher 2001: 56). Especially women who want to expand their farmland are often accused of witchcraft in order to deter them from their plans (Becher 2001: 63). The institutional frame and the politics of the 31st DWM was not opened towards the legal support of women and towards the change of gender relations and of social institutions. Examples from other African countries, however, show that ecological movements turned out to become political. A prominent example is the Greenbelt movement founded in 1977 with the leading person Matthai Wangari. The movement started with the planting of more than one million trees in the different districts of Kenya. Later on education and social welfare components were added, and it further turned out to become a political movement by criticising political power relations and has resulted in a problematic relationship with the government of Kenya.

Already in Tamale through the connection with the Ministry of Food and Agriculture, Elizabeth was asked by a German Development Organization to work as an organiser for them. Due to the outbreak of the war between the Konkombas and other ethnic groups in 1994 she was forced to leave with her children to Sunyani under the protection of soldiers. There Elizabeth continued to work in the office of the 31st DWM and gradually established herself again. By chance she met a development worker of the German Development Organization, who had also left Tamale, recognised her and employed her in Sunyani.

Experience as an Employee in a German Development Organization

Elizabeth's duty as an organiser was to form farmers co-operatives in three different villages around Sunyani. The programme of the organization is aimed at the enhancement and securing of food production, the improved storage of crops and the marketing of agricultural products to secure the food situation. Under the name of "post-harvest improvement systems" the conventional circle of selling maize at low prices directly after harvest should be broken by storing the crops until a later time when prices have been risen. Elizabeth's task was to go into the villages, to stay overnight and to explain the use of the program. She had no influence in its design. Apart from the frequent visits to the villages she was never involved in office meetings or in the organization of workshops. With her background in politics and development she was not recognised as a local expert as there had been recent changes in development co-operation programs. Those local experts have gained some importance and a certain degree of autonomy in the work of the organization especially as brokers between local and regional politicians and administration and the project leader (Illi, 2001). This situation was not applied to Elizabeth. Organization was the implementation of the programs, talking with the different employees at the Ministries of Food and Agriculture as well as with managers of the local banks, since the program had foreseen the involvement of bank loans. In her position as a broker she realised the ambivalent situation of being employed for development with a small salary and her own ambitions for educational progress. Her struggles for a higher salary, the struggle to get a car to get to the villages, and the lack of her own further education were ongoing discussion points, however, she never succeeded in implementing her own demands. Her small office which she shared with visiting students who were on short term exchange programs consisted only of two tables and a few chairs. Her suggestion of improving her education by taking computer courses[3] was not recognised as being worth financed by the organization. Behind everybody's back, however, she used the co-operation's infrastructure to experiment with the development of a solar-dryer.

The Hidden Agenda

Since she had partly been without any work at the office, she took the opportunity for experimenting on the demonstration plot of the organization with the drying of local pepper in a self-constructed solar-dryer. Those solar-dryers are simple constructions, made out of a flat sheet of bamboo and a simple wooden frame with a plastic cover. Collected pepper from her farm, which belongs to one farmer of the co-operation in a village, is dried for a few days. The dried pepper can be stored for weeks without being spoiled. Finally it is filled in plastic packages and sold in restaurants in Kumasi. Elizabeth demonstrated her own innovation at a seminar on Renewable Energies in Kumasi (1998), which was attended by a woman who reported on it later on at the Women's forum in Accra. The channelling of information among women went along forums and seminars as mediums for the exchange of experiences and of experiments. What is part of the individual stock of knowledge becomes part of the social stock of knowledge and permits permanent innovation. Elizabeth finally left the office in Sunyani, demanding a higher income to support her four children and her husband. Her demand was denied by the head of the office. Meanwhile she had contact with the country office in Accra, where she was offered a better paid job as a co-ordinator in another project concerning water and environment in the Volta Region. Her latest step shows that her power for demanding a higher salary was increased by opening choices by progressing with her career.

7.2 Every Human Being is a Political Person

The Failed Banking Career

Yaa Amina is the NCWD representative in Sunyani. Her age, which she did not tell, because *"women and men should not be dated"*, is around 60 years. She was born in Sunyani as the third of twelve children. Her father had an elementary education while her mother never went to school. Education

---

3 Computer courses at one of the computer schools cost around an average of 250,000 Cedis, which is a month's salary of a secondary teacher.

was of primary concern of her parents and apart from the eldest sister, who stayed at home to help the mother, all the children went to school. The education was financed by the father and mother together. After she finished primary school, she continued with her education in secondary school. Her education inspired her not to take over the trade of her mother. *"If I look at my mother, she did not go to school. So if I expected to be like my mother, this would have meant, growing up and taking her trade and that was all"*. Her first wish was to become a doctor, which she could not follow, because the school she attended did not offer science and maths. *"They did not offer science, but my interest was in science and maths. So when I finished I wanted to become a banker"*. After finishing her exams, Yaa Amina applied to different banks where her applications were rejected or she was told to wait for some time. Bored of sitting at home, she finally left after some months to go to a training college in Takoradi, a town at the coast. Becoming a teacher was a decision she rather took out of a lack of opportunities for women as she never actually wanted to become a teacher. She had to choose it because of this lack of choice. After one year of teaching she realised, *"[...] ah, if I am going to teach, I must do something higher than just with this qualification"*. She continued with her education at a special training centre in Winneba, where only twelve out of the sixty people were finally taken, including herself as the only woman. Despite the fact that all the students were men she did not experienced any problems, rather they protected her, because she was much younger than the average of her fellow students. After one year of training she went back to Sunyani and taught in the Secondary School. She married and followed her husband in 1967, who did his PhD in forest genetics, to the University of California, Berkeley. She passed the entrance examination at the California State University, where she studied applied statistics, and later economics. The scholarship she received was too small to live from, and in addition she taught lessons during the mornings, worked in a restaurant in the evenings, and she remembered that time as being hard work to support herself and her education. The time in the U.S., although it was at that time of the women's movement, she did not became engaged in it, but was concerned about social issues.

After four years in the U.S. she went back home to Ghana, where her husband had already returned one year earlier. There she expected to work at a bank. *"I wanted to work with the banks. Because I did a lot on finance, and money and banking"*. She was persistent with her applications to different banks, she went there personally, but she failed.

"Ohh, I was so frustrated. I applied and when they invited me for a interview, they sit down and talk and look at me. And they come and tell no vacancy. That was 23 years ago. And I attribute it to gender-inequalities. Because if you are a woman and have a higher qualification, it was almost impossible to get a job. But today it is not like that".

Gender at that time was a restriction on women to enter better paid and higher qualified jobs. Although women have entered higher professions in the last years, statistics indicate that men are still in leading positions within the banking sector. Data for the year 1995 reveal that out of 19 Heads of Departments in banks only 3 had been held by women (ISSER 1998: 117). For Yaa Amina it meant that despite her foreign certificate and professional experience, she had no choice of entering the formal banking sector, but had to return to working at a school as a teacher.

Teaching Science for Women

She continued to teach maths at a secondary school at Kumasi. She opened special morning classes for students, especially women, whom she encouraged to take maths, which is compulsory for entering the University to study science. "*You see, we have a lot of good women, but you have to encourage them. So what I did, I started an extra class in the morning as early as six o'clock*". Her experience with teaching in the morning hours was lasting. While she continued with it for many years, she realised the efforts of it. Former students of her, who once attended the classes, still come to see her and thank for the extra classes she gave. Through a friend she was made aware of an advert in the newspaper, that the National Council of Women and Development were looking for a co-ordinator. She hesitated about taking the opportunity. "*I did not really wanted to go into politics, but this work it is purely women and development affairs*". At this stage, she completely separated women and development from politics. Her conception of politics was restricted to political parties, on the other hand she admitted that, "*every human being is a political person. But going into active politics...I can tell you I do not support any party*". The paradigm which is inherent in her self-definition of politics follows the one of every day politics which she clearly distinguishes from party politics. "*In that process you come across a lot of politics. But as far as I do not do any active politics, I stand here not for any political party. I am standing for this and that. But what I am doing is something that will help the nation*". Her negative attitude against party politics was due to her husband's political activities who stood for elections to become a member of parliament, but failed to win the elections.

She realised however, that she can contribute in "*improving the living standard*". For Yaa Amina the beginning of her time of engagement in the women's movement was without any political involvement. After the divorce from her husband, she experienced her personal independence, financially and private, which is also expressed in her refusal to marry again "[...] *I found it not necessary to be married*". Both being single and without children is rather the exception in Ghana. She was turning to her job at the NCWD and moved back to Sunyani. From that time on, she supported the education of children who needed support within her extended family.

Starting in the Women's Organization

She describes her beginning in the women's organization as difficult from a logistic and financial point of view. The lack of staff and the uncertainty of financial matters were upcoming difficulties in the continuation of her work. At the beginning, the communication with the Head Office in Accra was less regular than nowadays. This offered her the chance of a kind of "de-programming" of the activities of the NCWD by creating space for self-interests and self-activities. She engaged herself in legal rights issues, in which she was supported by a female lawyer and in assisting women to get through court procedures. She further initiated a special STM (Science, Technology and Mathematics) course at the local secondary schools and additional workshops for girls concerning their education. STM is a nationwide course, which are not frequently taken by girls. It is however a compulsory prerequisite for the entrance exams at the Universities. To organise those extra courses has put her into a one year struggle with ministries and the administrative staff of schools. She describes this journey as,

"So I organised some STM courses for girls. And we got some school money from the District Assembly, for those who did well in school. And also, we had a strange system. Women went in for their exams, and even when they did well, they were not selected through this procedure. So I talked to the Principal to open another class for them. But he could not help me. So I went to the Regional Director of Education, who was not that helpful. Finally I went to Regional Minister and he had communicated with Accra. So I sat on their neck and finally the Minister of Education asked us to write formally. So we wrote and they did their part and a class was opened. And they give him a full class of 25. From the 13 women who were selected for the exams, 11 passed and went through. And only 4 boys fully passed".

Out of this short passage it becomes clear, that gender is not only detrimental for women to enter educational institutions, but gender discrimination is inherent in the institutional structures. The opening of classes was a step towards de-essentialising gender constructs and towards opening the space for higher educational progress of female students.

Informal Banking as a Hidden Development

On top of her engagement in education, another area of personal engagement outside the NCWD has been the financial support of small enterprises of women. Yaa Amina complained that the 31st DWM has monopolised income-generating projects in the area. However, due to her work in the rural parts, she realised that women in the villages complained about the problematic situation of establishing an enterprise or expanding an existing one. With a starting capital of 600 U.S. Dollars, she received from a friend in the United States, she established a private "bank". She gave an amount of 200 U.S. Dollars to a female baker, who used it for the technical improvement of her bakery. Although the bakery was running well, her efforts to get a loan from a local bank was refused as her own savings had been too small to make a capital intensive investment. The existing personal contacts of knowing each other for years without having established a deep friendship were sufficient for mutual trust in investing the money. This money was gradually repaid within one year, interest free. The intention of a seamstress to establish her own small shop after having worked as an apprentice is another example. She was looking for funds to buy the wood and the roofing sheets and to pay the carpenters for building the small shop. With the financial assistance she received she built it close to the market side and it is now a healthy enterprise. To date, Yaa Amina has not had any negative experience with her personal support of the business of women. The money loaned is normally paid back in small amounts and it takes years sometimes until the full amount is repaid. Being encouraged by her past experience, she is expecting some more money from a friend in the U.S. continuing to use it in the same way. Her personal interest in money and banking, which has accompanied her for forty years, is still present and she is trying to start up the African Women's Bank in Accra and to extend it to the rural parts of Ghana.

7.3 Women doing Development

Both women are engaged in different ways of "doing development". For Yaa Amina the motivation to become engaged in development was rather based on accident than on intention, since she was not conscious or aware of the women's movements. In contrary Elizabeth had been engaged in different activities since her early twenties with shifts from organization in the Church towards infrastructure, then within the political Youth Association and finally in the women's movement. Her experience in Cuba set her perspective into a global perspective. Despite the differences between both relevance of motivations of both women, one common aspect they share is their interest in their own professional progress in order to continue inducing social change. For both, the development of their own education and of professionalism was and still is a major factor for social mobility. It enables them to bridge and communicate between the worlds of women and to directly mediate to other political and social institutions, for instance through eliminating structural discrimination in education systems. Patterns of change include personal and systemic levels of society.

While both were active in the institutional structures of development organizations, they were extending their movements beyond its structures. For Elizabeth the experimenting with the solar-dryers was based on her own interest and in addition in getting another income to support the education of her four children. The experiments brought out new innovative elements on knowledge concerning the use of energy. Yaa Amina's interest has, in particular, been in the change of educational structures to open the space for women to continue with their education. The establishment as a founder of a single-purpose system of money-lending indicates that local knowledge is more critical than bureaucratic knowledge in acting on the economic situation of women. With this collaborative non-hierarchical form she reacts on financial insolvency by acting as a personal debtor. This specific form of money lending have been widespread in Africa as tontines in Cameroon, esusu in Nigeria or marounds Zimbabwe (Schneider 2001:210). The multiplicity of financial networking associations as ROSCAS (Rotating Savings and Credit Associations) contradicts the assumptions of Clifford Geertz who predicted a decline of its social importance in the progress and extension of the formal financial sector (Ardener 1995: 1,2). These associations are not pure reactions on financial situations although they are predominantly emerging at times of financial and economic shortages. The relations among members of one ROSCA are established outside the family context and are based on friendship in workplace situations such as between traders or between people of the same neighbourhood (Ardener/Burmann 1996: 1). Through financial networking across the family context they guarantee another form of social security, which can also be referred to at times of high money expenses due to funerals. The existence of ROSCAs which are termed as susu in Ghana are attractive to both men and women, but it can hardly be said that the logic of saving follows one pattern. Men, however, used to interact more often with the formal banks, while women use local clubs[4] to overcome money shortage and for informal money mobilisation. These clubs are open in their access to men and women, but in number they are dominated by women. Only recently, the possibilities of connecting informal saving with new self- created formal institutions have been taken up. World Women's Banking has set up programs on it to enhance the financial capabilities of women (Bortei-Doku/Aryeetey 1996: 92) as well as the African Women's Bank with its office at the well known Makola market in Accra has started to formalised these informal connections, by linking the informal banking system to its formal procedures.

The establishment of a new institution of individual money lending follows a non-bureaucratic logic in creating and expanding for wider innovations as the extension of businesses exemplified by the bakery. For Yaa Amina it was a hidden way to act on economic empowerment of women by establishing the access to credits outside the formal banking system. Even within the structures of the NCWD she has not succeeded in achieving loans through the Poverty Alleviation Schemes in Ghana, in which 20 % of its projects are considered to be addressed to women's organizations. The policy of most banks follows a high interest rate of an average of up to 30 % of the credit and avoided by women due to a lack of security. My landlady summarised her way of receiving money to buy items for her shop and the reason for avoiding banks, *"when I needed the money for my shop to buy the shampoo and the cream, I went to a woman on the market, and she gave me 100, 000*

---

4   For an analysis of different Clubs existing in the urban area of Accra see Bortei-Doku/Aryeetey (1996).

Cedis. I gave it to her within one year, after I have started with the shop. As for the banks, no. I will not go there. Soon you will be indebted for your lifetime. The men are doing it, as for me, no". The fear of insecurity due to changing interest rates and of paying back a higher amount of money than received, had been reasons for my landlady to borrow money from a person she frequently visited at the market, exchanges information, but had not established an in-depth friendship. Mutual trust is based here on a comparable anonyms relationship. Its constitution through "weak ties" a term Granovetter uses (1973: 1360 ff.) explains the effectiveness of its existence, is further characterised by channelling ideas and information without falling into future obligations. Its strength lies in bridging distances e.g. in linking members of different social groups (Granovetter 1973: 1371). The failing of obligations is usually accompanied with moral aspects such as a loss of personal reputation. So, the same amount of money she received, she paid back. For her, this was an informal, un-bureaucratic way of receiving a loan to start up with her shop.

Despite the single innovations taking place outside the organizations, they are used to feed in and for the distribution of gained knowledge to other women's organizations. It is a new societal feature, that women's organizations are establishing a "social apparatus" of knowledge (Schütz/Luckmann 1974: 295) in their function of infiltration and distribution of new elements of knowledge contributing to the formation of the translocal "stock of knowledge". Individual innovative knowledge does not turn to a specialisation into "experts knowledge", which specific feature is its cultural and social distance from everyday knowledge (Schütz/Luckmann 1974: 310) or secreted as secret knowledge, but remains practical within its permanence of feedback. Development in this sense is not a discourse, a programme, a project or a theoretical concept, but an active transformative practice of doing lifeworld adapted politics. The notion of politics is of importance, because it reflects the actuality of "doing" politics as a way of establishing on one hand new institutions and transforming old ones on the other. It is – apart form the personal – the systemic level of social institutions to which individual "doing development" activities refer to. In its meaning it discloses a separation from state institutions and from party politics. In the same way as Elizabeth, Yaa Amina and Queenmothers separate themselves from becoming members of parties, they define their work as *"we do development, but not politics"*. This seems contradictory, so why should I use the word politics ? Birgit Meyer, who studied the notion of politics among German women, concludes that the politics of women should not be seen from the reference point of male activities in party politics (1983: 13). Young women in Germany who are engaged in the environmental movement and in organizations such as Greenpeace are separating themselves from claiming to do politics. The turn away of women from parliamentary politics and party politics hints on their different use of the notion of politics. The form of politics within an established political frame entails the meaning of a structured – mostly hierarchical organised – system with a specifically defined programme within political action taking place. Politics in its wider its wider sense entails the connotation of keeping a high degree of personal freedom in developing ideas and in taking up pragmatic ways for realizing thereof. *"Doing development"*, however, is a political act in a strict sense concentrating on the opening of spaces from a ground outside political party systems, but it does not take place outside the wider socio-political arena. On the contrary, it is acting on the political administration, on ministries and on "traditional" institutions as well as eliminating gender constraints and gender discrimination inherent in these institutions.

8 DECENTRALISED POLITICAL INSTITUTIONS: KNOWLEDGE BETWEEN BUREAUCRATISING AND LOBBYING

Decentralisation has become a policy approach in many countries in the South as well as in the North in order to enhance participation of people through shifting political power and in order to bring politics closer to people. Decentralised political institutions are analyzes here from two sides. One side questions the relationship between the government and decentralised agencies of government with special reference to the production and reproduction of development discourses realised in the conceptualisation of programs and projects. The other side will draw on these organizations along the interface with women's organizations and their ability of "getting institutions right" (Goetz 1995: 1). Getting institutions right implies that something with institutions is wrong. This very general statement covers the accountability of state and development politics towards women and their activities in daily lives in agriculture or in trade or their social responsibilities in education or in children's health, yet it directly encounters between the production of knowledge in institutions in reference to local knowledge and the integration of the knowledge capacities of women's organizations. The analysis of the policy making process and the policy itself of national and international agencies has been a central topic to women's activists already before the emergence of the World-Wide Women's Web. In Ghana in particular, the debate has been taken up by female academics and activists in the field of development cooperation recently, maintaining a critical discourse and as a matter of scientific investigation. To date, the strength of interconnection of international and national bureaucratic cultures on development has hindered a systematic transformation of the formulation on the paradigms on development. The institutionalisation of gender in the form of isolated gender desks or of the integration of a gender/women perspective has not changed a male-dominated policy process and the hierarchical organization of development. Gender mainstreaming as a policy approach taken up in various development institutions has resulted in other techniques of gender-checklists (Tsikata 2001a: 331). Decentralisation as a formation of political order is constitutive for social relations in the organising of state-individual relations (e.g. participation) and in policy implications (e.g. distribution of resources) and implies the crucial aspects of control of policy makers and of accountability. Recently, national and international development organizations took up the process of decentralisation, too. Although data was not gathered on this specific aspect during the fieldwork, it is referred to since it is part of a new discussion on knowledge management in development co-operation having began with the World Bank in the late 1990s and is worth analysing in its structure.

8.1 Processes of Decentralisation

Decentralisation in all its varieties has been a constant process of political change since the independence of Ghana in 1957. Joseph Ayee who has critically examined the policy implementation of decentralisation programs in post-colonial Ghana and inquired that from independence on ten commissions dealt with its regulation, whereas eighteen laws and decrees were passed (1994: 133). The implementation of decentralisation programs in the past had been a "non-learning process" (1994: 47) since it was conducted during times of military regimes or one-party systems, which puts emphasis and efforts on representing state policies at all levels of society. In most attempts, decentralisation was a prolonged arm of state governance, aimed at installing local institutions to channel down government politics and to exercise political and social control. Decentralisation is a more complex process than a mechanical process of political translation. It can distinguish between deconcentration of the administrative bodies in which local bodies are instructed to assume responsibilities that have been carried out by state agencies and of devolution of the political bodies, in which local bodies are granted political and financial authority (Ayee 1994: 4). The current process of decentralisation has been initiated up by President Rawlings during the Third Republic (1979-1981) after two years of military regime under General Akuffo, and taken up in the Fourth Republic (1981-2000). The motives for political change and involvement of people in social and economic processes resulted from a rehabilitation of a declining and stagnating economy. The structuration process stood further under the pressure of Structural Adjustment Programs/Economic and Political Recovery Programs set up by the World Bank and the International Monetary Fund in 1983, which connected the conditions for financial support with a change in the political process, a change in fiscal policy and with the claim of privatisation of state owned companies. In 1992 it went along with a major political change under President Rawlings who decided to return to constitutional rule and a multi-party system (Ayee 1994: 122ff.). Those changes had been influenced by internal and external pressure and have resulted in a complex system of bureaucracy and decision-making processes. Another reason was the mobilisation of local support for winning the elections in 1993 by Rawlings by promising an enhancement of political integration of the widespread populations bodies (Ayee 1994: 133). Ayee resumes, that the feature of decentralisation in Ghana is a de-concentration of administration along three levels:

- Regional Ministries
- District Assemblies
- Town/Area Councils

I will however argue, that the process of decentralisation is both, a partial devolution to the level of town/area councils and of de-concentration to the district assemblies. Decentralisation should not mean a complete absence of state government. Both local and state interests are able to be channeled; state interests directly to local level and the channelling of local interests, which stops at the level of the district assemblies.

Along those vertical structures, Ghana is politically organised into ten regions, 110 district assemblies and 1106 town councils (Ayee 1994: 113). As a result, the building up of a new structure of institutions parallel to the "traditional" institutions leads to conflicts in many towns and villages, which are not referred to here in depth[1]. However, in some localities the co-existence has not caused any problems at all.

8.2 The Unit Committee Council in Susuanso

The formal concept of the Unit Committee Council separates Susuanso into four autonomous, artificially split units: two parts are on the right side of the street and two on the left side of the street. Each part forms a unit and is supposed to be composed of ten elected members and five members appointed by the government, all party members of the ruling NDC. Altogether it is supposed to include sixty members. The concept was introduced at town level in 1998 and faced the problem, that not sufficient candidates within each unit stood for elections. This was partly due to misinformation by the district assembly man in the town, who had failed to inform the town and to prepare the election. Several months before the elections he left the town and moved, due to business reasons, to Kumasi to settle there. The Unit Committee Council consists nowadays of 32 members, 20 appointed and 12 elected members, out of which three are women. Each smaller unit is responsible for internal development, which is the improvement of the surrounding infrastructure in particular such as the maintenance of water wells or the electricity lines. During my stay neither regular meetings of the complete unit nor of the smaller unit took place. Even at times of concern people did not assist each other within a unit, instead they relied on using family or friendship relations. The artificial creation and its mission of "making development" brought the rhetoric into another reality when walls of a house and parts of the roof were destroyed after a severe storm. Neighbours within one unit did not assist each when it came to rebuilding the house, on the contrary. When the farmer started to rebuilt his house, he relied on using his neighbour's mechanical stone machine

---

1 For examples of conflicts see Owusu (1996).

as he had the only one in the entire town. He did not give it to his neighbour for free, but charged him 1000 Cedis a day. When I asked him for the reasons of charging his neighbour, who has already felt into debt from purchasing sand and cement, he said that his neighbour belonged to a different political party. In this case, party membership was the refusal of mutual assistance, which could not have been overcome by belonging to the same unit.

On the contrary, at town level, the UCC as a common body has gained political importance as an independent institution in decision-making and as a counterbalance to the "traditional" institutions. During the only formal meeting which took place during my 10 months stay, the members decided about the offer of the Member of Parliament, who had visited the town two days before and gave the town the options of two gifts: one in the form of paint for one school and the other in the form of ten packs of cement. The UCC, reduced to twenty active members, formally decided about the paint. This decision was channelled to the Chief, who agreed on it. In case of disagreement, they would have entered a common decision-making process until a agreement was found. The relationship between "traditional" and "modern" institutions are not without tension, members of both institutions watch each other carefully. The UCC once blamed the Chief of Susuanso for the cutting of trees by a timber company which paid him 150, 000 Cedis. The UCC intervened with the argument, that he felt the trees were not the property of the Chief, therefore the money is supposed to be a donation for "development" of the town. This case made further it clear, that the UCC tried to influence the budget of the palace, which was definitely a delicate issue, since it never was transparent to the public. For them, financial matters kept on going as an important issue since they were not in charge of their own budget or any financial resources. The existence of being a dynamic body and a counterweight to the Chief was also exemplified when the UCC organised communal labour – which is usually a privilege of the Chief – for the construction of shelters for the local Catholic School, which was partly destroyed by the storm. Within two days, masons, carpenters and members of the UCC collaborated in building three shelters. Part of the material such as wood and nails had been donated by local companies as well as roofing sheets by a donation from the district assembly in Bechem. The existence of the UCC as a common body has gained political relevance, whereas in its division into smaller units it contradicts existing social ties and relations. As a body of political representation of the people in town to address personal issues or interests it was not considered of importance. People preferred to consult the members of the "traditional" institutions instead of members of the UCC.

Only three women formally joined at the very beginning, but all of them have withdrawn."*It is not working*" as one Subqueenmother once mentioned in attempting to channel the interests of women. Her expectations were part of a local forum for the channelling of the interests of the Subqueenmothers. Directly after the election many people left the UCC because expectations of resources in the form of money were not fulfilled. In addition, it gradually turned out to be an institution for party members, whether of the ruling NDC or the opposing NPP. The relations between the central government and local party members are still strong. In 1998 a special national programme for "Youth in Agriculture" was inaugurated by the Vice-President of Ghana, Atta Mills (NDC), to assist young men and women with equipment for agricultural production. Within the town ten young men and women were to be assisted each with a loan of 200,000 Cedis. The selection process was kept secret and finally it turned out that the head of the local NDC party, who is also a member of the UCC, distributed money to members of his extended family and close friends, and most were older than 35 years. This was just before election time. As a well known procedure it did not lead to any struggles in town, but people openly admitted that they knew the top-down and hidden manner of those programs, used to "buy" votes. It was also understood that the loan did not have to be paid back but was a hidden gift. For most women the fear of co-optation, was the argument not for avoiding joining the UCC and to getting into politics. Therefore many women refuse to stand for elections and showed a form of resistance against being captured and instrumentalised for government or party politics. The gendered communication was another reason for leaving the UCC meetings. "*Every time you open your mouth they will shout you down*" was an argument from a young woman for withdrawal.

Politically, the UCC of Susuanso forms one area council together with two neighbouring towns Afrisipa and Tanoso. The area council which also started up in 1998, is composed of one member from each unit and three district assembly men. Usually they meet once a month and discuss local improvements such as tarring of the road, renovation of the market-side or electricity connections. Those discussions are channelled to the district assembly which will then decide upon the proposals. Nowadays the area council has the power to decide on its own financial budget which can be used for improvements to the infrastructure. The money is part of a collection on taxes on a bag of maize. The concept also foresees that communal labour should be part of the improvements of reducing high costs. It is not yet the time to make any estimates regarding the future political relevance of the area council. As a forum composed of three neighbouring towns, it homogenises existing disadvantages between the towns. So was Susuanso, for instance, neglected in programs within the district for telephone lines, Afrisipa is still not connected to electricity lines and Tanoso has not yet been privy to a tarred road. As a political body it may influence future programs and projects within the area which are imposed on them. A British NGO came out with the plan to build a dam at the Tano river to secure water and electricity supply. In reaction to it, the people of Tanoso put pressure on the area council to investigate it whilst fearing the completion of the plan. I could not follow any further progress of it. The discussion just started right before I left. However it was clear that the argument of foreign NGO's to bringing "economic development" stood against the local interests of keeping the river part of their cultural heritage.

As such the area council is a forum of defence of local interests and a defence against external interventions.

8.3 The District Assembly Man: Linking Politics

Every town in the district is represented at the district assembly by a district assembly man/woman[2]. The current Susuanso representative has been a teacher by profession and employed in the district director's administrative office for education in Sunyani. He was born in Susuanso, where his father is one of the Subchiefs, but moved into the neighbourhood years ago teaching there at a secondary school. Although he does not live in Susuanso permanently, he visits the town every Saturday whether to go to his farm or to attend a funeral. Even during the week he frequently passes with his motorbike to visit his family, comes if anything special happens or passes by some personal messages he has received in Sunyani. He was elected by the people in town in a gathering at the Chief's palace, as the only candidate who stood for election, just before the election of the UCC, and since that time he has been in office. The job is done on a voluntary basis, without any payment or financial compensation. With his close relationship to the Chief, who is his maternal grandfather, he has the support of the "traditional" institutions in representing the town at the district assembly which also put the UCC in a disadvantaged position. This representation had been an advantage for the male side of "traditional" institutions. For a long time he directly passed information to the Chief and seldom interacted with the Queenmother or the Subqueenmothers. The Subqueenmothers, however as part of their self-empowerment process, put pressure on him to inform them, explaining that the Chiefs were hiding the information, something he was not aware of before. With their active lobbying, he took up in their argument and supported their struggle to enter the palace. Other women in town also began using him to lobby their interests. The market women who have long complained about their small market being squeezed in a place between some houses, constantly put pressure on him to get a new market side. He took up the initiative and brought it forward to the district assembly meeting, where it was put on a list for future programs. As such the district assembly man has become a mediator between district policy and the local actors, especially since no other mediums of channelling exist. He passes information of development programs and of the distribution of resources to the town as well as channelling local initiatives to the district assembly. Right after his election he organised a special towns meeting, where all the people gathered in the Chiefs Palace to explain his functions and the work of the district assembly. Together they decided that the building of a place of sanitation should be of priority. Already

---

2 Dependent on the size of the town, some larger towns have more than one district assembly man/woman.

some months later, with the money from the district assembly and with the communal labour a building was set up.

Women have gradually realised his political position between the town and the district assembly for using it to bring in their own politics of concern, whether in influencing the palace or towards the district assembly. Although they are dependent on his personal ability of establishing a successful relationship between the decisions of the district assembly and their interests; their "lobbying" strategies turn to an active appropriation of state resources and are a reaction to having a lack of choice to influence state politics directly.

8.4 The District Assembly

The district assembly is the basic political authority in each district by having executive and legislative functions (Ayee 1994: 121). It is separated into permanent administrative units, which prepare and implement the programs and plans, on which the district assembly meeting decides. Those meetings take place twice a year in a two day session discussing the loaded topic of "development" in the district. Before we go there I want to explain the processes of planning within government institutions.

8.4.1 Planning Development – Development Planning

Development in bureaucratic state structures is planned in two ways: First, within the district assembly itself and second, in implementing national programs and projects. Both levels are mutually related and its procedures can be summarised as planning development and development planning. Development plans for each district are elaborated at the district level in accordance with national and regional goals and are termed in a five year perspective. It encompasses four fields, which are selected by the executive body of the district assembly in accordance with general policy guidelines:

- Social: Improvement of literacy rates, provision of schools
- Environmental: Health, well-being of people
- Economic: Improvement of living conditions, education of farmers, poverty alleviation schemes
- Institutional: Education of people on their civic rights, adult education

Those plans which are described in detail in a four-hundred page book, are elaborated in a collaborative process by the district development planning officer, consultants of the Kwame Nkrumah University of Science and Technology (KNUST), as well as other planners and specialist in the region as doctors, forest engineers etc. The planning, implementing and evaluation process is guided under the responsibility of the district planning officer. The educational background of the district planning officers of the district assembly is academic. The district planning officer of the district assembly in Bechem has a University degree in professional planning whereas his deputy has a degree in law and philosophy. The lack of a social scientific perspective on development is expressed in their self-definition as they call themselves *"technocrats"*. The exercise of the profession goes along the economic and technocratic paradigm of the development planning process, starting with the procedure of information gathering. With pre-structured surveys they go to communities in the district and identify the needs of the communities, especially concerning infrastructure such as electricity, water or school-buildings. The gathered information is collected in map-like schemes, differentiating where improvement is most or least needed. Women's organizations are not involved in the planning process or only at the stages when additional information is needed such as on aspects of environmental issues by consulting the 31st DWM. The perspective of women is added as a piece of information, but not integrated as such in defining and designing programs. *"We seek their opinion"* to already predefined plans and *"we seek for their problems"* which shows continual ambivalence.

A technocratic approach towards development is also the framework in the district assembly in Sunyani, concentrating on infra-structural aspects in development. Development is measured using merely technical categories of the improvement of infrastructure, in technical planning terms, realisation and in content, and does not take sustainability in general and only partially local actors in the community into consideration.

The planning policy goes hand-in-hand with the policy focus of the district assembly meeting. The district assembly meeting is composed of 69 members headed by the district chief executive, virtually all of whom have been members of the NDC party. Out of the 69 members, 48 are elected directly through their task of being the district assembly man/woman. Also 17 members are ex-officio as departmental heads such as the director of the District Ministry for Food and Agriculture (MOFA). Four members are nominated for their function in "traditional" institutions. Altogether, four women are elected and seven ex-officio including the representative of the 31st December Women's Movement or the market women's association and two of the "traditional" institutions as two Queenmothers. The district assembly meeting in its composition does not represent political parties, whereas discussions during the meetings are not politicised, but are topic centred trying to obtain resources for the specific community of election. The topics are pre-given by the district chief executive, and the final decisions are made about which town or village takes part in the next step of technical improvement.

Out of the district assembly 1/3 is taken for the permanent executive body. It was discussed in the progress of decentralisation that one sub-committee should be for Women in Development. However, this was not achieved in Bechem, with the argument of the district assembly that *"women are not materialised"* and *"there is no sex discrimination"*. On the other hand it is institutionalised that within each sub-committee one woman should be present. The eight sub-committees are 1. Agriculture 2. Social security 3. Transport and Roads 4. Infrastructure 5. Finance 6. Development planning 7. Environmental 8. Social services. While those sub-committees enjoy continuity by administrative and policy, the sub-committees meet regularly with selected members out of the district assembly, the policy effect of gender mainstreaming is limited through being added, but not altering social relations.

8.4.2 The Policy of the District Assembly

During the year 1998 the district assembly of Bechem had a revenue of 636,249,000 Cedis as a common fund. Half of the amount have been collected through taxes and about 330,000,000 Cedis was obtained by a grant-in-aid from the central government. Apart from financial regulations prescribed by national programs, the financial investment was under the charge of the district assembly. The policy emphasises two main concerns:

(1) Infrastructural Projects
(2) Poverty Alleviation and Capacity Building Projects

(1) Infrastructural Projects

Infrastructural projects are selected by the planning unit of the district assembly and emphasises the improvement of school-infrastructure, lorry-parks, community centres and markets in the districts. Market projects have been criticised in recent times, since the rent for stores have been too high, and therefore could not be rented but remained unused. The costs of those projects were almost 1/3 of the budget.

(2) Poverty Alleviation and Capacity Building Projects

Poverty Alleviation Schemes are conceptualised on a national level and channelled through the district assemblies. Three programs have been designed with the aim of reducing poverty and enhancing capacity building. The rural enterprise project (REP) has the objective of reducing poverty in the rural areas by the creation of job opportunities. The over generalised frame of this projects which had no specified objectives was mainly used by the district assembly to support its administration such as by employing a social worker, a secretary and a driver.

The reduction of poverty is also the objective of the village infrastructure program (VIP), which is implemented in 48 districts in Ghana, aimed at projects on rural transport, rural water infrastructure, rural post-harvest and on the institutional level. The third one, the poverty alleviation schemes (PAS), has a slightly different approach. As part of the IFAD[3]-Loan scheme it is de-

---

3 IFAD is a special agency of the UN and was established as a international financial institution in 1977 as one of the major outcomes of the World Food Conferences. Its aim in 115 countries is to combat hunger and poverty.

signed to income-generating activities of organizations. 20 % of those organizations are supposed to be women's organizations or women's groups. The procedure follows, that every organization must apply to one of the rural banks which distributes at least an amount of 200`000 Cedis. This amount must be paid back within three years with an interest rate of 24 %. Women's organizations which are supposed to be part of the scheme have not succeeded at all in achieving any loan within the district. During a district assembly meeting its members complained that this form of poverty reduction program has in its efficiency not been successful, since the money was either too small or the credits were not paid back on time. Many organizations were rather within a short time, in debt and stuck in half of their projects, with an unstable currency and economy, a loan system rather increases the danger of putting people into a spiral of debt.

The conceptualising of all three programs along state interventions is named by Staudt as "goal displacement", meaning that agendas are reduced to implement and monitor, enhancing their own authority, resources and staff (1990: 17). The general framework towards poverty reduction remains an "empty" generalisation of the rural population, since a clear structure of how poverty mechanisms work is not revealed. Poverty reduction in a technical and financial matter around infrastructural concerns, thought as a symptom that can be cured through "injection" whereas the fundamental dilemma of its emergence and its abolishment is unrecognised.

The problem of national programs and its implementation does lie in its over generalisation of policy and its neglect of an evaluation of its results and its efforts in particular towards gender relations. Dzodzi Tsikata did an analysis of the politics of the district assemblies by taking up the national program Free Compulsory Universal Basic Education (FCUBE)[4] and concluded that the outcome helped a few individuals but has not resulted in an improvement of the quality of teaching and education (2001: 349). The budget has been mostly invested in travelling and transport, the maintenance of buildings, payment of employees. The scheme even has a negative effect on schoolgirls, since a scholarship program almost exclusively supports schoolboys. Whether district assemblies had been conscious in improving the management of education in the quality of education; nor could they address existing imbalances between urban and rural schools as well as between gender (Tsikata 2001: 349). The technocratic design as Tsikata called it "within the province of experts" (2001: 349) does not follow the establishment of a common policy dialogue and of agenda building as a process of negotiation between state politics and the politics and interests of women's groups and women's organizations. This example is representative of the other ongoing programs leaving the control of development in the hands of a few experts and politicians. At this stage "getting institutions rights" would imply a community and gender

---

4   The program was initiated by the Ministry of Education and the World Bank in 1996 to expand the access to education and to improve the quality (Tsikata 2001: 339).

perspective in development planning processes in the particular case here, in educational matters. The representation of women's organizations in the policy process is reduced to a sharing of information and not of transformation.

8.5 Planning at Regional Level

Development at regional level is conceptualised in the administration of the Development Planning Unit in the regional capital of Sunyani. The major task of the administration is the co-ordination of the policy between district level and central government in Accra as well as the monitoring of the districts. Information is gathered by standardised surveys, where results are used for the planning process.

The monitoring activities are co-ordinated in meetings between the district directors of the specific department, such as every first Tuesday all district directors of agriculture meet for a discussion at the regional department. Although agricultural production is dominated by women, out of the 13 directors, no women is among them and women's organizations who are active in the district in diverse agricultural project are not part of the meetings or invited by the district directors for their one or two day workshops as for example concerning ecological "green" farming or control of pesticides.

Women within the planning process are conceptualised as a target group along the question of *"how to get to the women"*. The bureaucratic design of implementation is built upon a social distance between expert knowledge and the knowledge of women. The conditions of many projects nowadays to reach and involve a certain percentage of women, however, is gradually changing yet it clearly implies the danger of instrumentalisation. The regional officer of development explained, "there was no special attention to make out an area for women as such. For instance with the SCIMP[5], no real attention was made for women as such, but after we started, we have come to realise that the women participation is low, and right now, when people are talking to farmers to co-operate they make special efforts between them" .

The gender-perspective was post-integrated into this specific program, whereas women originally should have been addressed to cover out of the total number 60 %. It is therefore the number that counted in a quantitative meaning and not a critical debate on the planning process as such, on the target of the project and its sustainability for women and men. As such it results in a paradox situation, that gender is recognised when based on conditions of numbers, and leaves the process of de-gendering as in other programs on livestock or extension services aside as another non-learning process. *"What I say is, that we normally do not differentiate between men and women"* as the regional officer. The pre-"fabrication" of knowledge (vgl. Knorr-Cetina, 1991)

---

5 SCIMP are Small Scale Input Marketing Projects, which have become a popular naming for many projects as food-processing and marketing of those goods.

within development institutions in its interactions with the moment of reflexivity on development as a social process and in particular as a gendered process.

At this level of coordination, monitoring, evaluation and planning, women's organizations are kept out as *"they are for the district level"*. The hierarchical level of planning attributes the spaces of women to the second lowest level. The culture of planning continuoues to be a form of exclusion of women's organization and their knowledge. It lacks not only political coherence, but might imply a reinforcement of gender asymmetries especially by continually marginalisation of female knowledge through superior claimed expert knowledge.

8.6 Reflecting on Women's Organizations: Changing Gender Ideologies?

Institutions are made up of rules, structures and ideologies (Goetz 1995: 1), whereas ideologies or constructs of gender refer to the borderlines of women's spaces. Men within the planning institutions are partly aware of the networking between women's organizations. On one hand they have realised that the "participation" of women in their programs and projects is rather low addressing it to the factor of education. *"Women in Africa are in a vast part backbenches of the house, education is low, so you will never be able to get them into politics"* as one mentioned. While bureaucracy has to date remained a hegemonic domain of men and government, excluding women with the argument of education, a few have recognised ongoing changes and address it to education and networking.

"So there is an education drive. Every women that is interested in politics. And even from the grassroots, some building themselves up to the national level. The network has been limited to the women who have already found themselves in politics. They are trying through the various women's organizations, they belong to whip up the interests of women in politics".

The drive of women's organizations is considered as a channel of women to, as one officer working in the agricultural department stated, yet gender mainstreaming the efforts of women within bureaucratic structures and roles remains untouched.

"Traditionally women do not want to come out, this is their attitude, but if you really want to know my opinion about emancipation. We are making a lot more progress than in the past ten years. Even now our police has established a "Women and Juvenile Unit" and there is FIDA, I believe, that in the next four years, women will start adventuring and pick up problems. The women, a lot of women are trying to get rid of the kind of mentality they themselves have. I do not think,they have not been able to finish that yet. And through their meetings and discussions, they are coming up gradually. And I think that in maybe ten, fifteen years time, you will get women able to speak on any topic free".

The awareness and recognition of women's organization and the establishment of their own institutions are part of the changing perceptions of a few men working in state departments. The personal balanced view on ongoing dynamics is recognised by a few expectional officers as an "outside" change, knowing the underlying reasons of networking between women's organizations. Apart from these verbal recognitions, these dynamics are not seen as part of development planning or as development as a process, but remain methodologically and in its consequences practically separated. The idea of planning remains such a technical issue, incompatible practically with women's organizations and social movements. Despite the mere recognition, the discursive marginalisation of women's organization as not being able to belong to the development arena creates a system of exclusion with no spaces for dialogue or common negotiations.

8.7 De-bureaucratising Development Knowledge

The process of decentralisation has led to a new emergence of political actors such as the UCC and the district assembly man as well as to the formation of new constellations with the "traditional" institutions at the village level. Through the institution of the UCC and the district assembly man it has opened channels for men and women to articulate, defend and integrate their interests. Since women are rather absent in the formal structures, they take up strategies such as lobbying by using informal channels in getting access to resources. Decentralisation has been realised as an ambivalent process between local channelling and the implementation of international and national politics. On the level of the district assembly both directions meet and rhetorics of development is reproduced and the definition of development takes place there. Although representatives of women's organizations are part of the decision-making process, the ability to change district policies or redirect it is limited since it is already pre-formulated and a ready made product for implementation. Local communities have, nowadays, the chance to decide about acceptance or resistance to these policies and even the financial capabilities to develop their own initiatives as on the area council level. The realisation of decentralisation has, up to now, turned out to be close to party politics making it understandable why women rather withdraw from it and turn to active lobbying. On the other hand they are not able to influence those politics which are detrimental to them especially if it is designed on a national level. The national policy framework follows in Ghana, according to Tsikata (2001: 12), the mainstream international discourse on development in a technocratic and neo-liberal market reform policy. Connell has called this regime the "international state" (1990) pointing at the strength of constellation between the state and the arena of multi- and bilateral development organizations such as the World Bank or UN related agencies. The criticism of Ghanaian academics to this policy constellation and its implementation within national structures hints at a form of development that helps a few working within these agencies or are part of a policy programme.

Bureaucratising is part of a planning culture which is based on a conceptual systematising of information and data within a technocratic oriented frame of logics and less on the everyday knowledge of those who are supposed to be reached. Bureaucratic development implicitly not only de-values local knowledge through its hierarchical development organization, but has not developed appropriate methods of evaluation integrating a process of reflexivity on "successes" and "failures" and the questioning of the relevance of collected data and information. A learning process is neglected while failures continue to be replicated.

The pressing question is, how can institutions address an analytical and practical policy which is not detrimental to women and which includes a gender policy ? Gender analysis in the development process has been brought up by different approaches as the gender roles framework developed by the Harvard Institute of International Development or the triple role framework which was elaborated between trainers at a British Development Planning Unit, some NGO's and donor agencies. Both have an emphasis on the economic activities of women in common. The gender roles framework in particular takes the household as the central unit and splits the economic activities of women into descriptions of their daily actions. The triple role framework splits the roles of women into productive, reproductive and community management roles. The productive role of women was recognised as work, while the community management role remained as "natural given" (Kabeer 1004: 274). A first overview of both approaches makes it clear that gender is treated in isolation and a wider structural perspective has not been addressed. Both approaches have been proved only partially for analysis and in the development of a transformative agenda (Acquaye-Baddoo/Tsikata 2001: 64). Since it is obvious that gender relations are interwoven into the broader context of social structures a practical framework of analysis must hint at existing rules, gender constructs, resources and power relations within institutions (Kabeer 1994: 281). With its special emphasis on power relations it makes it understandable that policies are part of power relations and power relations should be part of policies. What first sounds very abstract and as a product of rational machinery to achieve gender awareness is in reality a long durable and difficult process. Such theoretical approaches have been intensively discussed, critically reviewed, modified and refined by academic and practioners in Ghana. As a challenge to change institutions it has been of practical concern of academics of two Ghanaian universities in collaboration with women's organizations and activists. The efforts of collaboration were initiated within the TUC (Trade Union Congress of Ghana) the largest union consisting of 17 unions with overall membership of 500,000 out of which 25 % are women. The TUC is an organization of workers, a national player in influencing public policy and a mass movement. Like many other organizations, a low participation of women in management and decision-making bodies as well as forms of discrimination such as differences in salaries exist.

The first step was the integration of one women's desk, followed by an increase of women's organisers from two to four within the organizational department, which is the head office of the TUC. Gradually in all regions women's desks were established and covered seven out of ten regions in 1999. This structure spread to other unions, who are under the umbrella of the TUC. Through training on laws, of international conventions and with the asset of research results these women got to know the mechanisms of existing inequalities and on tools of mitigation. A critical mass of women within and outside the institution, and their commitment to women's empowerment, as well as the establishment of a culture of openness and communication has become an instrument for introducing a gender policy into the institutions despite forms of internal resistance (Graham 2001: 317). These mechanisms make it understandable how institutions can be changed, but needs the formation of alliances between women working in the institution, outside and women in workplace situations.

Such a mechanism of a "triple" alliance can, in its arrangement of collaboration, be one step towards integrating a gender analysis and policy into development institutions and into the processes of knowledge production. To change paradigms within institutions means to interact on the different levels of policy making process, local, regional and national as well as international.

The current trends of development organizations such as UNDP or GTZ towards a decentralisation of its structures and the shift of development planning from a centralised institution to decentralised country offices opens up opportunities to lobby at the local level through such an effective alliance building. New paradigms of development such as participation with actors of civil society are opening doors at the side of development organizations for women's organizations, who have long claimed for participation. At this stage, the negotiation of knowledge and a sharing of knowledge strategy concerning the various topics of development can lead to a new definition of development processes through involved women's organizations following a gender equality policy. This concern of the interactions of two knowledge systems in reference to development is part of a exceptional book on *Gender Training in Ghana* (Tsikata 2001). Mainly female Ghanaian researches and activists analyzed from a gender perspective the impact of national and international politics on gender relations, but also developed own perspectives. They follow the paradigm of a new politicising of knowledge in research, in training and in development politics. Their criticism is addressed to development agencies, which are still sticking to a de-politised, technical form of participation and the planning of programs and projects by referring to the Women in Development (WID) discourse. Part of the argument is, that development programs are not really aiming for and actually transform social relations, and through this remain fruitless. Participation in development cooperation must go back to the original meaning of transformation of social relations such as gender training and must follow a transformative approach. New approaches in training and in courses such as theatre and drama are open to integrate topics challenging manifested gender constructs and gender relations. Provocative theatre plays take up workplace or everyday situations which are familiar to rural communities. It should be without question, that those approaches should be recognized by the national and international development agencies.

The discourse on participation on knowledge has recently been rearticulated by female northern researchers[6] working in cross-cultural academia and politics, too. They re-politicise knowledge in development politics and in research. The cross-cultural exchange and the interactions however, bring about dilemmas. Since I have described the dilemma I experienced during my research in chapter 2, others will be mentioned and should contribute to the fact that development as a socio-cultural process encounters different dilemmas, making once more the complexities of interactions visible. Wendy Harcourt, who as a director of an international organization (Society for International Development), bridges research and politics, is confronted with dilemma situations as the translation of experiences into policy recommendations. Whose voice is talking and how can it be translated and to whom should it be addressed ? On the institutional level she realized that mainstream development organizations such as the British DFID (Department for International Development) have closed its doors to transformative recommendations.

General guidelines of projects are negative on the translation process as Charlotte Martin experienced in a research project on Muslim Women and Development in Sudan, a project which was implemented in seven African and Asian Countries as well as in the Netherlands. Research findings on the local level faced difficulties in being translated into action due to a lack of skill of the researchers in training and community mobilisation. A lack of reflexivity of power structures between researchers and researched were constantly evolving, which had not been given enough attention in the design. Donors implicitly had the right of ownership and the power to define the direction and the objectives of the project (Martin 2002).

A new approach of research has been developed in a project on sexuality and AIDS in Indonesia at the Institute of Social Studies in Den Hague. The project starts at the first step of empirical data collection in collaboration with local researchers following questions on sexuality and AIDS. The collected data enter a common process of reflection and is an asset for the design of the further project. Here lies the difference in the experience of Martin in Sudan,

---

6 They are part of the Gender and Development Working Group of EADI, as Prof. Dr. Gudrun Lachenmann, Dr. Saskia Wieringa, Dr. Charlotte Martin, Dr. Wendy Harcout, Dr. Joy Clancy, Dr. Irna van der Molen, Prof. Dr. Gabriella Rossetti, Prof. Dr. Antonella Piccio.

that the design is based on an in-depth research and not pre-defined before entering the locality. Research findings are directly fed in. In a second stage, those findings are discussed with women's organizations and with state officials. This should lead to a transformation through women's empowerment through their bodies and through political changes (Wieringa 2002). Such as form of cooperation builds on empirical data referring to local knowledge, which is the basis for designing projects connected with a paradigmatic approach of transformation. It becomes obvious, that alternative development concepts based on a idea of "sharing of knowledge" are emerging leading to new and more independent forms of cooperation through equal partnership overcoming the social distance between development experts and local actors.

Another recent trend which is of importance to the discussion on "getting institutions right" and on local knowledge is the change of structures within international development organizations towards the strategic orientation of knowledge management which goes almost hand in hand with decentralisation processes. This trend which began in the late 1990s with the discovery of the World Bank on "development through knowledge" (1998/99) aims at initiating development and erasing poverty through improved access to information within developing countries. The strategy of sharing knowledge could not deconstruct the assumption of a asymmetrical relation between northern and southern countries and the transfer of knowledge remains one-sided since the World Bank implicitly legitimates its policy through devaluating local knowledge. However, knowledge management as a form of organizing gained knowledge within development organizations and make it utilized for development experts, has been integrated by many development organizations in the North and South. With its claim to store accurate knowledge, the strategic concept of knowledge management is not a new concept of development cooperation but a strategy to strengthen competitiveness in a more and more competitive environment. Knowledge becomes an economic good, embedded in marketing strategies. Such trends which have not taken up the recognition of local valid knowledge in its holistic setting, but kept its self-reference, bear the danger of privatization and commerzialisation of the actual public good knowledge. Only partially in the progress of the discussion of knowledge management, the establishment of globalising structures based on social and technical information and communication (such as decentralised networks like Global Development Network and Global Knowledge Partnership, which are open to and composed by private actors, researchers, practitioners and politicians), are offering chances for local organizations to enter a globalised arenas of development. These new platforms are built on at regional and national level and are used for the exchange on knowledge and information concerning development. Since they are not only based on technology, but act as social networks they have the opportunity to formulate alternative visions on development whether from within or by using information from outside. The establishment of these new networks are supporting the plurality of actors and their approaches within the development arena, blurring the hegemony of "classical" development cooperation. Besides classical forms of development cooperation, these new networks, as well as women's networks, are now part of the "battlefields of knowledge" (Long/Long 1992) on development issues. The current situation within the development arena ranges from a privatizing to a politicization of knowledge.

9 GLOCALISED PRACTICES: TOWARDS A KNOWLEDGE SOCIETY

Women have organised themselves at local, regional, national and global level. This has been the starting point of the first Chapter. Along the interweaving of all the different levels, the organizations have formed pillars of knowledge generation, of knowledge production and of knowledge translation. At local level, the networking between Subqueenmothers across kinship system has created a female space out of which a discourse on the order of knowledge emerged. Everyday knowledge at this level is generated in daily practices, based on previous and new experiences. The important point is that local and translocal discourses on knowledge have melted into a common reflection process on observing, discussing and analysing the social environment of Susuanso. Part of the discourse is the re-definition of past female spaces, which have had a transformative effect on society and gradually have been socially marginalised. By taking up past spaces in a re-defined form and by integrating new elements of knowledge, Subqueenmother turn around the social marginalisation process and form a new knowledge repertoire. This new knowledge repertoire mainly consists of *everyday knowledge* and *historical knowledge.*

A politicisation of knowledge takes place by challenging the structures of "traditional" institutions and by defining new gender relation within adopting them to a changed social context. In this sense women are defending cultural specifies, which subversively first have to be transformed. The aim of politicising knowledge is to gain social power to make the re-defined spaces realise and to react on the social world, especially towards the young generation. The permanent feedback to the real and to change local realities is a process which creates its own culture of knowledge and development, making local knowledge independent from the implementation of external knowledge by development agencies or from externalized knowledge kept by experts and institution, thus maintaining it as internalized knowledge.

The new knowledge repertoire is legitimated in constituting a new identity of the *aberewa nyansafo*. At national level their common identity is also legitimating the actions of women within the (Sub-)Queenmothers' association. The specific feature here is, that everyday knowledge and *scientific knowledge* are politicized in order to act on the structure of "traditional" institutions. Individual knowledge gained in transnational experiences is fed in and disseminated back to the local level. On the basis of individual movements and in collaboration with other women's organizations at regional and national level, the (Sub-)Queenmothers have opened their knowledge repertoire towards mutual innovativeness. In strengthening and legitimating their own knowledge repertoire, they have formulated a pragmantic agenda of development, which is a partial counter-discourse to Western development by not adopting or just taking over Western practices.

Outside the "traditional" institutions, the umbrella organization NCWD has organized women into regional forums for the exchange of knowledge. This is done in a specific de-hierarchical form of learning from each other through sharing. Out of the common process of discovery a critical reflection on past and current social processes takes place leading to a re-politicization of knowledge and to a self-articulation of diversities of ways to react to negative consequences of modernization. Through personal networking, the connection between the regional co-coordinator of the forum with the pan-African network WiLDAF is given. Besides the repertoire of everyday and scientific knowledge, *informational knowledge* serves as a new source for agency along transnational spaces as well as being disseminated back towards the local level.

Along all levels, women's spaces are not isolated from each other, but overlap. Although women's organizations are defined metaphorically as pillars, the connectedness exists through social, individual and electronically supported networking. Knowledge within the process of networking is articulated, mediated, translated and circulated. Once again metaphorically, networking forms bridges between the pillars. The structure of networking at vertical and horizontal levels creates a new form of social cohesion between women's organizations.

The first specific feature of networking is, that along vertical and horizontal crossings new spatial structures across boundaries take place connecting the different locations of knowledge generation and production. Within networking as a medium, knowledge flows across ethnic, national and state borders, bridging rural-urban distances. The connections and interactions between the pillars form bridges structuring and extending spaces towards establishing a global knowledge architecture, turning local agencies into glocalised practices.

A second feature of networking is the establishment of an infrastructure in social sphere. In accordance with Habermas (1990) a social sphere can be defined as a space of social interactions in the public. Habermas analyzed the structural change of public sphere in accordance with the change in knowledge order from a historical perspective in Western societies. The historical emergence of a public sphere differs between Ghana and other western societies since for example literature, media or student's organizations have not had the same social meaning. With regards to women's organizations on all levels of society they have formed an infrastructure of public sphere and through politicizing of knowledge, turned the private sphere into relevance for the public sphere making it visible for everybody. Meetings, the media such as the radio and newspapers are only artificial objects, which women use to be present in the public. Own discourses and policies as well as action towards social institutions and the state, make women's organizations carriers of a "critical public sphere" (Habermas 1990: 32). Within this process is based a new definition of the boundaries between themselves and the state. Private matters such as violence against women turn to a public discourse, revealing social structural inequalities. With the acting on law for example they create a space, which leaves the dichotomy private-public behind. Building up own discourses and agendas on development is a further sign of resistance against mainstream development practices and against state politics. Resistance and the establishment of an infrastructure together form the object and the potentials of a change of knowledge order, between gender as well as between gender and institutions. Women in Ghana are not an exception in defending their social, cultural, political and economic localities while structuring and defining glocalities. Escobar/Rocheleau/Kothari (2002) examined women's organizations and their activities in three different parts of the world: India, Columbia and the Dominican Republic. In Columbia women in rural areas have organized themselves to defend their cultural specification attributed in their economic and ecological agencies, against practices of industrial companies within the region which are gradually destroying their natural environment (2002: 30). In the Dominican Republic, women of the Zambrana-Chacuey region are engaged in land struggle and environmental initiatives. Starting with the land struggle, they have built up gardens and forestry projects to demonstrate their broad knowledge of herbs, and use it to make others aware of the rapid destruction of forests, the misuse of pesticides and the contamination of water. Politically they have requested government reforms in land distribution and regulation, supported by other women's groups who deal with women's social and economic rights (2002: 32). Recently in South Asia women's organizations formed coalitions across national boundaries to challenge and resist macro-economic processes (Menon-Sen 2002: 132). These examples can be added with many more from other parts of the world. It indicates that women are negotiating globalization processes in defense and in defining new relations in social movements. At this stage it should become obvious, that local knowledge, politics, history, culture and identity analytically can hardly be separated from each other.

The Locality of Space

The meaning of a locality can be analyzed according to its specific configuration constituted by internal layers and by internal-external dimensions. Although a locality is constituted within a relational – glocal – context, meanings encompassing a certain locality are spatially bounded. For most, the locality of space remains as the world within its actual reach of impact for its actors. Despite all flows across borders and external influences, the actual reach of impact shapes the main horizon for its inhabitants. The meaning of this world within its direct reach is threefold and deals around the notion of governance characterizing a local politics of knowledge:

In its first meaning, a locality is a *space of regulation* of the social organization of knowledge: the main generation processes of knowledge are still acquired, transmitted and exchanged within the kinship and family context. This knowledge is characterized by the fact of being recursive, meaning open for innovation. However, the regulation of the knowledge repertoire follows the logic of an integration of those external produced elements of knowledge which are socially relevant for the local context. Newly defined cultural practices stand in reference to constructed history as a means of legitimating, disseminating and securing knowledge.

In its second meaning, a locality is a *spaces of negotiation*: in reference to knowledge, negotiations concern the definition of social competences necessary for the regulation of knowledge. Along these definitions processes of negotiation have its beginning and its consequences in the forms of political inclusion or exclusion. The negotiation of boundaries provokes "taken for granted" power constellations and hierarchies whether between or within gender. Negotiations refer to the individual level of the mutual construction of gender-identities and at the societal level to social institutions. The factor of time – as historical time – is inherent in present discourses on the change of "tradition" and "traditional" institutions. Negotiation also means a critical process with consequences of modernization affecting individuals through an increase of external induced risks.

In its third meaning, a locality is a *space of control*: social relevant knowledge needs control, meaning that generated elements of knowledge and contents of knowledge are not only the outcome of societal activities, but become now a matter of independence from other forms of external or externalized knowledge. A continuation of the orientation towards own capacities of knowledge and defense thereof is one form of control of knowledge as well as critically dealing with external produced elements of knowledge such as Western imposed development knowledge. Such a strategy in securing and controlling experienced knowledge aims at minimizing risks and maximizing self-reliant problem solving. A growing independence and autonomy through moments of reflexivity are not only rooted in individual agency, but in a newly defined social structure.

Towards a Knowledge Society

Discussions on knowledge societies have mainly taken place in reference to Northern countries and to ongoing changes precisely concerning economy, technology and science (Lane, 1966; Bell 1985; Drucker 1993; Willke 1998; Stehr 2000). Hardly anyone has attempted to characterise a Southern country as a knowledge society. One reason may be attributed to the fact, that the content of knowledge has been much more important for development oriented research than the dynamics constituting the processes of "how to know" and how knowledge becomes reality. The importance of the focus on the content, might be due to the orientation given within development cooperation and discourse on its practical utilization of local knowledge for development and less on its societal constitution. To refer only to content of knowledge is not sufficient for characterizing a society as a knowledge society, even more, it is an anthropological condition that knowledge is necessity for the existence of a society.

In reference to the ideas of academic scholars who have taken up the matter of knowledge for their scientific investigation in Northern countries, Nina Degele suggests that there are three features characterizing a knowledge society: knowledge, science and technology (vgl. Degele 2002: 163). The empirical findings indicate that on a societal level, the knowledge repertoire in present Ghana is composed of three main sources: historical and everyday knowledge, scientific knowledge and informational knowledge. Of concern now is less the individual level or the specific content of knowledge, but the systemic level of society. To set the empirical findings into an analogy with the scientific categories proposed by Degele the following scheme visualizes the correlation:

Table 1: Sites of Knowledge Production

Knowledge	Science	Technology
Everyday and historical knowledge	Scientific knowledge	Informational knowledge

There are two structural mechanisms found in each category underlying the density of communication within and among the three sources of knowledge : the first one is the explication of knowledge and the second one the communicability of knowledge. Both mechanisms go beyond a discussion on the content of knowledge, but even more, build a completely new level which is *knowledge on knowledge*. What is established through both mechanisms is therefore a meta-level: it is a second-order. It is this new particular feature of a second-order knowledge characterizing the dynamics of a knowledge society and making knowledge a relevant factor for present and future social change in its feature of becoming an integrative and regulative principle within the social organization and its order. The emergence of knowledge societies is not a theoretical construct of scientific knowledge production, but an empirical observable reality. Knowledge seen from this perspective rises up to become the main principle of the constitution of society, turning it into what it can be called now: a knowledge society.

BIBLIOGRAPHY

Abu-Lughod, Lila (1991): »Writing against Culture«. In: Fox, Richard G. (Hg.) Recapturing Anthropology, Santa Fe, New Mexico: School of American Research Press.

Acquaye-Baddoo, Naa-Aku/Tsikata, Dzodzi (2001): »Gender Training and Trainers in Ghana«. In: Tsikata, Dzodzi (Hg.) Gender Training in Ghana, Accra: Woeli Publishing.

Aidoo, Agnes Akosua (1981): »Asante Queenmothers in Government and Politics in the Nineteenth Century«. In: Steady, Filomina Chiomaa (Hg.) The Black Woman Cross-Culturally, Rochester, Vermont: Schenkmann Books.

Albrow, Martin/King, Elizabeth (1990): »Introduction«. In: Albrow, Martin/King, Elizabeth (Hg.) Globalization, Knowledge and Society, London, Newbury Park, New Delhi: Sage Publication.

Allman, Jean (1996): »Rounding up Spinsters: Gender Chaos and Unmarried Women in Colonial Asante«. In: Journal of African History, 37, S. 195-214.

Allo, Fatma (1999): »Information Technology and Cyberculture: The Case of Zanzibar«. In: Harcourt, Wendy (Hg.) Women@Internet, London: ZedBooks.

Amponsem, George K. (1996): Global Trading and Business Networks among Ghanaians: An Interface of the Local and the Global, unpubl. PH.D. Thesis, Bielefeld: University of Bielefeld.

Antweiler, Christoph (1995): »Lokales Wissen, Grundlagen, Probleme, Bibliographie«. In: Honerla, Susan/Schröder, Peter (Hg.) Lokales Wissen und Entwicklung, Saarbrücken: Verlag für Entwicklungspolitik.

Anyidoho, Agnes (1994): »Tradition and Innovation in Nnwonkoro, an Akan Female Verbal Genre«. In: Research in African Literatures, Vol. 24, No. 3, S.141-159.

Appadurai, Arjun (1998): Modernity at Large: Cultural Dimensions of Globalization, Minneapolis and London: University of Minnesota Press.

Appiah, Kwame (1995): »The Postcolonial and the Postmodern«. In: Ashcroft, Bill/Griffiths, Gareth/Tiffin, Helen (Hg.) The Post-Colonial Studies Reader, London, New York: Routledge.

Appiah-Donyina, Evelyn (2000): »Ghana's Annual New Year Schools: Five Decades of an Experiment in Adult Education«. In: Adult Education and Development, No.54, S. 245-258.

Arbeitsgruppe Bielefelder Soziologen (1973): Alltagswissen, Interaktion und gesellschaftliche Wirklichkeit, Band 1 und 2, Reinbek: Rowohlt.
Ardener, Shirley (Hg.) (1993): Women and Space, Oxford, Providence: Berg.
Ardener, Shirley (1995): »Women Making Money Go Round: ROSCAs Revisited«. In: Ardener, Shirley/Burman, Sandra (Hg.) Money-Go-Round, Oxford/Washington: Berg.
Arens, William/Karp, Ivan(1989): »Introduction«. In: Arens, William/Karp, Ivan (Hg.) Creativity of Power, Washington, London: Smithsonian.
Arhin, Kwame (1983): »The Political and Military Roles of Akan Women«. In: Oppong, Christine (Hg.) Female and Male in West Africa, London: Allen and Unwin.
Ashcroft, Bill/Griffiths, Gareth/Tiffin, Helen (1995): »Introduction«. In: Ashcroft, Bill/Griffiths, Gareth/Tiffin, Helen (Hg.) The Post-colonial Studies Reader, London, New York: Routledge.
Assimeng, Max (1989): Religion and Social Change in West Africa, Accra: University Press.
Auslander, Marc (1993): »Open the Wombs !«. In: Comaroff, Jean/Comaroff, John (Hg.) Modernity and its Malcontents, Chicago: University of Chicago Press.
Awumbila, Mariama (2001): »Women and Gender Equality in Ghana: A Situational Analysis«. In: Tsikata, Dzodzi (Hg.) Gender Training in Ghana, Accra: Woeli Publishing.
Awusabo-Asare, Kofi (1990): »Matrilinity and the New Intestate Succession Law of Ghana«. In: Canadian Journal of African Studies, No. 24, S.1-16.
Ayee, Joseph (1994): An Anatomy of Public Policy Implementation, Avebury: Aldershot.
Bachmann-Medick, Doris (1998): »Einleitung«. In: Bachmann-Medick, Doris (Hg.) Kultur als Text. Die anthropologische Wende in der Literaturwissenschaft, Frankfurt am Main: Fischer.
Basu, Amrita (Hg.) (1995): The Challenge of Local Feminisms: Women's Movements in Global Perspective, Boulder, San Francisco, Oxford: Westview Press.
Becher, Cathrin (2001): »"According to our tradition a woman can not own land": Die geschlechtsspezifische Einbettung von Land und Ökonomie in Nord-Ghana«. In: Lachenmann, Gudrun/Dannecker, Petra (Hg.) Die geschlechtsspezifische Einbettung der Ökonomie, Hamburg: Lit.
Beck, Ulrich (1994): »The Reinvention of Politics: Towards a Theory of Reflexive Modernization«. In: Beck, Ulrich/Giddens, Anthony/Lash, Scott (Hg.) Reflexive Modernization, Cambridge, Oxford: Polity Press.
Behar, Ruth (1995): »Introduction«. In: Behar, Ruth/Gordon, Deborah A. (Hg.) Women's Writing Culture, Berkley, Los Angeles, London: University of California.
Beneria, Lourdes (1981): »Accumulation, Reproduction and Women's Role in Economic Development: Boserup Revisited«. In: Signs: Journal of Women in Culture and Society, Vol. 7, No. 2, S. 279-298.

Berg, Eberhard/Fuchs, Martin (1993): »Phänomenologie der Differenz. Reflexionsstufen ethnographischer Repräsentation«. In: Berg, Eberhard/ Fuchs, Martin (Hg.) Kultur, soziale Praxis, Text, Frankfurt am Main: Suhrkamp.

Berger, Peter L./Luckmann, Thomas (1966): The Social Construction of Reality, New York, Anchor Books.German Translation Berger, Peter L./ Luckmann, Thomas (1980) Die gesellschaftliche Konstruktion der Wirklichkeit, Frankfurt am Main: Fischer.

Bell, Daniel (1985, orig.1973): Die nachindustrielle Gesellschaft, Frankfurt/New York: Campus.

Berger, Peter (et al.) (1973): The Homeless Mind: Modernization and Consciousness, New York: Vintage.

Bierschenk, Thomas (1999) »Lokale Entwicklungsmakler. Entwicklungshilfe schafft neue Formen des Klientelismus in Afrika«. In: Thiel, Reinold (Hg.) Neue Ansätze zur Entwicklungstheorie, Bonn: Deutsche Stiftung für Internationale Entwicklung.

Blumer, Herbert (1973): »Der Methodologische Standpunkt des Symbolischen Interaktionismus«. In: Arbeitsgruppe Bielefelder Soziologen (Hg.) Alltagswissen, Interaktion und gesellschaftliche Wirklichkeit, Band 1 und 2, Reinbek: Rowohlt.

Bortei-Doku, Ellen/Aryeetey, Ernest (1995): »Mobilizing Cash for Business: Women in Rotating Susu Clubs in Ghana«. In: Ardener, Shirley/Burman, Sandra (Hg.) Money-Go-Round, Oxford/Washington: Berg.

Bourdieu, Pierre (1976): Entwurf einer Theorie der Praxis, Frankfurt am Main: Suhrkamp.

Bourdieu, Pierre (1991): Language and Symbolic Power, Cambridge: Polity Press.

Bourdieu, Pierre (1995): »Narzistische Reflexivität und wissenschaftliche Reflexivität«. In: Berg, Eberhard/Fuchs, Martin (Hg.) Kultur, soziale Praxis, Text, Frankfurt am Main: Suhrkamp.

Braig, Marianne (1999): »Fraueninteressen in Entwicklungstheorie und -politik. Von Women in Development zu Mainstreaming Gender«. In: Thiel, Reinold (Hg.) Neue Ansätze in der Entwicklungstheorie, Bonn: Deutsche Stiftung für Internationale Entwicklung.

Bruchhaus, Eva-Maria (1988): »Frauenselbsthilfegruppen: Schlüssel zur Entwicklung aus eigener Kraft oder Mobilisierung der letzten Reserve?«. In: Peripherie, Nr. 30/31, S. 49-61.

Brydon, Lynne (1994): »Women's Chiefs and Power in Volta Region«. In: Brempong, Nana Arhin/Ray, D./van Rouveroy van Nieuwaal E.A.B. (Hg.) Proceedings of the Conference on the Contribution of Traditional Authority to Development, Human Rights and Environment Protection: Strategies for Africa, Leiden: African Studies Centre.

Busia, Kofi (1968): The Position of the Chief in the Modern System of Ashanti, London: Cass.

Butegwa, Florence/Nduna, Sydia (1995): Legal Rights: Organizing for Women in Africa, Harare: WiLDAF.

Cicourel, Aron V. (1981): »Notes on the Integration of Micro and Macrolevels of Society«. In: Knorr-Cetina, Karin/Cicourel, Aron V. (Hg.) Advances in Social Theory and Methodology: Towards an Integration of Micro- and Macro-Sociologies, Boston, London, Henley: Routledge & Kegan Paul.

Clark, Ann Marie/Friedmann, Elisbeth, J./Hochstetler, Kathryin (1998): »The Sovereign Limits of Global Civil Society: A Comparison, of NGO Participation in UN World Conferences on the Environment, Human Rights, and Women«. In: World Politics, Vol. 51, No.1, S. 1-36.

Clifford, James (1986): »Introduction«. In: Clifford, James/Marcus, George E. (Hg.) Writing Culture, Berkley, Los Angeles, London: University of California Press.

Clifford, James (1995): »Über Ethnographische Allegorie«. In: Berg, Eberhard/Fuchs, Martin (Hg.) Kultur, soziale Praxis, Text, Frankfurt am Main: Suhrkamp.

Comaroff, Jean/Comaroff, John (1993): »Introduction«. In: Comaroff, Jean/Comaroff, John (Hg.) Modernity and its Malcontents, Chicago: University of Chicago Press.

Dausien, Bettina (1996): Biographie und Geschlecht: Zur biographischen Konstruktion sozialer Wirklichkeit in Frauenlebensgeschichten, Bremen: Donat.

Deere, Carmen Diane (1986): »Foreword«. In: Golde, Peggy (Hg.) Women in the Field, Berkley: University of California Press.

Degele, Nina (2002): Einführung in die Techniksoziologie, München: Fink.

Diawarra, Mamadou (1985): »Les recherches en histoire orale menées par un autochthone ou L'inconvénient d'etre du cru«. In: Cahiers d'Etudes africaines, 97, 15, S. 5-19.

Drucker, Peter F. (1993): Die postkapitalistische Gesellschaft, Düsseldorf, Wien, New York, Moskau: Econ.

Durkheim, Emile (1985): Die Regeln der soziologischen Methode (Erstausgabe 1895), Frankfurt am Main: Suhrkamp.

Eder, Klaus (1988): Die Vergesellschaftung der Natur, Frankfurt am Main: Suhrkamp.

Elwert, Georg (1987): »Die gesellschaftliche Einbettung von Schriftgebrauch«. In: Baecker, Dirk/Markowitz, Jürgen/Stichweh, Rudolf/Tyrell, Hartmann/Willke, Helmut (Hg.) Theorie als Passion, Frankfurt am Main: Suhrkamp.

Elwert, Georg/Evers, Hans-Dieter/Wilkens, Werner (1983): »Die Suche nach Sicherheit: Kombinierte Produktionsformen im sogenannten Informellen Sektor«. In: Zeitschrift für Soziologie, Jg.12, 4, S. 281-296.

Escobar, Arturo (1999): »Gender, Politics and Networks: A Political Ecology of Cyberculture«. In: Harcourt, Wendy (Hg.) Women@Internet, London: Zed-Books.

Escobar, Arturo/Rocheleau, Dianne/Kothari, Smitu (2002): »Environmental Social Movements and the Politics of Place«. In: Development, SID, Vol. 45, No.1, S. 28-36.
Evers, Hans-Dieter/Schiel, Tilman (1988): Strategische Gruppen: Vergleichende Studien zu Staat, Bürokratie und Klassenbildung in der Dritten Welt, Berlin: Reimer.
Evers, Hans-Dieter (1999): Globalisierung der Wissensgesellschaft – Ansätze einer neuen Entwicklungstheorie, Working Paper No. 310, Sociology of Development Research Centre: University of Bielefeld.
Evers, Hans-Dieter/Kaiser, Markus/Müller, Christine (2002): »Entwicklung durch Wissen: eine neue globale Wissensarchitektur«. In: Soziale Welt, Zeitschrift für sozialwissenschaftliche Forschung und Praxis, S. 49-70
Fairclough, Norman (1985): »Critical and Descriptive Goals in Discourse Analysis«. In: Journal of Pragmatics, 9, S. 739-763.
Fairclough, Norman (1992): Discourse Analysis and Social Change, Cambridge, Oxford: Polity Press.
Fals Borda, Orlando (1990): »The Application of Participatory-Action Research in Latin America«. In: Albrow, Martin/King, Elizabeth (Hg.) Globalization, Knowledge and Society, London, Newbury Park, New Delhi: Sage Publication.
Farrar, Tarikhu (1997): »The Queenmothers, Matriarchy and the Question of Political Authority in Precolonial West African Matriarchy«. In: The Journal of Black Studies, Vol. 27, No.5, S. 579-597.
Farwell, Edie/Wood, Pelegrine/James, Maureen/Banks, Karren (1999): »Global Networking for Change«. In: Harcourt, Wendy (Hg.) Women@ Internet, London: Zed-Books.
Finnegan, Ruth (1970) Oral Literature in Africa, Oxford, New York, Toronto: Oxford University Press.
Fortes, Meyer (1962): »Kinship and Marriage among the Ashanti«. In: Radcliffe-Brown, A.R./Forde, D. (Hg.) African Systems of Kinship and Marriage, London: Oxford University Press.
Fraser, Arvonne S. (1987): The U.N. Decade for Women, Boulder, London: Westview Press.
Garfinkel, Harold (1973): »Das Alltagswissen über soziale und innerhalb sozialer Strukturen«. In: Arbeitsgruppe Bielefelder Soziologen (Hg.) Alltagswissen, Interaktion und gesellschaftliche Wirklichkeit, Band 1 und 2, Reinbek: Rowohlt.
Geertz, Clifford (1983): Local Knowledge, Further Essays in Interpretive Anthropology, New York: Basic Books, Inc. Publisher.
Gerhard, Ute (1996): »Atempause: Die aktuelle Bedeutung der Frauenbewegung für die zivile Gesellschaft«. In: Aus Politik und Zeitgeschichte, B 21-22.
Geschiere, Peter/Konings, Piet (1993): Itinéraires d'accumulation au Cameroun, Paris, Leiden: Karthacha.
Geschiere, Peter (1995): »Local Knowledge and Imported Knowledge:

Witchcraft, Healing and New Forms of Accumulation«. In: Meyns, Peter (Hg.) Staat und Gesellschaft in Afrika, Schriften der Vereinigung von Afrikanisten in Deutschland (VAD e.V.): Lit.

Gibson, Kathrine (2002): »Women, Identity and Activism in Asian and Pacific Community Economies«. In: Development, SID, Vol. 45, No. 1, S. 74-80.

Giddens, Anthony (1990): Consequences of Modernity, London, Polity: Blackwell Press. Dt: (1995) Konsequenzen der Moderne, Frankfurt am Main: Suhrkamp.

Gilbert, Michelle (1989): »Sources of Power in Akuropon-Akuapem: Ambiguity in Classification«. In: Arens, William/Karp, Ivan (Hg.) Creativity of Power, Washington, London: Smithsonian.

Glinga, Werner (1989): »Mündlichkeit in Afrika und Schriftlichkeit in Europa«. In: Zeitschrift für Soziologie, Jg. 18, Heft 2, S. 89-99.

Gluck Berger, Sherna/Patai, Daphne (Hg.) (1991): Women's Words, The Feminist Practice of Oral History, London, New York: Routledge.

Göring, Christina (1979): Strukturanalyse traditioneller und moderner Herrschaft in Ghana, Göttingen: Klaus Renner.

Goetz, Anne-Marie (1991): »Feminism and the claim to know: contradictions in feminist approaches to Women in Development«. In: Grant, Rebecca/ Newland, Kathleen (Hg.) Gender and International Relations, Bloomington: Indiana University Press.

Goetz, Anne-Marie (1995): »Institutionalising Women's Interests and Accountability to Women in Development«. In: IDS Bulletin, Vol. 26, No.3, S. 1-21.

Golde, Peggy (1986): »Introduction«. In: Golde, Peggy (Hg.) Women in the Field, Berkley, Los Angeles, London: University of California Press.

Graham, Yao (2001): »Changing the United Brotherhood: An Analysis of the Gender Politics of the Ghana Trades Union Congress«. In: Tsikata, Dzodzi (Hg.) Gender Training in Ghana, Accra: Woeli Publishing.

Granovetter, Marc (1973): »The Strength of Weak Ties«. In: American Journal of Sociology, 78, S. 1360-1380.

Granovetter, Marc (1985): »Economic Action and Social Structure: The Problem of Embeddedness«. In: American Journal of Sociology, 91, S. 481-510.

Grau, Ingeborg (1989): »Frauen in Geschichte und Geschichtsschreibung Afrikas. Zur Historischen Aufarbeitung früher antikolonialer Bewegungen nigerianischer Frauen. Ein Beitrag zur Frauenforschung«. In: Zeitschrift für Afrikastudien, Wien, S. 9-24.

Grohs, Elisabeth (1980): Kisazi – Reiferiten der Mädchen bei den Zigua und Ngulu Ost-Tanzanias, Berlin: Reimer.

Gupta, Akhil/Ferguson, James (1992): »Beyond "Culture": Space, Identity, and the Politics of Difference«.In: Cultural Anthropology, 7,1, S. 6-23.

Habermas, Jürgen (1981): Theorie des kommunikativen Handelns, Band 1 und 2, Frankfurt am Main: Edition Suhrkamp.

Habermas, Jürgen (1990): Strukturwandel der Öffentlichkeit, Frankfurt am Main: Edition Suhrkamp.

Haddad, Lawrence (1991): »Gender and Poverty in Ghana: A Descriptive Analysis of Selected Outcomes and Processes«. In: IDS Bulletin, Vol. 22, No.1, S. 5-13.

Hagemann, Karen (1990): »Ich glaube nicht, dass ich wichtiges zu erzählen habe- Oral History und historische Frauenforschung«. In: Vorländer, Herwart (Hg.) Oral History, Göttingen: Vandenhoeck & Ruprecht.

Halbwachs, Maurice (1967): Das kollektive Gedächtnis, Stuttgart: Ferdinand Enke.

Hanisch, Rolf (1976) Ghana and the Cocoa World Market, Saarbrücken: SSIP-Schriften.

Harding, Sandra (1991): »Subjectivity, Experience and Knowledge: An Epistemology from/for the Rainbow Coalition Politics«. In: Nederveen Pieterse, Jan (Hg.) Emancipations, Modern and Postmodern. In: Development and Change, Vol. 23, No.3, S. 175-194.

Harcourt, Wendy (Hg.) (1997): Power, Reproduction and Gender: The intergenerational transfer of knowledge. London: Zed-Books.

Harcourt, Wendy (Hg.) (1999): Women@Internet, London: Zed-Books.

Harcourt, Wendy (2002): Confessions of a Border Crosser: At the limits of Disciplines, Missions, Passions, and Languages. Paper presented at EADI workshop (15-16 March), Rome.

Harcourt, Wendy/Escobar, Arturo (2002): »Women and the Politics of Place«. In: Development, Vol.45, No.1, S.7-14.

Hasan, Dahabo Farah/Adan, Amina H./Warsame, Amina Mohamoud (1995): »Poetry as Resistance against Colonialism and Patriarchy«. In: Wieringa, Saskia (Hg.) Subversive Women, London, New York: Zed-Books.

Hirschauer, Stefan/Amann, Klaus (1997): »Die Befremdung der eigenen Kultur. Ein Programm«. In: Hirschauer, Stefan/Amann, Klaus (Hg.) Die Befremdung der eigenen Kultur, Zur ethnologischen Herausforderung soziologischer Empirie, Frankfurt am Main: Suhrkamp.

Hirshman, Mitu (1995): »Women and Development«. In: Marchand, Marianne H./Parpart, Jane L. (Hg.) Feminism/Postmodernism/ Development, London, New York: Routledge.

Hitzler, Ronald/Reichertz, Jo/Schröer, Norbert (1999): »Das Arbeitsfeld einer hermeneutischen Wisenssoziologie«. In: Hitzler, Ronald/Reichertz, Jo/ Schröer, Norbert (Hg.) Hermeneutische Wissenssoziologie, Konstanz: Universitätsverlag.

Hobart, Mark (Hg.) (1993): An Anthropological Critique of Development, London: Routledge.

Holthaus, Ines/Klingebiel, Ruth (1998): »Vereinte Nationen – Sprungbrett oder Stolperstein auf dem langen Marsch zur Durchsetzung von Frauenrechten?«. In: Klingebiel, Ruth/Randeria, Shalini (Hg.) Globalisierung aus Frauensicht, Bonn: Dietz.

Honer, Anne (1989): »Einige Probleme lebensweltlicher Ethnographie«. In: Zeitschrift für Soziologie, Jg. 18, Heft 4, S. 297-312.
Honerla S./Schröder, P. (Hg.) (1995): Lokales Wissen und Entwicklung: Zur Relevanz kulturspezifischen Wissens für die Entwicklungsprozesse. Saarbrücken: Verlag für Entwicklungspolitik.
Hountondji, Paulin J.(1995): »Producing Knowledge in Africa Today«. In: African Studies Spectrum, Volume 38, No.3, S. 1-10.
Illi, Holger (2001): Development Experts at the "Interface", Research Report, Sociology of Development Research Centre: University of Bielefeld.
ISSER (1998): Women in Public Life in Ghana, University of Ghana (Legon): ISSER.
Jommo, Rosemary Berewa (1993): »African Women's Indigenous Knowledge in the Management of Natural Resource«. In: Steady, Filomina Chioma (Hg.) Women and Children First, Rochester, Vermont: Schenckmann.
Kabeer, Naila (1994): Reversed Realities, London, New York: Verso.
Kaplan, Flora Edouwaye (1997): »Introduction«. In: Kaplan, Flora Edouwaye (Hg.) Queens, Queenmothers, Priestesses and Power. Case Studies in African Gender. New York: New York Academy of Science.
Keller, Reiner (1997): »Diskursanalyse«. In: Hitzler, Ronald/Honer, Anne (Hg.) Sozialwissenschaftliche Hermeneutik, Oplanden: Leske und Budrich.
Kerner, Ina (1999): Feminismus, Entwicklungszusammenarbeit und Postkoloniale Kritik, Hamburg: Lit.
Klein-Hessling, Ruth (2000): Methodology of Gender Research and Local Development Concepts. Report on Workshop 11-12 November 1999. Working Paper No. 331, Sociology of Development Research Centre: University of Bielefeld.
Klingebiel, Ruth/Randeria, Shalini, (Hg.) (1998): Globalisierung aus Frauensicht, Bonn: Dietz.
Klingshirn, Agnes (1971): The Changing Position of Women in Ghana, Dissertation, Marburg/Lahn.
Knorr-Cetina, Karin (1981): »Introduction«. In: Knorr-Cetina, Karin/ Cicourel, Aron V. (Hg.) (1981) Advances in Social Theory and Methodology: Towards an Integration of Micro- and Macro-Sociologies, Boston, London, Henley: Routledge & Kegan Paul.
Knorr-Cetina, Karin (1989): »Spielarten des Konstruktivismus«. In: Soziale Welt, 40 (1/2), S. 86-96.
Knorr-Cetina, Karin (1991): Die Fabrikation von Erkenntnis: zur Anthropologie der Naturwissenschaft, Frankfurt am Main: Suhrkamp.
Knorr-Cetina, Karin (1999): Epistemic Cultures, Cambridge, London: Harvard University Press.
Knorr-Cetina, Karin/Bruegger, Urs (2002): »Global Microstructures: The Virtual Societies of Financial Markets«. In: American Journal of Sociology, No.4, S. 905-950.
Korf, Benedikt (1998): »Local Self-Reliance im Kontext der Dezentralisierung in Ghana«. In: Trialog, Vol. 59, S. 31-35.

Kyeremateng, Nkwasa (1996): The Akans of Ghana, Accra: Sebewie.
Lachenmann, Gudrun (1982): Entkolonialisierung der Gesundheit, Theorie und Praxis der Gesundheitsversorgung in Namibia und Benin, Konstanz: Rüegger.
Lachenmann, Gudrun (1989): Frauenpolitik in der Entwicklungspolitik, Berlin: Deutsches Institut für Entwicklungspolitik.
Lachenmann, Gudrun (1992): »Von der Unsichtbarkeit zur Verletzlichkeit zur Pflichtorganisation«. In: Hofmeier, Rolf/Tetzlaff, Rainer/Wegemund, Regina (Hg.) Afrika-Überleben in einer ökonomisch gefährdeten Umwelt, Münster, Hamburg: Lit-Verlag.
Lachenmann, Gudrun (1993): Selbstorganisation sozialer Sicherheit von Frauen in Entwicklungsländern, Working Paper No. 191, Sociology of Development Research Centre: University of Bielefeld.
Lachenmann, Gudrun (1994): »Systeme des Nichtwissens«. In: Hitzler, Ronald/Honer, Anne/Maeder, Christoph (Hg.) Expertenwissen: Die institutionalisierte Kompetenz zur Konstruktion von Wirklichkeit, Opladen: Westdeutscher Verlag.
Lachenmann, Gudrun (1995): "Methodenstreit" in der Entwicklungssoziologie, Working Paper No. 241, Sociology of Development Research Centre: University of Bielefeld.
Lachenmann, Gudrun(1995a): »Einleitung«. In: Meyns, Peter (Hg.) Staat und Gesellschaft in Afrika. Erosions-und Reformprozesse, Hamburg: Lit.
Lachenmann, Gudrun (1996): Weltfrauenkonferenz und Forum der Nichtregierungsorganisationen in Peking – Internationale Frauenbewegungen als Vorreiterinnen einer globalen Zivilgesellschaft, Working Paper No. 251, Sociology of Development Research Centre: University of Bielefeld.
Lachenmann, Gudrun (1997): »Zivilgesellschaft und Entwicklung«. In: Schulz, Manfred (Hg.) Entwicklung. Die Perspektive der Entwicklungssoziologie, Opladen: Westdeutscher Verlag.
Lachenmann, Gudrun (1998): Frauen und Globalisierung: aktuelle Entwicklungen und kritische Diskurse, Working Paper No. 284, Sociology of Development Research Centre: University of Bielefeld.
Lachenmann, Gudrun (1998a): »Frauenbewegungen als gesellschaftliche Kraft des Wandels. Beispiele aus Afrika«. In: Ruppert, Uta (Hg.) Lokal bewegen – global verhandeln: internationale Politik und Geschlecht, Frankfurt am Main, New York: Campus.
Lane, Robert (1966): »The decline of politics and ideology in a knowledgeable society«. In: American Sociological Review 31 S. 649-663.
Lash, Scott (1994): »Reflexivity and its Doubles: Structure, Aesthetics, Community. In: Beck, Ulrich/Giddens, Anthony/Lash, Scott (Hg.) Reflexive Modernization, Cambridge, Oxford: Polity Press.
Latour, Bruno (1999): »Actor-Network Theory«. In: Law, John/Hassard, J. (Hg.) Actor Network Theory and After, Oxford: Blackwell.

Lebeuf, Annie M.D. (1963): »The Role of Women in the Political Organization of African Societies«. In: Paulme, Denise (Hg.) Women of Tropical Africa: Routlegde & Kegan Paul.

Lefébvre, Henri (1991): The Production of Space, Oxford, Cambridge: Blackwell.

Lentz, Carola (1998): Die Konstruktion von Ethnizität: Eine politische Geschichte Nord-West Ghanas, ca. 1870-1990, Köln: Köppe.

Lentz, Carola (1999): »Youth associations und Ethnizität in Nordghana«. In: afrika spektrum, 34, 3, S.305-321.

Lenz, Ilse (1990): »Geschlechtsymmetrische Gesellschaften«. In: Lenz, Ilse/Luig, Ute (Hg.) Frauenmacht ohne Herrschaft, Orlando: Berlin.

Little, Kenneth (1972): »Voluntary Associations and Social Mobility among West African Women«. In: Canadian Journal of African Studies, 5, S. 275-288.

Long, Norman (1992): »Introduction«. In: Long, Norman/Long, Ann (Hg.) Battlefields of Knowledge, London, New York: Routledge.

Long, Norman (1996): »Globalization and Localization: New Challenges to Rural Research«. In: Moore, Henrietta L. (Hg.) The Future of Anthropological Knowledge, London, New York: Routledge.

Löw, Martina (2001): Raumsoziologie, Frankfurt am Main: Suhrkamp.

Luckmann, Thomas (1986): »Grundformen der Gesellschaftlichen Vermittlung von Wissen: Kommunikative Gattungen«. In: Kölner Zeitschrift für Soziologie und Sozialpsychologie, Sonderheft Nr. 27, Westdeutscher Verlag.

Luig, Ute (1984): »Probleme bei der Erforschung Oraler Traditionen«. In: Kölner Zeitschrift für Soziologie und Sozialpsychologie, Sonderband Nr. 26, Westdeutscher Verlag.

Luig, Ute (1990): »Körpermetaphorik, Sexualität und Macht der Frauen«. In: Lenz, Ilse/Luig, Ute (Hg.) Frauenmacht ohne Herrschaft, Orlando: Berlin.

Luig, Ute/von Oppen, Achim (1995): »Einleitung: Zur Vergesellschaftung von Natur in Afrika«. In: Luig, Ute/von Oppen, Achim (Hg.) Naturaneignung in Afrika als sozialer und symbolischer Prozess. Forschungsschwerpunkt moderner Orient. Arbeitshefte No.10, Berlin: Das Arabische Buch.

Luig, Ute (1997): »Ethnographische Anmerkungen zum Verhältnis von Fruchtbarkeit, Geschlecht und Macht in Afrika«. In: Braig, Marianne/ Ferdinand, Ursula/Zapata, Martha (Hg.) Begegnung und Einmischung, Stuttgart: Hans-Dieter Heinz Akademischer Verlag.

Lutz, Cathrine (1995): »The Gender of Theory«. In: Behar, Ruth/Gordon, Deborah A. (Hg.) Women's Writing Culture, Berkley, Los Angeles, London: Universitiy of California.

Mac Laughlin, Andrée Nicola (1995): »The Impact of Black Consciousness and Women's Movements on Black Women's Identity: Intercontinental Empowerment«. In: Pala, Achola (Hg.) Connecting Across Cultures and Continents: Black Women Speck out on Identity; Race and Development, New York: UNIFEM.

McCaskie, Tom C. (1995): State and Society in pre-colonial Asante. New York: Cambridge University Press.

Martin, Charlotte (2002): Acts of Translations: Reflections on Action Research and Policy. Paper presented at EADI workshop (15-16 March), Rome.

Mensah-Kutin, Rose (1994): »The WEDNET Initiative: A Sharing Experience between Researchers and Rural Women«. In: Riano, Pilar (Hg.) Women in Grassroots Communication, Thousand Oaks, London, New Delhi: Sage Publications.

Meyer, Birgit (1983): »Sind Frauen unpolitisch ?« In: Die Frau in unserer Zeit, J. 22, Nr.1, S. 11-18.

Meyerowitz, Eva (1958): The Akan of Ghana: Their Ancient Beliefs, London: Faber and Faber.

Middleton, John (1983): »One hundred and fifty years of Christianity in a Ghanaian town«. In: Africa, S. 1-25.

Mikell, Gwendolyn (1985): »Expansion and Contraction in Economic Access to Rural Women in Ghana«. In: Rural Africana, 21, S. 17-27.

Mies, Maria (1989): »Methodische Postulate zur Frauenforschung«. In: Beiträge zur feministischen theorie und praxis, Nr.11, S. 7-25.

Mies, Maria/Bennholdt-Thomsen, Veronika/Von Werlhof, Claudia (1988): Women: The Last Colony, London: Zed-Books.

Mohanty, Chandra Talpade (1991): »Under Western Eyes: Feminist Scholarship and Colonial Discourse«. In: Mohanty, Chandra Talpade/ Russo, Ann/Torres, Lourdes (Hg.) World Women and the Politics of Feminism, Bloomington and Indianapolis: Indiana University Press.

Moore, Henrietta L. (1986): Space, Text and Gender, Cambridge: Cambridge University Press.

Moore, Henrietta L. (1994): A Passion for Difference, Cambridge, Oxford: Polity Press.

Moore, Henrietta, L. (Hg.) (1996): The Future of Anthropological Knowledge, New York, London: Routledge.

Moore, Sally Falk (1986): Social Facts and Fabrication, Cambridge: Cambridge University Press.

Mudimbe, Valentin Y. (1988): The Invention of Africa, Bloomington, Indianapolis: Indiana University Press.

Müller, Christine (2002): Conceptualising Knowledge: Reflections on Research and Social Change in Ghana. Paper presented at EADI Gender and Development Workshop, (15-16 March), Rome.

Müller, Christine (2003): »Knowledge between Globalization and Localization: The Dynamics of Female Spaces in Ghana«. In: Current Sociology, Vol. 51, No.3/4, S. 329-346.

Nageeb, Salma (2000): Stretching the Horizon: New Spaces and Old Frontiers: Women's Construction of Social Space in Sudan, unpubl. Ph.D. Thesis: University of Bielefeld.

Nana Odeneho Oduro Numapau II. (2000): »Chieftaincy. An Age-Old Institution«. In: Scheidetweiler, Thomas (Hg.) Human and Economic Development – The Importance of Civil Society and Subsidiarity, Bonn: KAAD.

Neidhart, Friedhelm (1985): »Einige Ideen zu einer allgemeinen Theorie sozialer Bewegungen «. In: Bolte, Karl Martin (Hg.) Sozialstruktur im Umbruch, Opladen: Leske, Buderich.

Nelson, Nici/Wright, Susan (1995): »Participation and Power «. In: Nelson, Nici/Wright, Susan (Hg.) Power and Participatory Development, Theory and Practice, London: Intermediate Technology Publications.

Newland, Kathleen (1991): »From Transnational Relationship to International Relations: Women in Development and the International Decade for Women«. In: Grant, Rebecca/Newland, Kathleen (Hg.) Gender and International Relations, Bloomington: Indiana University Press.

Nederveen Pieterse, Jan (1995): »Globalization as Hybridization«. In: Featherstone, Mike/Lash,Scott/Robertson, Roland (Hg.) Global Modernities, London, Thousand Oaks, New Delhi: Sage Publications.

Nederveen Pieterse, Jan (1995b): The Development of Development Theory towards Critical Globalism. Working Paper No. 187, The Hague: Institute of Social Studies.

Noller, Peter (2000): »Globalisierung, Raum und Gesellschaft. Elemente einer modernen Soziologie des Raums«. In: Berliner Journal für Soziologie, Nr. 1, S. 21-49.

Okali, Christine (1983): Cocoa and Kinship in Ghana, London, Boston, Melbourne: Kegan Paul International.

Okonjo, Kamene (1976): » The Dual-Sex Political System in Operation: Igbo Women and Community Politics in Midwestern Nigeria«. In: Hafkin, Nancy J./Bay, Edna (Hg.) Women in Africa, Stanford: Stanford University Press.

Ong, Walter (1982): Orality and Literacy: The Technologizing of the World, London: Methuen.

Owusu, Maxwell (1996): »Tradition and Transformation«. In: Journal of African Studies, 34, 2, S. 307-343.

Padmanabhan, Martina Aruna (2002): Trying to Grow – Gender Relations and Agricultural Innovations in Northern Ghana, Münster: Lit.

Parpart, Jane (1995): »Deconstructing the Development "Expert". In: Marchand, Marianne/Parpart, Jane (Hg.) Feminism/Postmodernism/ Development, London, New York: Routledge.

Parpart, Jane/Marchard, Marianne (1995): »Exploding the Canon: An Introduction/Conclusion«. In: Marchand, Marianne/Parpart, Jane (Hg.) Feminism/Postmodernism/Development, London, New York: Routledge.

Parrinder, Geoffrey (1973): West African Religion: A Study on the Beliefs and Practices of the Akan, Ewe, Yoruba, Ibo and Kindred Peoples, London: Epworth Press.
Peleikis, Anja (2003): Lebanese in Motion, Bielefeld: transcript.
Polany, Karl (1978): The Great Transformation. Politische und Ökonomische Ursprünge von Gesellschaften und Wirtschaftssystemen. Frankfurt am Main: Suhrkamp.
Porter, Fenella/Verghese, Valsa (1999): »Falling between the Gaps«. In: Porter, Marilyn/Judd, Ellen (Hg.) Feminists doing development: a Practical Critique, London: Zed-Books.
Porter, Marilyn (1999): »Caught in the web? Feminists doing development«. In: Porter, Marilyn/Judd, Ellen (Hg.) Feminists doing development: a Practical Critique, London: Zed-Books.
Powdermaker, Hortense (1966): Stranger and Friend: The Way of an Anthropologist, New York: Norton.
Powell, Walter/Smith-Doerr, Laurel (1994): »Networks and Economic Life«. In: Smelser, Neil J./Swedberg, Richard (Hg.) The Handbook of Economic Sociology, Princeton: Princeton University Press.
Prah, Kwasi (1997): »North/South Parallels and Intersections«. In: Critique of Anthropology, Vol.17 (4), S. 439-445.
Rathgeber, Eva, M. (1990): »WID, WAD, GAD: Trends in Research and Practice«. In: Journal of Developing Areas, No. 24, S. 489-502.
Rattray, R.S. (1923; 1969): Ashanti, London: Oxford University Press.
Ray, Donald (1995): »Chief-State Relations in Ghana – Divided Sovereignty and Legitimacy«. In: van Rouveroy van Nieuwaal, Adrian/Zips, Werner (Hg.) Sovereignty, Legitimacy and Power in West African Societies: Perspectives from Legal Anthropology, Hamburg: Lit.
Richards, Paul (1985): Indigenous Agricultural Revolution: Ecology and Food-Production in West Africa, London: Hutchinson.
Robertson, Roland (1992): Globalization, London, Thousand Oaks, New Delhi: Sage Publications.
Robertson, Roland (1995): »Glocalization: Time-Space and Homogeneity-Heterogeneity«. In: Featherstone, Mike/Lash, Scott/Roberston, Roland (Hg.) Global Modernities, London, Thousand Oaks, New Delhi: Sage Publications.
Rodenberg, Birte (1999): Lokale Selbstorganisation und globale Vernetzung: Handlungsfelder von Frauen in der Ökologiebewegung Mexikos, Bielefeld: transcript.
Roe, Alan/Schneider (1992): Adjustment and Equity in Ghana, Paris: OECD.
Rosander Evers, Eva (Hg.) (1997): Transforming Female Identities – Women's Organizational Forms in West Africa, Uppsala: Nordiska Afrikainstitutet.
Rott, Renate (1992): »Entwicklungsprozesse und Geschlechterverhältnisse«. In: Rott, Renate (Hg.) Entwicklungsprozesse und Geschlechterverhältnisse, Saarbrücken, Fort Lauderdale: Verlag Breitenbach Publishers.

Ruf, Anja (1996): Weltwärts Schwester ! Von der Weltfrauenkonferenz in die globale Zukunft, Bonn: Dietz.

Ruf, Anja (1998): »Frauennetzwerke im Spannungsfeld von Globalisierung und Vielfalt«. In: Klingebiel, Ruth/Randeria, Shalini (Hg.) Globalisierung aus Frauensicht, Bonn: Dietz.

Rupp, Leila J. (1997): Worlds of Women – The Making of an International Women's Movement, Princeton: New Jersey.

Sackey, Brigid Maa (1986): Spiritual Churches, and Politics on Ghana, Ann Arbor: Bell and Howell Company.

Sarpong, Peter (1977): Girl's Nubility Rites in Ashanti, Tema: Ghana Publishing Cooperation.

Schäfer, Rita (1995a): »Geschlechteraspekte der Wissenssysteme und Wissenskommunikation in westafrikanischen Agrarkulturen«. In: Honerla, Susan/Schröder, Peter (Hg.) Lokales Wissen und Entwicklung, Saarbrücken: Verlag für Entwicklungspolitik.

Schäfer, Rita (1995b): Frauenorganisationen und Entwicklungszusammenarbeit, Pfaffenweiler: Cenaurus-Verlagsgesellschaft.

Schäfer, Rita (1998): Guter Rat ist wie die Glut des Feuers, Pfaffenweiler: Centaurus-Verlagsgesellschaft.

Schäfer, Rita (1999): »Frauenrechtsorganisationen im südlichen Afrika«. In: Nord-Süd aktuell, 2. Quartal, S. 301-311.

Schlee, Günther (1990): Ritual Topography and Ecological Use. Working Paper No. 134, Sociology of Development Research Centre: University of Bielefeld.

Schmidt, Heike (2002): »Entangled Memories. Bindung and Identiy«. In: Yehuda, Elkana/Krastev, Ivan/Randeria, Shalini (Hg.) Unraveling Ties – From Social Cohesion to New Practices of Connectedness, Frankfurt am Main: Campus.

Schneider, Gerlind (2000): Auf der Suche nach Sicherheit und Gemeinschaft: Die Wirtschaft der Frauen in Harare, Simbabwe, unveröff. Dissertation, Fakultät für Soziologie: Universität Bielefeld.

Schneider, Gerlind (2001): »Zur sozialen Einbettung von Frauenarbeit in Harare«. In: Lachenmann, Gudrun/Dannecker, Petra (Hg.) Die geschlechtsspezifische Einbettung der Ökonomie, Hamburg: Lit.

Schönhuth, Michael/Kievelitz, Uwe (Hg.) (1993): Partizipative Erhebungs- und Planungsmethoden in der Entwicklungszusammenarbeit: Rapid Rural Appraisal, Participatory Appraisal, GTZ, Wiesbaden: Universum.

Schrijvers, Joke (1995): »Participation and Power«. In: Nelson, Nici/Wright, Susan (Hg.) Power and Participatory Development, Theory and Practice, London: Intermediate Technology Publications.

Seebode, Jochen (1998): Aduro kum aduro: Ritual, Macht und Besessenheit in Asante (Südghana), Münster: Lit.

Schütz, Alfred (1962): The Problem of Social Reality, Collected Papers 1, The Hague, Boston, London: Martinus Nijhoff.

Schütz, Alfred (1967): The Phenomenology of the Social World, Evanston: Northwestern University Press.
Schütz, Alfred/Luckmann, Thomas (1974) Die Strukturen der Lebenswelt, Neuwied: Luchterhand.
Schütze, Fritz/Meinefeld, Werner/Springer, Werner/Weymann, Ansgar (1973): »Grundlagentheoretische Voraussetzungen zum methodisch kontrollierten Fremdverstehen«. In: Arbeitsgruppe Bielefelder Soziologen (Hg.) Alltagswissen, Interaktion und gesellschaftliche Wirklichkeit, Band 1 und 2, Reinbek: Rowohlt.
Schuler, Margaret (1990): »Introduction«: The 1989 WLD Interregional Meeting. In: Schuler, Margaret (Hg.) Women, Law and Development – Action for Change. Washington: OEF International.
Schweizer, Thomas (Hg.) (1988): Netzwerkanalyse, Berlin: Dietrich Reimer Verlag.
Sen, Gita/Grown, Caren (1987): Development, Crises and Alternative Visions, New York: New Feminist Library.
Silitoe, Paul (1998): »What, know Natives ? Local Knowledge in Development«. In: Social Anthropology, 6, S. 203-220.
Simmel, Georg (1983): »Soziologie des Raumes« (1903). In: Simmel, Georg (Hg. Dahme, Heinz-Jürgen/Rammstedt, Ottheim) Schriften zur Soziologie, Frankfurt am Main: Suhrkamp.
Soeffner, Hans-Georg (1999): »Strukturen der Lebenswelt – Ein Kommentar«. In: Hitzler, Roland/Reichertz, Jo/Schröer, Norbert (Hg.) Hermeneutische Wissenssoziologie, Konstanz: Universitätsverlag.
Speiser, Sabine (1995): »Tradierung von Wissen, Lehren und Lernen«. In: Honerla, Susan/Schröder, Peter (Hg.) Lokales Wissen und Entwicklung, Saarbrücken: Verlag für Entwicklungspolitik.
Stacey, Judith (1991): »Can there be a Feminist Ethnography ?« In: Gluck Berger, Sherna/ Patai, Daphne (Hg.) Women's Words, The Feminist Practice of Oral History, London, New York: Routledge.
Staudt, Kathleen (1989): »The State and Gender in Colonial Africa«. In: Charlton, Sue Ellen/Everett, Jana/Staudt, Kathleen (Hg.) Women, the State and Development, Albany: State University of New York Press.
Stehr, Nico (2000): Die Zerbrechlichkeit moderner Gesellschaften: Weilerswist: Verlbrück Wissenschaft.
Stehr, Nico (2003): Wissenspolitik, Frankfurt am Main: Suhrkamp.
Stoeltje, Beverly J. (1994): »From Durbar to Development: Asante Queenmothers«. In: Brempong, Nana Arhin/Ray, D./van Rouveroy van Nieuwaal E.A.B. (Hg.) Proceedings of the Conference on the Contribution of Traditional Authority to Development, Human Rights and Environment Protection: Strategies for Africa, Leiden: African Studies Centre.
Stoeltje, Beverly J. (1995): »Asante Queenmothers: A Study in Identity and Continuity«. In: Reh, Mechthild/Ludwar-Ene, Mechthild (Hg.) Gender and Identity in Africa, Münster, Hamburg: Lit.
Stoeltje, Beverly J. (1997): »Asante Queen Mothers: a Study in Female Au-

thority«. In: Kaplan, Flora Edouwaye (Hg.) Queens, Queen Mothers, Priestesses and Power, Case Studies in African Gender, Vol. 810: Annals of the New York Academy of Science.

Strauss, Anselm L. (1994): Grundlagen qualitativer Sozialforschung, München: Fink.

Thomas, Dorothy O. (1994): »Keynote adress«. In: Strengthening Linkages for Women's rights in Africa, A report of the Women in Law and Development in Africa, Harare: WiLDAF.

Tonah, Steve (1994): »Agricultural Extension Services and Smallholder Farmers' Indebtedness in Northeastern Ghana«. In: Journal of Asian and African Studies, 1-2, Vol.24, S. 119-129.

Tsikata, Edzodzinam (1989): »Women's Political Organisations 1951-1987«. In: Hansen, Emmanuel/Ninsin, Kwame E. (Hg.) The State, Development and Politics in Ghana, London: Codesira.

Tsikata, Dzodzi (2001): »Gender Equality and Development in Ghana: Some Issues Which Should Concern a Political Party«. In: Tsikata, Dzodzi (Hg.) Gender Training in Ghana, Accra: Woeli Publishing.

Tsikata, Dzodzi (2001a): »The Politics of Policy-Making: A Gender Perspective«. In: Tsikata, Dzodzi (Hg.) Gender Training in Ghana, Accra: Woeli Publishing.

UNDP (1995): Bericht über die menschliche Entwicklung, Bonn: Deutsche Gesellschaft für die Vereinten Nationen.

Van Gennep, Arnold (1972): The Rites of Passage, London: Routledge & Kegan.

Vansina, Jan (1985): Oral Tradition as History, Madison: University of Wisconsin Press.

Von Braunmühl, Claudia (1998): »Frauenanfragen an Enwicklungspolitik«. In: Ruppert, Uta (Hg.) Lokal bewegen – Global verhandeln: Internationale Politik und Geschlecht, Frankfurt am Main, New York: Campus.

Vorländer, Herwart (Hg.) (1990): Oral History, Göttingen: Vandenhoeck & Ruprecht.

Waibel, Gabi (1998): Sesshaftwerdung und sozialer Wandel bei den Tuareg Zinders (Niger), Hamburg: Institut für Afrika Studien.

Weber, Max (1980): Wirtschaft und Gesellschaft, Grundrisse einer verstehenden Soziologie, 5. revidierte Auflage, Tübingen: J.C.B. Mohr.

Weingart, Peter (2001): Die Stunde der Wahrheit?: Zum Verhältnis der Wissenschaft zu Politik, Wirtschaft und Medien in der Wissensgesellschaft, Weilerswist: Velbrück Wissenschaft.

Westermann, Verena (1992): Women's Disturbances: Der Anlu-Aufstand bei den Kom (Kamerun), 1958-1960, Münster: Lit.

Whitehead, Ann (1984): »Women's Solidarity- and Divisions among Women«. In: IDS Bulletin, Vol. 15, No. 12, S. 6-11.

Wichterich, Christa (1984): Frauen in der Dritten Welt. Bonn: Deutsche Stiftung für Internationale Entwicklung.

Wichterich, Christa (1999): »Global Sisterhood – Women Time Go Come«. In: Beiträge zur feministischen theorie und praxis, Nr. 53, S. 111-127.
Wichterich, Christa (2000): »Glokalisierung von Frauenbewegungen«. In: Lenz, Ilse/Mae, Michiko/Klose, Karin (Hg.) Frauenbewegungen Weltweit, Opladen: Leske und Buderich.
Wieringa, Saskia (1995): »Methods and Power: Epistemological and Methodological Aspects of a Feminist Research Project«. In: Wieringa, Saskia (Hg.) Subversive Women, London, New Jersey: Zed-Books.
Wieringa, Saskia (2002): Women's Sexual Empowerment in Indonesia. Paper presented at EADI workshop (March 15-16), Rome.
Wilks, Ivor (1975): Asante in the Nineteenth Century. The Structure and Evolution of a Political Order, London: Cambridge University Press.
Willke, Helmuth (1998) Systemisches Wissensmanagement; Stuttgart: UTB.
Williams, Patrick/Chrisman, Laura (Hg.) (1994): Colonial Discourse and Post-colonial Theory, New York: Columbia University Press.
Woodford-Berger, Prudence (1997): »Associating Women«. In: Rosander, Eva (Hg.) Transforming Female Identities, Women's Organizational Forms in West Africa, Uppsala: Nordiska Afrikainstitutet.
World Bank (1989): World Development Report, Washington: Oxford University Press.
World Bank (1998/99) Development through Knowledge, Washington: Oxford University Press.
Youngs, Gilian (1999): »Virtual Voices: Real Lives«. In: Harcourt, Wendy (Hg.) Women@Internet, London: Zed-Book.

Homepages: Web Addresses

APWIP: http://www.ipc.apc.org
CLADEM: http://www.derechos.org
DAWN: http://www.dawn.fj
ISIS: http://www.isis.org
REFAD: http://www.focusintl.com
WEDO: http://www.wedo.org
WIDE: http://www.eurosure.org
WLD: http://www.wld.org
WiLDAF: http://www.wildaf.zb

LIST OF ABBREVIATIONS

31stDWM	31st December Women's Movement
AAWORD	African Women's Association for Research on Development
ACP	African, Carribbean, Pacific Countries
APWIP	Asian Pacific Women in Politics
APWLD	Asian Pacific Women in Law and Development
ATRAC	African Training and Research Centre
BANGO	Brong-Ahafo Network of NGO's
CEDAW	Convention on the Elimination of all Forms of Discrimination against Women
CIDA	Canadian International Development Agency
CLADEM	Comité de America Latina y el Caribe para la defensa de los derechos de la mujer
CPP	Convention Peoples Party
DAWN	Development Alternatives with Women for a New Era
ENDA	Environment Development Action in the Third World
EU	European Union
FAO	Food and Agricultural Organisation
FIDA	International Federation of Lawyers
GO	Government Organisation
GTZ	German Technical Cooperation
IFAD	International Fund for Agricultural Development
IMF	International Monetary Fund
ISSER	Institute of Statistical, Social and Economic Research, Legon
NCWD	National Council of Women and Development
NDC	National Democratic Congress
NGO	Non Governmental Organisation
NPP	National Peoples Party
PRA	Participatory Rural Appraisal
REFAD	Réseau Sous-Régional Femmes Africaines et Droits Humainés
RHoC	Regional House of Chiefs
RRA	Rapid Rural Appraisal
UGCC	Unites Gold Coast Convention

STM	Science, Technology, Mathematics
TUG	Transport Union of Ghana
UCC	Unit Committee Council
UN	United Nation
UNCED	United Nation Conference on Environment and Development
UNDP	United Nations Development Programme
UNIFEM	United Nations Development Fund for Women
WAD	Women and Development
WEDNET	Women, Environment and Development Network
WEDO	Women, Environment and Development Organisation
WID	Women in Development
WIDE	Women in Development Europe
WiLDAF	Women in Law and Development Africa
WLD	Women, Law and Development
WLSA	Women and Law in Southern African Research Trust